EDUCATIONAL TOURISM

EDUCATIONAL TOURISM

Vikash Choudhary

CENTRUM PRESS
NEW DELHI-110002 (INDIA)

CENTRUM PRESS
H.O.: 4360/4, Ansari Road, Daryaganj,
New Delhi-110002 (India)
Tel: 23278000, 23261597, 23255577, 23286875
B.O.: No. 1015, Ist Main Road, BSK IIIrd Stage,
IIIrd Phase, IIIrd Block, Bangalore-560085 (INDIA)
Tel: 080-41723429
Email: centrumpress@gmail.com
Visit us at: www.centrumpress.com

Educational Tourism

First Edition, 2010

PRINTED IN INDIA

Printed at Mehra Offset Press, Delhi

Contents

Preface

What is Education Tourism? The term education tourism or edu-tourism refers to any "program in which participants travel to a location as a group with the primary purpose of engaging in a learning experience directly related to the location". It is comprised of several sub-types including ecotourism, heritage tourism, rural/farm tourism, and student exchanges between educational institutions. The notion of travelling for educational purposes is not new and its popularity in the tourism market is only expected to increase Sub-Saharan African countries can increase their tourism earnings by tapping into this growing market phenomenon.

Tourism was used at key points in British history to educate people. It is possible to argue that it was filling an educational role most of the time, at least in its early stages. Virtually all forms of tourism began for educational reasons. Most currently available work underplays this fact, with the possible exception of discussions on the Grand Tour. Holloway makes a statement about "tourists and locals alike widening their horizons" almost as an afterthought to a short discussion of sociocultural problems. Cooper et al refer to myths surrounding tourism which "should be broken", pointing out "Tourism is not purely for the purposes of leisure. It also includes business tourism, pilgrimages and tourism for health purposes" A later chapter on "The Future of Tourism" makes only passing mention to `new' tourists looking for "rewarding activities to fill their leisure time and to satisfy their cultural, intellectual and sporting interests", but it is only in the context of the needs of certain market segments in "multi-interest travel". Voase in an interesting and useful book touches on many aspects of tourism which relate to education, without dealing with it as a perspective. A chapter about the future discusses economics, global warming, people in tourism, sustainability, transport and fashions, but not tourism as an educative activity.

Ryan's "The Chase of a Dream, the End of a Play" refers to tourism as an educative process within the context of sociological discussion. The historical references consider tourism largely as leisure and escapism. Hollinshead's "Heritage Tourism Under Post-modernity: Truth and the Past" in the same collection as Ryan shows how great a gap there is between the sociological critic on the one hand and the teacher of history on the other, as the scholarship of Samuel's "Theatres of Memory" illustrates. Hollinshead paints a pessimistic picture of a world in which all history teaching outside the classroom or library appears impossible since it long ago succumbed to a conspiracy by various forces of darkness. There is little illumination in this kind of writing for the history teacher working out of the classroom. History teachers know well that all interpretations - including books and academic papers - of the world take particular viewpoints, selecting, interpreting and presenting reality as they see it. Even so, a reassessment of tourism which hopes to be accepted at a higher academic level will have to establish a credible, theoretical and practical counter-argument to the Hollinshead kind of view.

Weiler and Hall edited a collection of papers in "Special Interest Tourism" which look at a number of case studies and review some sectors. They point to the "diversity of market segments and products ... encompassed within the rubric of `special interest tourism'" and "the limited amount of research that has been done" The book unfortunately suffers from being more a collection of snapshots of relevant areas, but the opening chapter does attempt an overview. Sadly, it remains only a collection of separate perspectives such as marketing, ethics and green tourism, rather than shining a well-focused new light on the whole issue.

Tourism is a good source of learning from various religious places, historical buildings and forts, mosques, temples, besides hydroelectric projects, dams and urban centres. Tourism leads to cultural development in many ways while as for students from educational institutions it is directly responsible for education in the national integration and social awareness for adults, it is helpful in bringing changes in their professions and social behaviour.

This book tries to explore the instructional value of tourism and tries to assess the influence on the people of the ideas, values, customs and habits of the developing world. The fact that the developing countries are targets of the people from the Western world, because of the cheap money of the developing world and it is very convenient and affordable for the western man to visit developing countries. In fact tourism and cultural developments are interdependent terms and the impact of tourism on cultural development is tremendous. Sports events, cultural gatherings, music festivals, are nowadays very popular. The book will be found to be of immense value to the teaching community and the general public alike."

—*Vikash Choudhary*

1

Academic Learning and Teaching in Educational Tourism

Summary of Key Findings

Educational Tourism as Lifelong Learning

- Intentional, experiential, and structured learning are perceived by scholars, clients and companies as the defining features of educational tourism.

Evidence from Academic Scholars Indicates that:

- Over half of those surveyed have already engaged in a form of educational tourism.
- Three quarters of those surveyed would do so in the future.
- Participation in educational tourism changes the way they think about their work.
- Participation in educational tourism enhances their communication and teaching skills in and beyond the classroom.
- Participation in educational tourism enhances their research both directly and indirectly through securing funds, accessing unique or important sites, and engaging with a learning community.

Evidence from Educational Tourism Providers Indicates that:

- Participation by academics is highly valued.
- Participation by academics can occur in a variety of ways, not just leading tours.
- Cutting edge knowledge content created by academics creates a marketable educational tour product.

Evidence from Educational Tourism Clients Indicates that:

- Group learning is preferred over independent learning.
- History, cultural heritage, and natural landscapes were the most highly valued content of educational tours.
- Meaningful contact with the local communities is a highly valued experience in educational tours.
- Clients rate prior educational materials for their research highly and like to research their trip in advance.
- Maps and handbooks are the educational aids most highly valued by all respondents, before, during and after the tour.
- Novels and informal meetings are also highly valued as post tour educational aids.

Background

In July 2007 Associate Professor Susan Broomhall, Mr. Tim Pitman, and Dr. Ela Majocha from The University of Western Australia (UWA), funded by a grant from the Australian Learning and Teaching Council (ALTC) commenced a study into educational tourism in Australia: "Articulating Lifelong Learning in Tourism: Dialogue between humanities scholars and travel providers". The aims of the study were to:

- Improve communication between scholars and the tourism sector, with a particular focus on the adult educational tourism market and Arts and Humanities scholars;
- Support the development of educational tourism as a facilitator of lifelong learning;
- Equip scholars with the skills necessary to contribute to educational tourism; and
- Improve the learning experience of tour participants on educational tours.

The project commenced in July 2007 and will be completed in June 2009. A full project time line is available at. This interim report details the analysis of literature, interviews, and on line surveys. It is disseminated in its current form for feedback from academic stakeholders. Data used in this analysis come only from publicly available documentation, and from interview subjects and survey respondents who have given express permission to have their data circulated to this readership.

This consultation discussion paper is a work in progress, and feedback received will shape the final report to be submitted to the ALTC and made available for public release. Please do not cite publicly from this document. A final report will be made available to all stakeholders at the end of the project.

Support for this report has been provided by the Australian Learning and Teaching Council Ltd, an initiative of the Australian Government Department of Education, Employment and Work place Relations. The views expressed in this report do not necessarily reflect the views of the Australian Learning and Teaching Council. The project team gratefully acknowledges the participation of the following organisations:

- Academy Travel,
- Alumni Travel,
- Australians Studying Abroad,
- Centre for Continuing Education, University of Sydney,
- Odyssey Travel,
- Renaissance Tours,
- UWA Extension.

Data Collection Methods

Educational Tour Provider Literature

Qualitative and quantitative content analysis was conducted on a range of publicly accessible forms of documentation that is produced by educational tour companies. These texts included website material, advertising flyers and brochures, specific tour itineraries, and detailed tour handbooks. This literature was collected during late 2007 and early 2008.

Online Surveys

Responses for this aspect of the study were collected via an online survey. Two surveys were conducted. The "client survey" collected data from individuals who identified themselves as having had previous experience of educational tours as well as from those who had not. These individuals were approached via an email invitation to a combination of existing company client records, from the UWA Extension database, and from an open invitation on the travel/place website.

Because of the last category, it was not possible to determine the total number of people who were contacted. A total of 612 participants and potential participants completed this survey, of which 465 agreed to share their responses with educational tourism providers. A second survey was constructed for academic scholars in the Arts and Humanities fields in Australian universities. 1552 academics were invited by email to complete the survey. 228 completed the survey, and 183 agreed to share their responses with educational tourism providers. Responses to all questions were optional, in an effort to encourage people to complete the survey. This explains the varying sample sizes across the questions.

Interview Data

Six Australian educational tour providers were approached for interviews. Personnel from five companies agreed to recorded interviews. Detailed interviews were conducted, including company directors, tour program developers, tour leaders, tour managers and trainers, operations managers, marketing and sales staff. A range of academic scholars, currently employed in Australian universities, were also interviewed in depth. Some had extensive experience as tour leaders, program designers or course material designers, while others had experience of organising study tours and volunteer tourism for university students. Finally, some academic scholars were interviewed as interested future leaders.

Work place Observation

The project team visited the offices of all six companies and observed working practices and structures. Project researchers also observed tour leader training and discussed the research themes with prospective and current tour leaders.

Defining Educational Tourism

Clarifying academic, provider and client understanding of what educational tourism is and can be, was a fundamental starting point for the project, as well as a springboard to the team's other research questions. The idea that learning occurs in non formal environments, such as travel, is not new. Putting aside discussions in Herodotus, or the role of the Grand Tour in eighteenth and nineteenth century Europe, one can look at seminal discussions of the role of education that played out in the 1960s and 1970s. Global education lobby organisations such as UNESCO and the OECD observed that education should be dispensed through a multiplicity of means; what was important was not the path that an individual had followed, but what learning had occurred as a consequence.

The general increase in leisure time since the Second World War, plus the increase in disposable income and relative decrease in the cost of travel has given many more people the opportunity to engage in "intellectual improvement". With a widening in people's interests and appreciation of cultural values, many individuals have come to look upon vacations as a means of developing these interests (ibid). Tourism is, arguably, one of the few contemporary sites outside of the education industry where explicitly designated, non vocational learning about other times, places, and peoples takes place.

The 1980s witnessed the appearance of new tourism designs that both recognised tourism's negative impacts and imagined a more positive role for tourism. These new designs include ecotourism, ethnic tourism, nature tourism and adventure travel. The informal learning that occurs in these environments can often be translated back into a formal curriculum. Sesow and Wunder (1995) have explored how teachers have been able to use their travel experiences to enhance their students' learning.

Much of the discussion has centred on theories of experiential learning, such as those expounded by Kolb (1984) and Mezirow (1990, 1991). Guy, Curtis and Crofts (1990) explored the factors influencing the rate and degree of environmental learning of first time visitors to an international destination. The relative contributions of direct experience and direct and indirect sources of information were examined. Their empirical study concluded that the immersive experience of travel was the primary correlate of learning in terms of scope, accuracy, and detail. Similarly, Schmeink and Thurston (2007) found that travel experiences enhanced the ability of children with spatial cognition.

However the power imbalance inherent in many tourist/local interactions means that usually it falls to the traveller to choose who to interact with, where to go, and what to consume. Consequently, the validity of what is learnt is always contestable. Yet there is evidence that learning and benefit can occur in both directions. For example, the almost accidental development of tourism in the Longsheng county of Guangxi, China, has resulted in the revival of previously vanishing aspects of local culture and the strengthening of community education programs for the local community. Much of the analytical interest in educational tourism to date, particularly in the form of mature age tours, has come from practitioners and the market. The most significant in depth studies of the field stem from research commissioned by companies themselves about their client markets and their learning needs, as well as influential intellectual investigations into their ontology conducted by company personnel. Although a relatively under researched scholarly field, establishing a theoretical framework for touristic learning could assist in the development of products that better fulfil both consumers' needs and providers' objectives and perhaps illuminate our understanding of forms of learning which are more incidental. Beyond this, a greater understanding of touristic learning may also provide new insight on why people travel at all.

Academic research into educational tourism, however, has been slow to emerge. A recent collection of scholarly papers in contemporary niche tourism does not include adult educational tourism. This may be because it requires synthesis of two areas of scholarship: education and tourism. Scholars are increasingly observing that education facilitates mobility whilst learning has become an increasingly important part of the tourist experience. Using broad definitions, their work has allowed for the analysis of people not usually classified as tourists travelling to seek an educational experience.

For example, Cooper and Latham (1988) consider schoolchildren visiting a museum to be potential educational tourists. Cushner (2004) considers the "travelling teacher" to be the master of experiential learning, by using his or her travelling experiences (as well as encouraging this intrepidness in her or his students) as the ideal way of acquiring multicultural skills. In fact, anyone combining travel with their normal duties (soldiers, diplomats, spies, journalists, politicians) could be said to be undertaking educational travel. Ritchie has argued, "the concept of travel for education and learning is a broad and complicated area, which explains why tourism academics and industry have to date largely ignored this field."

As such, definitional issues dog the field. Hecht, Starosielski and Dara Abrams (2007) use the term "information centric" tourism to describe a range of touristic experiences that are motivated by a desire or need to learn. This includes "alternative" tourism: a touristic activity that attempts to negate negative aspects whilst retaining the positive ones; "heritage" or "cultural" tourism; "literary" tourism or "eco tourism". This project analysed provider literature and websites to assess the use and meanings of the term in current Australian practice. Surveys canvassed the perceptions of a broad range of potential clients and academics. Finally, our more detailed follow up interviews directly posed the question of defining this term to educational tour directors and employees, and to the academics with whom they worked.

Educational Tourism and Learning

The Australian tourism sector that identifies itself as providing educational tourism offers many kinds of educational experiences through travel, from a broad range of mature age study tours and programs, to participation in academic research programs such as archaeological digs and ecological fieldwork, for credit on site university units, school group tours, and professional development tours. Provider literature identified learning or enquiry as a key differentiating point of its niche in the tourism market: from the passive "audience interested in travelling to learn", to the more dynamic "enquiring minds" which focus on "stimulating … the active, inquisitive traveller". Companies' advertising material promoted the notion of an in depth engagement with other cultures through the opportunities they provide to gain contextualised knowledge as well as a deeper (often longer) appreciation of particular sites. One company proposed a quote that summarised its target audience identity: "I want to have time to absorb the environment and to learn something about what I'm seeing."

Similarly, learning was unmistakably the dominant outcome defined by survey respondents who returned 609 responses to the question "What does the term 'educational tourism' mean to you?" The responses ranged from the succinct to the expansive: A holiday with a strong learning component.

Travelling so as to learn more about a place, culture, activity, period of history, rather than just have fun or relax. It can be guided by people &/or books &/or lectures etc, before, during & after the actual travel. It is primarily for personal pleasure rather than formal education, though that could be a component in some tours. Ideally it demonstrates great respect for the people who live in the place & their environment eg by them owning the tour company, being specialist guides etc. It involves a relationship, not just looking at people.

The concept of learning appeared in more than 83% of the definitions. For example: Travelling with the aim of learning rather than just having fun alone. Seventeen definitions identified all tourism, indeed travel in general, as being educational: I guess that all tourism has something of an educational dimension to it.

Visiting other 'places' either physically or virtually where you will encounter 'different' perspectives, experiences, cultures, countries and projects for the purposes of learning and reflection.

The definitions expressed three key ideas about the form of learning in educational tourism:

1. It is intentional (e.g. "Taking a trip specifically to broaden my horizons or enhance my knowledge."; "Travel with a purpose; an enriched travel experience that provides food for your brain"
2. It is experiential (e.g. use of word/phrases such as included "immersion", "hands on", "vivid" and "evidence", "engaging with ideas in their original context" and "being exposed to politics, society and economy")
3. It is structured. (e.g. "It is the combination of travel with a structured educational program." "Going overseas to learn something in a structured way."

These three elements were also highlighted in definitions provided in interviews. One director saw his company's focus as " travel experience through learning for fun." Academics defined the provision of an explicit structure to pursue learning as the significant feature of educational tourism. One academic tour leader expressed it as: "Tourism, or travel which is structured, has a theme to pursue and requires some background knowledge of the sites being visited and some attempt to analyse on the spot." Another highlighted "the desire to acquire information about that place and that information can be on, you know, I think anything to do with architectural history, art, it can be broader history. It can be to do with laying out of gardens, it can be cookery, it can be all sorts of things. It's the sense of information." One experienced female academic leader offered: "education tourism is for those people who want to take it seriously, who want to learn from it, rather than those who just want to come along for a holiday." Statements such as these emphasised the intent required by clients to learn on such tours as an important definitional feature of educational tours.

However, a marketing manager of an educational tourism company highlighted one of the challenges of marketing this form of tourism as learning: "From the client's perspective you have to be careful how you approach educational tourism because some people think that they're not smart enough." Indeed, experienced tour leaders recognised that clients wanted different types and quantities of information, as one male academic leader observed: "they all want to learn … but there's a certain amount that they want to learn".

Another reflected: "I don't know how serious some of these people are, they like to think that they are interested in educational tours, they're interested to a degree." Others emphasised the importance of the traveller identity that participation in such a tour might convey for clients. One academic tour leader surveyed for this study considered that: people [who] go on an educational tour want to see themselves differently from normal tourists. In fact they may not be that different, you're still travelling on buses, you're still staying in quite fancy hotels and so on. It's not that different from all the other tourists but they want to see themselves as there for a different purpose. And they, I think, have a genuine interest in engagement with the local culture.

Educational Tours and Personal Development

For most survey respondents, educational tourism suggested the idea of an intentional, structured, *in situ* learning experience. Overwhelmingly, both academic and client respondents' definitions pointed to the need for a conscious or deliberate learning component as part of this form of travel. So how was learning described in company literature? As seen above, explicit references to provision of an educational component, in depth information, cultural contact, and mental stimulation were central to the marketing strategies of educational tour organisations.

Several companies indicated that their tours could be claimed as professional development or used for academic credit, however the generally accessible educational tours are typically designed for the satisfaction of individuals rather than professional or scholarly requirements.

"Experience", "explore", "discover" were the key descriptors of the educational experience within company literature. "Learning" was not commonly used and was often replaced by less directed (and less quantifiable) verbs such as "enquiring".

In general, the learning described was implicitly about personal development rather than testable information. Companies emphasised that no specific academic qualifications were necessary to participate in a tour – rather a willingness to explore another culture in detail. Attitude rather than qualifications was thus a key requirement for clients. The degree of knowledge attainment was up to the individual, with phrases such as "broadening your knowledge" conveying learning that was measurable only at the level of each participant.

Educational tours contributed to a participant's personal and intellectual lifelong learning. Because of the individual nature of the learning, and the need to avoid quantifiable knowledge outcomes that cannot be guaranteed for each participant, there was in general no attempt to provide specific learning outcomes for an individual tour.

The humanistic perspective of lifelong learning contends that learning throughout life, and via varied fora, is a means by which individuals develop personally and socially. Lifelong learning, travel and personal development are linked by the acknowledgement that the experientially based, informal learning that can occur in touristic events can be beneficial in these terms. At the level of the individual tourist, the primary goals of a leisure trip are likely to be experiential. Lifelong learning via tourism is becoming increasingly important to many individuals:

> *But it is not only older people who are going on tours and overseas holidays—it is people of all ages who travel abroad for holidays and not all just seek the sun and the sand, many do go to places of historical and cultural interest and seek to understand more of this cultural heritage. But it is not only a matter of understanding but preserving this heritage that is important and as concern for the planet grows, so this role becomes more important. Tour guides and guides to sites of such interest and importance are playing a significant liberal adult educational role.*

Events experienced whilst on a leisure trip can not only cause individuals to change their perception about the country being visited but also the way in which they view their own country. Some forms of tourism place a specific emphasis on lifelong learning as a focus of their activities. Moscardo (1996) explores the idea of the "mindful" tourist and argues that their experiences with heritage tourism allow them a greater understanding of the wider environment. Thacheen and Lauzon refer to learning tours as "organized conversations" in which an individual's experiences can change his (sic) life as well as those around him. Elderhostel, an American tourism provider to the over 55s ("baby boomers"), has conducted research on learning habits of the over 55 age group. The research concluded that "a sustained commitment to learning" was seen as a way of achieving successful aging by the baby boomers. Furthermore, the learning combined "blending intellectual stimulation, social engagement, physical activity, and creative expression". Participation in an educational tour meets at least the first three of the four criteria of lifelong learning for some seniors.

Australian tour company personnel interviewed for this project saw explicit learning objectives as off putting to clientele who might be of different educational levels and experience. These were also perceived to be hallmarks of degree or university study. With educational tours, they insisted, learning must be progressed in an enjoyable way.

The director of one educational tour company described the learning that they provide as "what we're about is continuing education, lifelong learning. So it's about learning for fun without examinations attached." As one tour designer articulated for her company: We do think of them as educational experiences because they do come away from it having learnt something and having very special experiences that I think helped aid their learning and ... the sort of experiences that we provide really enhance their whole travel experience.

Educational Tourism and Expertise

Explicit academic connections matter to educational tour company marketing. Provider literature, such as tour programs and brochures, make clear the academic qualifications of its personnel. The previous teaching appointments at secondary and tertiary level of employees, from directors and office staff to tour leaders, were typically provided in website and brochure literature. Previous tours led by the staff members were commonly noted as a form of recognition of prior experience in this domain. The use of tertiary scholars as leaders was frequently noted in addition to other forms of expertise (although how this would be identified was unspecified): "led by academics or experts in the focus of the tour." Companies defined their tourism therefore as one engaged with academic or other expertise.

Most definitions offered by clients and academics in the survey did not include an aspect of the facilitator, guide or leader of the learning experience, but where the leader was mentioned, they were most commonly described as being an "expert":

The opportunity to learn more about areas and places through visits accompanied by expert guides.

Importantly, one marketing manager in an educational tourism company saw the involvement of academics and experts as crucial in the distinction of their company from other tourism providers: "we believe educational tourism is having group leaders that know more about the place and can put it into a sense of its era and the perspective of where it's come from." One experienced male tour leader reflected that it was the careful structure, unique locations, as well as the expertise of the leader expertise that attracted clients: "because you have worked there for 35 years and also because you are a professional'. He reflected on feedback from tour participants that indicated that: they want to be informed by someone that they think they trust knows the material. And I think that's the reason they look at them and say okay, this person's worked there that long, they lecture at this university so we can rely upon what they say.

Educational Tourism or Travel

Educational tourism providers did not generally refer to their activities as tours and the participants as tourists. The preferred terminology includes travel, travellers and programs. The tourist traveller dichotomy goes back at least to the end of the eighteenth century and first quarter of the nineteenth century, when travel both domestic and foreign gained popularity. Previously, the experience of travel by young aristocrats in the seventeenth and eighteenth centuries was described as "tour" derived from the Grand Tour, and those who participated were called "tourists". With the emergence of a broader section of the population able to participate in tourism, the nineteenth century saw vigorous debate on the subject of the true "Traveller" as opposed to the "Vulgar Tourist".

While the words "tourism" and "travel" are used by some scholars interchangeably, for others they are quite distinct. Russians use the same word (tourist) to describe both the broad and the narrow: a tourist can be either a traveller for pleasure, enlightenment or excitement, or simply anyone who travels, for a purpose, using their own physical powers.

Similarly, in his examination of sustainable tourism in Nepal, Zurick (1992) uses the terms "adventure travel" and "adventure tourism" interchangeably. Yet for Daniel Boorstin tourists are a particular – and inferior – type of traveller, who have shifted their gaze from authentic travel to unauthentic tourism.

> Most of us aren't travellers at all – we're tourists, vulnerable to the process of commodification as the places we visit. A homogenous group of dopey beasts, who take cattle class flights at 3am, organise stag nights in Prague, and demand egg and chips and a beer whose name we can easily pronounce on a sunny beach in Spain. The smaller the world gets, the more we seem to want it to be as much like home as possible.

Gorusch (2003) suggests that tourism often implies a controlled experience driven by a hidden agenda and uses by way of example the promotion of domestic tourism in post war Russia to advance the Stalinist regime's own xenophobic interpretation of world events. Others link definitions to the behaviour of the individual: whereas the act of taking a photograph is likely to signify a tourist, that of writing is more often associated with travellers, perhaps due to it being more commonly linked to professional activities such as journalism. Consequently the terms travel and tourism can be synonymous for some scholars and conflicting for others. This is in part a consequence of definitions being driven from both the demand side (consumer) and supply side (industry) of tourism. Whilst some definitions describe those with whom the industry wishes to engage, others reveal how individuals wish to perceive themselves. Researchers themselves often construct definitions of tourism in order to define their own, specific subject of enquiry.

It is notable that a significant number of both academic scholars and education tour company practitioners appeared to display some aversion to use of the word "tourism". Feifer, succinctly observes that "no one wants to be called a tourist". Generally within the travel provider literature terms such as "travel," "journey" or "adventure" were preferred – seemingly, as a broader, more intellectual and less explicitly commercial definition of their practices. One brochure used a quote from a participant: "The program contained a good mix of information and activities meaning that I felt like a traveller rather than a tourist." In particular, in defining the identity of a typical company client, tour provider literature highlighted the distinction between travel (what they do) and tourism (what something else unspecified – perhaps mass tourism does). This was achieved by the choice of adjectives to describe tour principles and clients, by implication indicating what it was not. Thus, there was the perception that something was wrong with being a tourist.

The description of tours emphasised the provision of more detailed information and cultural engagement than was possible in "mass tourism". Clients should therefore have the desire to have "greater involvement in another culture, than merely observing it from a coach window" and were "those who want more out of travel than simply a catalogue of places." Features included "extended stays" to "get to know the places you visit". Mass tourism was portrayed either as the absent other against which comparisons were made, or through phrases which critiqued other modes of touristic engagement: spend your time actually looking at the things you've travelled to see, rather than straining to listen to a local tour guide. Through the background talks you'll also build up a coherent understanding of the country you're visiting, not just a fragmented set of facts.

Educational tourism, these brochures claimed, was for "those who want to move beyond mass tourism" or "beyond the worn tourist trails." The experience that these tours provided was perceived to be "unique and privileged" and might sometimes involve "some unusual sectors" as well as "all the classic travel experiences".

This notion of a deeper and intentional effort to form a richer or deeper understanding of a place or culture echoed survey responses. One marketing manager explained: "while we offer similar…destinations, we tend to offer a more comprehensive approach to the history and the sense of place". An employee in one educational tour company described his company's niche learning approach in the following terms: "it gives tourists an opportunity to step outside the regular old box of a tourism experience and gives them an insight into educational aspects and certainly would... develop knowledge and satisfaction of visiting a destination instead of just seeing the elementary sights and sounds."

Moreover, the organised tour structure could itself be advantageous, as a content developer at one company identified: "we offer very good value for money because the experience that people are paying for is something quite unique, and something they most certainly couldn't achieve on their own." For the following phases of the research, we elected to keep the term "educational tourism" in order to make the direct connection to the format of the educational experience we were most commonly analysing in this study – both in the sense that it concerns the organised tour, and to reflect the fact that these are commercial operations. Our interviews with academic scholars and educational tour company representatives suggested diverse views both within and between these groups about the meaning of this term and its coverage of 'paid for' tourism practices in Australia.

Indeed, within the interview context, directors of companies referred more commonly to intellectualised notions of travel as mind broadening, eschewing the explicit commercial dimensions of their company practice. Moreover, one director of a not for profit company had consciously rejected the terminology of "a tour" for the following rationale: "we run programs, educational programs, basically, instead of tours. It's to differentiate a little bit what we do from what the commercial world does". The use of participant feedback statements as above which distinguished between travel and tourism served to reinforce a difference in these modes of practice.

When asked the same question, some scholars perceived the use of the term "tourism" to be problematic or conceptually incompatible with education. In the survey, several respondents – all academic provided negative definitions of educational tourism, centring either the quality of the learning experience or a belief that tourism itself was negative: Travel can be educational, but tourism per se is not educational Sounds a bit sus. The exploitation by the tourist industry of peoples better instincts toward the planet. A marketing ploy When asked about their engagement with educational tourism, some scholars explained their disinterest in terms of perceived exploitation of the tourist mode:

The idea of "tourism" has negative connotations for me; it signifies to me a type of intrusion. I realise that some places rely upon tourism economically, but I feel suspicious about claims made about the type of learning that can occur as a tourist. Because I don't think mediated encounters with living people or places that are pre defined as "other" will conduct to those peoples' or places' welfare. This perception has been noted in scholarly literature. Werry (2008, 14), for example, refers to the "paradox of tourism": The more cultural capital the travel consumer wields and accrues (through tourism), and the deeper her belief in travel's potential to inform and transform, the more deep seated her prejudice against tourism as a "bad cultural object" is likely to be. For such consumers, tourism is a byword for superficiality, in authenticity, wilful ignorance, political irresponsibility, exploitation, and cultural prostitution.

In interviews, while one academic linked educational tourism to the tradition of the Grand Tour, a number of other academic responses saw tourism as a limited or limiting term. As one male academic and tour leader argued: "by using the word tourism, you're limiting yourself to one part of the phenomenon. If you use the word "educational travel", you would be widening that." As another explained: "there is also, almost a contradiction in terms: educational tourism, isn't there? Because tourism often necessitates a sort of blinkered view of the world, what I call cocooned existence we've all seen tourist buses with people who seek to stay within their comfort zone... You're in a bus, you're in a nice hotel, you don't have to learn the language." Yet the same academic concluded his response by reconciling the possibilities of learning within a commodified genre: "I think educational tourism, if it's to be packaged as a commodity, is tourism with a particular focus and the focus is to engage with aspects of the place where you are touring. In other words, it's beyond looking."

Educational Tourism Knowledge

To examine educational tourism learning further, survey respondents were presented with a series of statements concerning factors contributing to knowledge acquisition and were asked to indicate the degree to which they did, or did not, agree with the statements. Some of the statements were contradictory and others similar, to allow triangulation and cross checking of answers. Respondents scored the statements from 0 to 5: with 0 meaning they thought the statement not applicable, 1 meaning they disagreed strongly and 5 meaning they agreed strongly. Clients were asked to think about themselves, as an educational tourist, when considering the statements. Academics, however, were asked to respond as educators. Some statements were unique either to academic or client surveys.

A series of statements tested the importance of elements such as repetition, novelty and reinforcement in the learning involved in educational tourism. New experiences (which could be either a new subject matter or destination) were clearly preferred by tour clients, over reinforcement of destinations or content with which they were already familiar. Female clients displayed a stronger preference for new experiences than males. Academics appeared ambivalent as to whether new experiences or repetitive ones were superior in terms of learning.

Respondents were also asked what sort of experiences and knowledge were important in an educational tourism experience. The answers reveal responses to two different aspects of the question: the kinds of experiences and the type of knowledge desired. Experiencing a different culture was seen by some as a means of understanding, or re examining their own or themselves:

> *Travel that extends me physically and mentally so that I learn both about myself and the area of travel. Some respondents were careful to express the difference between overt, touristic cultural experiences and engagement with the daily life of the country being visited: For me, educational tourism could hold two meanings: Tourism while discovering the Culture Tourism while discovering the culture (living with people from one specific culture, sharing their table, etc) Understanding contexts was seen to be the type of knowledge to make sense of that. In terms of concrete knowledge genres, history and cultural heritage were the preferred elements of an educational tour. Understanding natural landscapes also rated highly.*

It enriches tourism by providing travellers with a greater appreciation for the histories of the locations that they visit. These histories can bring to life otherwise overlooked aspects of a location, and create connections that enrich the experience of visiting a place When I travel, I always want to learn more about the place I am in and the way that present is informed by the past. 3.7 Conclusions Although academics tended to hold more diverse ideas of what educational tourism could be than did clients, a number of key findings were apparent between the groups:

- The primary outcome of the educational tourism experience is learning and furthermore, that the learning is intentional.
- Tour operators contend that they will provide particular knowledge, expertise or experience so as to distinguish their product within the broader tourism sector.

- "Tour" and "tourism" appear problematic terms because they can convey mixed messages to both tour clients and academics.
- "Travel" is frequently substituted to connote both the exploration of physical places and the personal development journey.

Engaging with Educational Tourism

In what ways do academics currently engage with this form of education to communicate with new audiences and to develop their knowledge? Why do they do so? How does it challenge them intellectually as teachers and researchers?

Approximately half the academic scholars surveyed (92 out of 183) had previously participated in some form of educational tourism, according to their own definition of the term. Almost half of these had participated as either a guest lecturer or tour leader. A sizeable proportion had also presented information sessions, or authored educational tourism materials.

Other forms of educational tourism experiences included:

- Acting as an impromptu tour leader for visiting family, friend, students or colleagues.
- Program coordinator.
- Using travel to further one's own teaching and research.
- Lecturer in a course with tourism related material.
- Giving adult courses.
- Lecturing on study (credit) tours.
- As a participant themselves.

Embedded Knowledge Experts

A well qualified tour leader was clearly an important part of educational tour marketing. Travel company literature emphasised the care and consideration of tour groups in "sourcing" an appropriately trained program leader. But what does qualified and trained mean in this context? Content expertise or knowledge was the most commonly discussed feature of tour leaders.

They were "informed", "experts", and "specialists" with "extensive knowledge". As noted above, the academic qualifications of tour leaders were frequently highlighted in company literature and their academic titles commonly used. Leaders' current or present positions within higher education institutions were noted, as well as other work roles relevant to the tour content.

Surveyed academics and clients were asked "When taking part in educational tourism, what are the qualities that would make a person a good tour leader?" There were 427 free form responses to this question. Knowledge was clearly the most sought after quality of a tour leader (included by two out of every three respondents). However, most respondents did not expand upon their definition of knowledge skills. Close examination of the responses revealed that underlying the vast majority of definitions was the assumption that the tour leader will be appropriately qualified to speak on the subject matter of the tour:

Friendly, welcoming, I would take for granted that they would be qualified Where survey respondents did clarify what qualified might mean, most sought experiential knowledge in a tour leader, defining it as knowledge stemming from first hand experiences of the tour content, including local integration, language skills and personal connections.

Interviews with educational tour personnel were consistent in their agreement that the involvement of knowledge experts was a key feature of their ethos, and marketing edge. Academic qualifications were widely considered to signal knowledge expertise (although not exclusively). Experiential knowledge of a location was also highly valued, matching the views of survey respondents above. A manager at one educational tour company defined a good leader as having "an expertise either in a particular country they are going to, they will know the local language, they can speak the local language, they've had either study of that particular country or lived in that country so it's not just someone who is a tour expert as such. They're someone with far higher qualifications." The director of one educational tour company did connect expertise to academic recognition: "Our tour leader for our tours has to be an expert in his or her field so they must bring with them an educational standard of some level. ... they have to be an expert in that field, recognised expert, not a self proclaimed expert."

In addition to the leader, tour companies provided a suite of other knowledge experts such as "local guides", "local lecturers" or "on site experts", who were responsible for "enhancing" the tour experience. Tour literature suggested that these personnel were "authoritative" typically because they either provided scholarly knowledge or possessed unique professional expertise. This gave participants a particular, in depth or unusual insight into the locality because of the guide's access to off limit or off the beaten track sites, or the perspective of a well informed local on the tour's theme. One leader saw the inclusion of local experts as an important way in which educational tourism could foster local communities and knowledge development: when it actually comes to walking around and looking at things, whether it's inside an art gallery or whether it's on site, whatever it might be, … the main interpretation automatically is left to the local person. It's part of their employment, it's obviously a very good thing for them to develop those skills and they bring, I would have to be honest, not just more detailed knowledge of their local political and social context, they also may visit a site a hundred times and I may have only visited it four times and so they may know more recent excavation, more interpretative history. And it's their right to talk about their country of course. But what I will do, will be to add some comments of what we're looking at, with their permission of course and we try and do it in a very friendly way.

Leaders drew distinctions between their role and that of local experts in terms of the material and contexts they provided: The local guy, if we have one travelling with us, might talk about social, gender, political issues of the current day which are things which he or she would know in more detail than I would. Then I might talk a bit about the sites that we're visiting and their cultural impact. So I will try and do that every couple of days on the bus. … Certainly the interpretation of that I can bring, and hopefully it's appreciated, is by putting these things in a much wider cultural, political, historical context which you know which is, I would imagine, beneficial for people to enjoy hearing in that sort of way.

Academic engagement as knowledge experts on tour was perceived to add value not just by tour providers and their clients, but also by scholars. One male academic reflected: I think you could say therefore there's an onus upon us to put that back... into the community. But I think there's a lot of people in the community who are really interested in this so it's not like oh well, we have to do this. I think there are people out there, lots of people, who are interested in all sorts of things… I think it's enjoyable.

Moreover, by providing his expertise on tour, one academic leader felt: "I'm able to pursue what I'd say is my personal interest which is the same as my professional." Participation in educational tourism assisted scholars' own understanding of their teaching strategies and research. One male academic reflected: "not all that I do personally in my research leads into my teaching... but a lot of it does". More than one academic explained their involvement in terms of advancing their own research agenda through the opportunity to explore new or unique destinations, or to revisit sites of interest. Practically speaking, involvement with a tour company had enabled some scholars to develop their research interests with the funds the company provided. One academic indicated that the company had donated funds to his team's ongoing excavation. One company involved in this study is in fact a not for profit organisation, comprised of 25 members universities and colleges, part of whose income is allocated to support university based research programs.

Learning Facilitators

Enthusiasm was another quality of note for leaders. They had "passion" for their subject and "love" for the places to be visited; indeed these were "their favourite places". They possessed "skills in communicating this knowledge to an interested audience". This signified an important facet of educational tourism as it was marketed by companies: that the learning should be made both accessible and fun.

It was not surprising therefore that companies also highlighted the people skills of their leaders. They were "caring" and "willing to adapt to the pace of the group". Leaders' sensitivity to the diversity of knowledge and experience of tour participants could be emphasised in the lifelong learning market of educational tourism. This was reflected in the personal qualities desirous in a tour leader rated in the survey: A good sense of humour… very perceptive so they can read the mood of the group and understand what is required for that particular session.

Knowledge was considered by survey respondents not as a quality, but as a non negotiable pre requisite for a tour leader. No company staff member referred to knowledge expertise independent of communication and social skills. One director summarised the best tour leaders as: "Excellent qualifications, be good at their tour leader experience and social coordinator." Indeed, communication rated as the most valued personal skill in a tour leader, across all respondents: Good at communication i.e. also in eye contact and rapport with people. They don't sound like they are bored and have said the thing a 1000 times, but genuinely interested in what they do, teach.

This passion to communicate knowledge defined the excellent tour leader, as the director of one educational tour company observed: "somebody who is deeply involved, intimately involved with the country or the theme of a particular tour, who can share that enthusiasm with others but who also has an empathy for travellers who may not be experienced". These qualities marked those who were "the best in their field," an employee of one company commented: "the knowledge of their subject, their confidence in their subject... They have to be able to impart the knowledge to their clients in a way that people are going to appreciate while they're away". One male academic reflected: "For teaching I would say because it broadens your communication skills."

To cater for the range of skills required in tour leader, some companies have created a division between an organiser/manager role and the accompanying expert. This is in addition to the on site guides who might also be provided. As one designer put it: "the tour manager is really somebody who assists with the tour arrangements. The tour leader is responsible for the educational and the social aspects of the tour really. ...what we've done is divided the expectation and the needs of tour members." However it is notable that the social aspects of group cohesion and dynamics (if not practical arrangements) were seen as the role of the intellectual expert. One academic leader described his input as leader on a photography tour in the following terms:" I was there as a kind of creative mentor, I suppose, that is the term that I like to use. And that worked very well."

Leaders were defined as flexible thinkers. When asked to consider how they delivered content on tours, leaders' responses consistently highlighted the key characteristic as adaptability: "we are flexible in that we will ask people on the group that we take at the moment, what are you interested in? What would you like us to talk about? We have got a series of topics that we think you should get information on, but if you have particular components, let us know." Leaders commonly spoke of the need to be sensitive to the different ways and environment in which learning occurred: "the experience of good teaching is to be mindful of what people are bringing to the classroom and to make sure that in the discourse we have some are not being alienated by only talking to others." The importance of observing the variety of learning styles and levels in a tour group was noted by one female academic leader: "several of them will be taking notes. And with some of them they will also come up to you later and ask for clarification of certain of the points that you've made." The opportunity to pose questions with the leader was highlighted by many leaders as a common feature of participant learning. One brochure, for example, quoted a participant: "I found the lectures on culture & history excellent & informative. Good to have opportunities to ask questions." This suggests that beyond the formal delivery of lectures, an important aspect of client learning takes place in informal settings. These may be places where the participants felt comfortable and supported, unafraid to ask questions, to verify their learning or to reflect upon the sites visited and their meanings.

In addition to the challenge of clients' differing levels of subject familiarity, learning styles, and abilities, catering to different degrees of interest in learning was a critical feature for most leaders. One described his method for responding to different learning styles and degrees of prior knowledge: "while we do start up with a generalised kind of thing, you know that not everyone will perhaps want to walk down that path of more detailed or more specific knowledge that's what those before departure or before evening meal sessions are for… equally of course as a tour leader you're available for discussions whenever people want. … what I will do is walk on the bus and talk and then sit with people." Another described his approach as follows: I prepare comprehensive notes for myself which I take and then you really play it by ear… If they're particularly interested sometimes we will have a meeting in the evening. If they initialise it. I don't organise that. If they say, "We'd like to learn more about this." I say, "Okay let's get together after dinner." As these examples suggest, tour leaders' skills include not just knowledge expertise but also critical social skills in detecting levels of engagement and responding appropriately to them.

Being "on site" was seen for many to provide distinct pedagogical insights, both for clients and for academic scholars as well. The delivery required and the value of being in place was articulated by one academic tour leader: "there is a different dynamic and you can draw on that shared experience without having to spell it out". Another observed that it was unlike classroom lectures because of the immediacy of the content: "depending on what we've seen that day, they may be more focused perhaps on what they've just seen. For instance … you know what XYZ looked like, you've just been down it, therefore you can visualise it. So there's a difference." A number highlighted overlap between their work in the institution and beyond. One academic observed that "A lot of what I do is taken straight out of what I do in lectures. And then a lot goes back in to the lectures afterwards." The variety of the teaching environments on a tour was a feature that attracted some leaders, as one academic explained: " always intriguing, trying to teach in different places, in different contexts, in different ways. I think teaching in universities is... well, it's the same, rather repetitive."

The influence that being in place has on the production of new knowledge cannot be underestimated, according to tour leaders. As one academic observed: "the impact of it there in person – stays in your memory very much better. You can see it in context, explain better how something got there, which really can't happen on a page in a book." A female tour leader reflected: "you take them to the monuments, then you go around the monuments with them, they can actually see it… They've got it in all it's glory so to speak and they can walk about. The significance of the "real" over visuals, as well as the ability to move through the spaces, to be active in them, not just passive." One academic explained: "doing it in situ, absolutely there are things that you can teach only when you are there. It's partly indescribable, just the sense of place… that you can't convey in the classroom. There's also an intensity to the teaching".

Academics were able to advance their own learning and research through tour locations: the company "can gain access – because of their contacts and reputation to sites that you wouldn't be able to see yourself." Another academic reflected that "they've given me access to opportunities I never would have had".

Beyond "being in place" however, academics observed important learning which clients experienced outside of site visits. "Most of the time you are there on the site and then in the evening there is a discussion, sometimes, over dinner. If someone wants to know something I'm happy to explain it to them". Others however utilised such informal times to promote reflection, much like a tutorial or workshop. One academic tour leader articulated his technique: everybody on that tour is going to have a different story, from just from the day's journey. And so over dinner at night I'd go round the table. I mean, I'd still run a constructed sort of workshop, if you like. … And then that becomes quite interesting because we've all seen the same things and yet they've all had different experiences of the same things. That's what leads to the creative discourse. A tour leader for one company used these sessions as an opportunity to extend learning and cater to those of different learning interests and levels: what I will do every second morning or every second evening is get our guide and say, "whoever wants to join me for half an hour straight after breakfast or half an hour before dinner will come and we'll talk through the progress of what we've doing. We'll talk through what we've seen, where we've been and where we're going, and that will enable me to cater to a more advanced interest if that's the requirement.

In such contexts, the leader acts as a facilitator of client learning, using the relationships built over the length of the tour. This also distinguished the role of the leader and of local guide who might deliver a one off lecture. Most leaders described their experiences and practices in ways which suggested a strong emphasis on tutorial type teaching, rather than as formal lectures.

The idea of creating a tour learning community is suggested through phrasing such as "sharing experiences with like minded travellers" which is commonly found in provider literature. A learning community can be defined as a group of people who share some values and beliefs, and are actively engaged in learning together from each other. Learning communities include concepts of membership ("belonging"), shared experiences and emotional connections. Much of the work on learning communities has focused on alternative teaching strategies for students, or professional. Three assumptions underlie the support for learning communities: that they will a) create a group that will work together b) increase intellectual interaction and c) enhance learning. More recently, the rise of the internet has seen the emergence of "virtual" learning communities. Whilst research has been conducted on learning communities using tourism to further their goals, educational tourism itself as a learning community appears to have been somewhat overlooked. In survey responses for this project, leaders and clients both identified the group experience as a valuable learning resource and rated group learning/travel experiences higher than individual experiences. A tour leader for one educational tour company described the advantages of the group learning environment: "that person is sharing all their excitement and enthusiasm and knowledge for what they're looking at. They're also sharing that experience with like minded enquirers". One male academic who ran tours for independent groups of travellers, friends and companies explained his motivation: "I enjoy the interaction with other people and it's really good when you have a group of people who share the same interests. You can sit around the hotel at drinks times and discuss what we've seen". Academics, as well as clients, have found the sense of learning together an enriching feature of their work in this domain. One female academic leader explained: I enjoy meeting the people and I certainly enjoy imparting the knowledge that I have to those people. And some of them are extremely interested, they will come up with questions, no doubt about it, so I enjoy that aspect of it… on the whole I enjoy it, I thoroughly enjoy it, I enjoy meeting them, being with them. Another male scholar, experienced in tour leading, reflected on distinctions between the insights gained on tours with mature learners and his undergraduate classroom teaching experiences: I think from my point of view that the more people you talk to about this you get lots of different perspectives from them and you learn. I think we learn from talking to them because we can go into a student classroom here, particularly if it's first or second level, you don't get any feedback. A female academic leader commented: "It's not only looking at the monuments yet again, seeing perhaps new monuments. That would help, but no, interaction with the people on the tour would enhance my understanding of my research."

Authors

Beyond participating as tour leaders, the project research has highlighted a range of other opportunities for academic input. Many do not require scholars to travel on, or lead, tours. Organising travel itineraries; identifying seminal historical moments, architectural features, geographic regions; writing travel literature; speaking at information sessions are also all educational tourism opportunities for engagement of the expertise of the academy. A significant facet of academic engagement with educational tourism occurs off tour, writing preparatory materials and designing tours. Tourist information has been shown to have an important influence on the choice of vacation destinations by travellers. Despite the advent of new technologies such as the internet, great quantities of money are still being assigned to the publication of more traditional texts, such as guidebooks (ibid).

There has been much scholarly research on the role of such publications in the decision making process of potential travellers. Robinson and Anderson (2002) explore the ways in which authors and their books can influence people's choice of destination and how they perceive them. However, research is scant concerning the role guidebooks play in education. Werry does however refer to travel literature as a "de facto teacher" of tourism's knowledges and ways of knowing. Botterill and Crompton (1996) have noted that how the tourist "vacates" their normal space and creates an understanding of the new, holidaying space is an area where intermediaries, such as tour guides and travel writers, can be important in enabling the traveller. This research is mirrored in our project's findings. Responses investigating educational aids highlighted the fact that the educational tourism experience was not confined to the actual travel component, but extended to encompass learning opportunities either side of the tour. There were significant opportunities for scholarly interactions in off site educational tour opportunities.

Clients were asked to rank in importance a series of statements regarding preparation for tours. The results indicated that prior information (such as handouts, books, other educational aids) was highly valued. Female clients showed a much stronger preference for preparing their learning. Survey participants were also asked to consider what types of educational aids they would find useful for learning on an educational tour, and the point at which they would be most useful (i.e. before, during or after the tour). Almost unanimously, maps were considered to be the most valuable educational aid, consistently ranking highly at all stages of the educational travel experience. Handbooks were almost as highly valued as maps pre and during tour. One leader reflected on how his group used their textual resources on tour: if we're walking around we have these available to us, people can jot notes down in that sort of way or above all when we meet in the evening we've got this shared resource to actually work with. So these take the place fairly obviously of visuals, overheads, things like that which we would use in the teaching classroom setting. So it does enable people to, I think, have a fairly good and comprehensive aid memoir for what's going on, a bit of resource which can actually be used in the field, in the hotel to enhance their knowledge.

Participant feedback was often used in company marketing to highlight the quality of materials provided to clients: I have just received … preparatory material, and wish to convey my pleasure at receiving such a beautifully presented package, full of clear, detailed and fascinating material. This package would have to rank as one of the best ever. Superb!

The inclusion of such a comment demonstrates that the educational tourism experience extends beyond the time of the tour itself. Within such materials, a participant might find more identifiable "Objectives of the Program" although these were noticeably broader and measured against one's own personal starting point in comparison to most university units: "At the conclusion of our program…. we will have developed: "a greater understanding" "an appreciation", "a sense of wonder", "a greater knowledge".

Apart from introductory information and details about the sites to be visited, such course handbooks often included a suggested reading list that may contain novels as well as scholarly textbooks. A manager at one educational tour company described the documentation prepared by their company:

The preparatory material is quite a large document which can be anything up to sort of 33 pages, and gives details on where they're going to be going to, it gives them the history of the places they're going to, and it gives them more detail on the places that they're going to visit….we also offer a reading and reference list and that's given to them as soon as they deposit on a program so that they can begin to read about the program… We encourage them in their welcome letter to go the library, use the resources at the library. A tour leader for one educational tour company described the materials he prepared for participants of his tours as: Good solid introductions to daily visits that we're doing in that way. Extensive bibliography which everyone gets of course a month or so before. But I think perhaps more importantly and as a very important teaching aid what all these books contain are maps which can be used as historical discussions points… Or they might include individual plans of buildings.

How such material is used was highly variable, as one male academic leader observed from his experience: "the people that come on these tours don't want to go overseas for three weeks and study in the way that we would think it. They don't really want to do much reading in the evening. They... a few of them will prepare themselves, the majority will not."

Another academic took a different (and unusual) approach to providing literature for the clients to use on tour however: "At the beginning we took the decision that the city was the text, and the handbook just accompanied that... but the internet has changed everything. There's just so much more that they can access now, wherever they are." Interestingly, the web appeared to play little part in post tour reflection according to respondents, although at least one academic interviewed had extended the educational experience both before and beyond the on site engagement with his group: "on my website I keep the reports from the tours and I've given detailed notes beforehand and I keep them on the site as well, so I think it makes a huge difference." A number of academic scholars interviewed had been asked to compose the content for tour handbooks. One academic described his motivation for writing such texts: "I thought it would be interesting, to see if I could... I came to the realisation not only that I could do it, but that it was quite interesting to write for a general audience." Asked what is involved in pitching to this audience, one academic responded: "I think you do have a duty to be interesting and to write reasonably clearly." How this has impacted academics' other scholarly writing was also explored.

As one male academic put it: I found it quite interesting. It made realise that this was something that I could do and that it's quite enjoyable doing it ... The point is: everything you do is a dialogue with an audience that is either there, or is a potential audience. And so many times the dialogue comes back to you unexpectedly, without you planning or even knowing it. You don't know who you're writing for, you never know who you're writing for. And I find that extraordinarily interesting, that you can get something out of the blue... So you're always learning new stuff out of the blue. And of course it feeds into your teaching.

Conclusions

Academic engagement with educational tourism has occurred in a variety of roles, both on and off site.

- The educational roles of a tour leader are distinct from those of local lecturers and guides.
- Social skills, as well as knowledge expertise, are vital in tour leaders because these enable leaders to identify levels and degrees of capacity and engagement in the clientele and to respond accordingly.

- Most leaders act as learning facilitators, teaching in a variety of formal and informal contexts on tours.
- Preparatory and post tour phases are important complementary opportunities for enhancing learning in educational tourism.

Related Work in Narrative Intelligence

In the narrative intelligence framework laid out by Mateas and Sengers (1999) and Mateas and Sengers (2003), the Minotour narrative generation system draws most heavily from the then-state-of-the-art (1999) body of work designed to support human narrative intelligence. Indeed, the key presumption in Minotour is that there is inherent value-increased cohesion, improved recall and comprehension, the ability to overcome certain cognitive obstacles, increased synergy with how tourism is experienced, closer alignment with geography education, etc.-in providing information to users in a form that is easier to interpret as a narrative than in the dominant manner in which Internet information is accessed.

In order to provide narrative support, however, we make a concrete assumption as to the definition of narrative, at least in the context of our system. This definition, outlined in section 4, is used to generate stories, thus placing our work also well within Mateas and Sengers' Storytelling Systems category of work, and within the story-centric sub-category.

While Minotour's feature base lies firmly in narrative support and Storytelling Systems, Mateas and Sengers' Interactive Fiction and Drama category also applies to Minotour. Users interact with Minotour in both spatial and non-spatial ways: they are only allowed to obtain tours beginning in their present spatial location and end destinations are chosen via the medium of the mobile device.

The Narrative Generation Algorithm

In order to understand Minotour's narrative generation algorithm-the computational methodology we use to generate tours such as that is necessary to first highlight some properties. In their review of narrative intelligence research, Mateas and Sengers (2003) note that, with narrative being such a rich and complex concept, it is critical for narrative intelligence scholars to be explicit about their approach. As an interdisciplinary team bridging the sciences, engineering and the humanities, our approach to narrative is based in narratology, a field of narrative theory developed from the analysis of literature, film and other media.

Much work that is adopted from this field draws from structuralist authors and their rigorous interpretation of underlying narrative structures. Structuralist approaches translate these underlying structures into sets of variables, codes, and functions that reside in the text. One of the earliest examples of this approach is Vladimir Propp's *Morphology of the Folktale* (1928), which delineated 8 basic character types and a series of possible functions that each character could enact. Structuralist theories assume that one can define narrative as a text that aligns to a certain set of rules, such as the depiction of characters, plot, and cause-effect relationships. The problem with adopting this model in narrative intelligence research is that these approaches often sidestep the psychological and spatial conditions that influence narrative experience.

We draw our narrative approach, rather, from recent research in narratology that is influenced by cognitive science, including the narrative theories of David Bordwell and Edward Branigan. These theories are grounded in the same rigorous interpretation of structures as Structuralism, but rather than defining "narrative" as the sum of these structures, they locate narrative as a perceptual activity.

Edward Branigan writes that narrative is a "perceptual activity that organizes data into a special pattern which represents and explains experience". It is this understanding of narrative that we use to develop our ideal narrative function.

According to Bordwell, a precondition for understanding a fiction film as narrative is the unity of the text as a formal system. He writes that, in the most formally unified films, "every element present has a specific set of functions, similarities and differences are determinable, the form develops logically, and no element is superfluous. In turn, the film's overall unity gives our experience a sense of completeness and fulfilment". Thus, for a reader or viewer to understand the narrative as unified, they must perceive the individual elements as interrelating and nothing must seem "out of place." As is also noted in this passage, a sense of development is also key to a sense of unity. Bordwell defines formal development as a progression moving from beginning through middle to end. Simply including unity and development, also termed "progression," will not designate a given text as a narrative. However, they are two of the most common narrative cues that elicit a narrative mode of organization. Bordwell delineates this narrative comprehension process as follows: cues are organized "to encourage the spectator to execute story construction activities. The film presents cues, patterns and gaps that shape the viewer's application of schemata and the testing of hypothesis".

Unity in the Ideal Narrative Function

However, as noted above, unity is a critical narrative cue. As such, unity must be an important characteristic of the ideal narrative function, the function against which all possible narratives between two 3D articles are evaluated. Of course, the most obvious way that we provide unity is by linking 3D article *a* to 3D article *b* through a series of other articles. Before the user reads the narrative, these articles were likely perceived as distinct entities; afterwards, they are inherently connected. But this form of unity is weak and only informs our ideal narrative function in the most basic way.

More significantly, we provide unity by highlighting the themes in the user's space. This approach to unity is informed by our educational tourism focus. A critical element of geography education is the highlighting of themes embedded in the geography of a region. In fact, a key element of regionalization – a backbone of the United States National Geography Standards – is being able to reduce the complexity of a diverse area through the construction of thematic regions.

While it might seem that incorporating a number of themes might disconnect the narrative, the presence of multiple themes can unify the narrative experience as a whole. Each theme serves to draw a conceptual link between two or more snippets. For example, in our sample narrative, issues about German freedom, unification, and community are directly referenced in the snippets about the "Brandenburg Gate," "Hans Modrow," "Strausbourg," and "Humbolt University of Berlin." The themes of German freedom, unity, and community thread together these snippets. On the other hand, the intersection of the academic institution with political and religious forces is present in the snippets from "Strausbourg," "Martin Luther," and "Humbolt University of Berlin."

The need to quantify the thematic requirement is the reason we chose in-links as the defining variable in the ideal narrative function. In the context of Wikipedia, in-links are a highly accurate proxy for generality. When an author working on one entry links to another entry, that author is essentially saying "this entry is important to my entry". Articles that are more important to more entries are more general articles.

For instance, in the German, the article for "Poker" has far more in-links than the article for the "1990 World Series of Poker". We make the assumption-proven to be mostly true experimentally-that more general articles have more thematic content. Given the in-links/generality/theme relationship and the ideal narrative function's focus on high in-links articles, the reason for the appearance of themes in our ideal narrative function becomes clear. It is important to note that we include in the narrative function a maximum number of in links that is less than the actual maximum number of in links. We found through experiments that articles with extremely high in-link totals are too broad to carry much interesting thematic significance. The most common example of excessive in-links are the articles about days of the year, i.e. the "October 5" article. In the English Wikipedia, this article has thousands of in-links, but has little to no thematic content.

Development in the Ideal Narrative Function

If we were just focused on theme, it would be ideal to find a set of articles with a high number of in-links (but not too high) and present these to the user. However, it is critical to the narrative foundation of our tours that the reader understands the snippets of the text as developing in a certain direction.

As was the case with unity, there is an obvious answer to the question of how our ideal narrative function incorporates development: each snippet is linked to the next snippet. However, just as with unity, the function also includes conceptually deeper models of development. We accomplish this by incorporating a *small* positive slope in the first two-thirds or so of the function. In this part of the function, each snippet becomes only slightly more general than the next.

As such, the reader gains a sense of movement toward generality. She can then question and form hypotheses about the broader themes of her space and how they will connect her start to her destination. This activity mirrors the experience of the traditional narrative reader.

In the traditional narrative text, conflict builds to a climax, followed by a resolution. In the context of our ideal narrative function, this conflict is manifested in the question "What does this snippet from this thematic article have to do with the specific space in which I am moving"? As such, before the user is returned from wiki-space to a 3D article, the broadest theme of that space – the climax – is revealed. Then, the movement from the broadest theme back to the concluding 3D article – the resolution – provides a sense of completeness and closure to the experience. In the case of our sample narrative, the climax occurs at the Martin Luther snippet. At this point, we expect that the user is maximally wondering what a highly broad article like "Martin Luther" has to do with the specific space in between the Brandenburg Gate and Unter den Linden.

Since Minotour's generated texts are designed to be delivered as the user travels from feature *a* to feature *b*, they are accompanied by the plotline the user is experiencing by moving through the space. The progression of this two-trajectory context in which the stories diverge at the beginning (at *a*) and rejoin at the end (at *b*), is one that the user is used to perceiving within a narrative, and thus aids development. Thousands of examples of this context exist in pop culture media. For instance, nearly all Seinfeld episodes begin with one narrative that splits into two (or more) at the beginning and intersects at the end.

Implementation

We have taken a basic client/server approach to our implementation, an approach that maximizes the individual flexibility of the client and the server. All of the narrative generation work takes place on the server, while all of the narrative delivery is done by the client. When a narrative is desired, the client, sends the article id number of 3D articles *a* and *b* to the server, and the server returns the optimal narrative between these two features.

In addition to extracting links, snippets, and other critical data, this parser is responsible for identifying the existing geo-information in Wikipedia, as well as doing the rudimentary georeferencing and tagging of purely temporal articles. We have written the parser to support any of the hundreds of languages for which a Wikipedia version exists, but so far, only the English Wikipedia and the German Wikipedia have been tested. The client side of this project is the lesser-developed side, and we are exploring delivery platforms other than hand-held devices. That said, our current hand-held software, developed in C# and the Windows Mobile Native C++ API, is effectively a mini-geographic information system (GIS) with GPS capabilities, customized for the various features and desired user experience of Minotour. Because no suitable open-source code could be located, it was necessary to write this software from scratch. A screen shot of a software-emulated version of the application can be found.

Conclusion and Future Work

In this paper, we have presented a novel, narrative theory-informed approach to data mining from a Wikipedia corpus within the context of educational tour generation. While we have completed a proof-of-concept system, we have many more research avenues to explore. First and foremost, we intend to rigorously investigate both theoretical and artistic methods for increasing the narrative pleasure of our generated narratives. One idea currently in the works is eliminating spatially-referenced articles (in addition to temporally-referenced articles) from the body of the narratives. Spatially-referenced articles play a critical role as the start and the end points of our narratives.

However, we have found that when they have snippets that appear in the body, these snippets suffer from the same semantic weakness problems as purely-temporally referenced articles. For instance, the implicit "lies on" relationship between Humboldt University and Unter den Linden is a rather uninteresting and non-educational one, and one that would be obvious to any user who looked at the map on their mobile device client. Other possible avenues for increased narrative pleasure include providing theme-based tours and using Wikipedia's link structure to include more articles in the narratives that are closely tied to the space in which the user is travelling.

Secondly, we are exploring different narrative theoretical constructs with which to examine and improve our generated narratives. We aim to develop further research in the area of cognitive science-based narrative theory with the goal of proposing better strategies for the interdisciplinary adoption of contemporary narratology.

We are also excited about the possibilities for client-side development. Raw text presentation is not the best delivery format for our narratives. We are exploring many possibilities for ways to utilize the presentation as a means to aid narrative interpretation, either through the increase of unity and development, or via other theoretical constructs. One idea on the table includes audio. We are also looking into turning the faceless narrator of our stories into a more explicit character, perhaps even similar to that in or. We have many ideas for using the properties of Wikipedia to enact Person's suggestion to closely integrate character behaviour and presented content. This might include placing greater emphasis on the real life Wikipedia users who input content, as well as considering article conflict statistics.

Following, we are taking steps towards designing an appropriate evaluation for Minotour. We will determine the average user's reliance on narrative schema for the comprehension of a random series of linked snippets (our baseline) as opposed to Minotour generated narratives. Finally, we also plan on implementing spatial feature contribution functionality. Ideally, users should be able to enter information about a spatial feature on which Wikipedia has no information and, immediately afterwards, receive a tour with that feature as the start or end destination. This would add a whole new level of interactivity to our current system.

Minotour is currently heavily customized towards its educational tour narrative generation test platform. However, the ideas behind the implementation can be utilized in other areas and with different goals. Most apparently, the concept can be applied to generating narratives, spatial or not. In initial tests, the authors learned a lot from narratives generated between biographies and even between two mathematical concepts. More broadly, we are considering how this idea could be employed on the Internet as a whole. While we have not explored the narratology implications of such non-spatial and/or non-Wikipedia applications, these are vital further research directions.

2

Foreign Students as Tourists

Under a democratic dispensation South Africa has become a favourable destination for foreign students, especially from African countries, to further their academic qualifications. This trend has given prominence to a market segment in the tourism industry, namely, educational tourism. Given the relative underdevelopment of technology in most African countries, opportunities for scholars to enter a worldwide web of learning (e-learning) is at present not a possibility.

Temporary migration for study purpose to another country remains the only way in which Africans can obtain specialized education. Though the main travel motive of student tourists is education, international students have time to travel during university breaks and in this event they visit tourist spots in the host country making a contribution to the growing tourism market. Little is however known about the non-educationally related time spent in a foreign country, moreover, their leisure, recreational and tourist activities. This paper will shed some light on the concept educational tourism and hopefully contribute to the emerging body of literature on this tourism market segment. After a statistical overview of foreign students in South Africa, will we use data collected in a survey among foreign students at the University of the Western Cape in Cape Town to deliberate the potential for this market segment.

Internationally, educational tourism has been recognized as an important market segment in the tourism industry and is indeed not a new concept. Although definitions of educational tourism abounds, the best way to conceptualise the market segment is to look at the broad range of activities. These include the classic education-like school trip and study tours (referred to as a model for benign tourism by some scholars), sabbatical and exchange programmes, under and postgraduate study programmes, short courses, and language courses where tourism and English is considered a powerful combination.

Expatriates working at overseas universities are also known to arrange compulsory fieldtrips for students during their summer vacations. Interwoven with cultural tourism are educational tourists now visiting Buenos Aires to learn to tango, foreigners are being enticed to visit Cape Town for a photographic week "during which they snap the city's most beautiful people *au naturel* in picturesque natural landscapes, taking cooking lessons in France, and learn about the Gorillas in the misty mountains of Rwanda. Ecotourism or enviro-education is an added overlapping aspect of this market segment.

Educational travel providers are in most cases religious organizations, non-profit organizations, private institutions, private and public sectors, educational institutions such as universities, and private language schools. Despite the seemingly, abundant educational tourism activities, do numerous authors acknowledge the absence of qualitative and quantitative research done on this topic.

What is clear though is that educational tourism is becoming a major potential growth market as the international student population expands annually. Current figures estimate for example a total of 540 000 foreign students in the USA whereas in Western Australia, 20,000 overseas students contributed to an estimated $ 430,000 in domestic spending and other tourism related activities. Another study in Australia estimated the annual expenditure by international students in 1997 as 3.337 billion Australian dollars, almost three times higher than the 1992 figures.

Globalisation has directly contributed to an increase in special interest tourism (such as educational tourism) as boundaries, work opportunities and a new international division of labour emerges. In this regard an IAU statement tabled at the UNESCO World Conference on Higher Education in 1998 emphasized that "higher education and research are among the primary forces that create the conditions of globalization. Through scientific discovery and their contributions to technological progress in communications, information and transportation, universities have been key actors in bringing about globalization in trade and production of goods and services. Through education and training they also prepare the individuals who can best take advantage of these new conditions".

In Australia for example a concerted effort by the national government through the Australian Tourist Commission (ATC) resulted in the signing of an international educational memorandum of understanding to promote Australian international education. The ATC states that there are many opportunities to develop this segment such as strategic partnerships and industry involvement (such as airways). National prestige is seemingly a major recruitment strategy adopted by Australia. Autonomous universities are however in competition to attract foreign students and according to Knight and de Wit recruitment can be divided into four categories: "(a) academic grounds related to the institution's prestige; (b) economic and financial motives; (c) cultural, social, political, and diplomatic considerations; and finally, (d) fear of being outperformed by a competitor or of simply appearing outmoded". It is therefore likely to expect that in the next decade the number of international students may double and hence there is 'great promise for the consumption of tourism products'.

Educational tourism in South Africa Visser recently published a comprehensive review of tourism related research in South Africa between 1973 and 2003. The report however makes no reference to studies covering educational tourism as a market segment. So too, has a study on migration patterns of students from Lesotho to South Africa in *Africa Insight*, not made a direct link between tourism and foreign students. The International Educational Association for South Africa (IEASA) was established in 1997 in view of the need for South African institutions of higher learning "to respond to the unprecedented interest from the international community in the tertiary education sector in this country".

The Association argued, for the country "to remain competitive within the global economic and political environment, it is imperative for higher education in this country to provide opportunities for local staff and students to obtain a global perspective to their study and research activities, and to promote the country's tertiary education sector amongst the international academic community". South Africa is thus not only in the educational production side of tourism but also exporting its own students.

Lubbe gave the example of an agreement signed between the government and Cuba to train medical students. IEASA also pointed out that South Africa offers quality education at a lower cost, and that, especially African students do not have to leave the continent. Educational tourism is also said to result in the mobility of professionals, multilateral networks and the kind of international feel, which is helpful in combating xenophobia and racial tensions.

It does not matter from which point of view this tendency is debated, education has become an export commodity. During 2002 a total of 6 459 916 foreign travellers entered South Africa of which 0.6% (94 015) indicated entry for study purpose. A breakdown according world region of origin, clearly shows that most educational tourists are from Africa constituting more than three quarters of educational tourists. There is, however, no huge discrepancy between other regions with Europe and Asia and North America producing the majority educational tourists. Mashinini and Mashinini made reference to the SADC Protocol on Higher Education and Training that stresses the importance of developing human resources that would facilitate "free mobility of human capital. They further argue that South Africa will bear the brunt of this protocol. A closer look at the tourists coming from Africa reflects a spatial nucleus coming from the SADC region: Botswana (38 471), Swaziland (8 530), Lesotho (7 565), Zimbabwe (66 44), Namibia (5 841), Mozambique (5 076), Angola (2 786) and Zambia (1 536). With the exception of a few countries are students from all over Africa studying in the country.

Agreements between certain South African universities and African countries have become a distinct feature of the tertiary educational sector after 1994. For example, agreements between the Botswana Government and the unbundled Vista University saw a great number of students enrolling at various Vista campuses in the country in the early 2000s.

The above figures from Statistics South Africa in relation to an official estimate of 47,000 international students studying in South Africa in 2004 made by the International Education Association of South Africa (IEASA) reflects a general inconsistency in using numbers to illustrate accurately a market segment such as tourism education..

Data was also collected from the Department of Education on the number of all foreign students registered at South African tertiary institutions. The dramatic increase in intake over a three year period, especially at South Africa's universities.

Majority of the foreign students are from SADC countries followed by over 7000 from all other continents and lastly over 6000 from other parts in Africa. The percentage of foreigners as registered students at tertiary institutions increased by 2% between the 2000-2003 period. The intake of students from the North Americas doubled over this period whilst the intake from Botswana increased by more than 6000 students.

Although the University of South Africa (UNISA) has the greatest number of foreign students is it the University of Cape Town where the percentage of foreign students in relation to local students is the highest. The University of Port Elizabeth has shown the greatest decline in foreign student intake whilst the University of the North-West experienced the biggest growth, probably attributed to an intake of students from neighbouring Botswana.

It was not possible to determine the specific courses students are enrolled for but the percentage of foreign students studying towards a post-graduate degree. It is the traditionally well-off former advantaged institutions such as UCT, University of Pretoria, University of the Witwatersrand, and Free State that attract a high percentage of postgraduate students. The University of the Western Cape also attracted a high percentage of foreign students. It is to this institution where the remaining focus of this paper will shift.

Case Study: University of the Western Cape

Against the background of the above the remaining sections of this paper will focus on findings from a case study survey conducted among foreign students based at one of the universities in Cape Town. The survey focused on a broad range of issues that included an investigation into the potential economic contribution of international students, why they have chosen this institution in particular, how much they spent on travel related activities, and on living expenses. In addition tourist travelling patterns and means of getting information about tourist places were also investigated. A total of forty questionnaires were distributed to international students via a snowball sampling technique. An attempt was made to get representation of students staying on and off campus. The questionnaire was divided into four sections: demographic information, UWC as study destination, student spending patterns, social cultural and recreational aspects, and organisational matters.

Foreign Student Numbers

The international student population at the University of the Western Cape increased dramatically over the past five years. Student enrolments increased from 162 in 1998 to 1169 in 2004. This reflects a percentage growth of 621% over a 6 year period.

The region of origin for international students is summarised in. Majority of the students are from Africa, but the greatest percentage growth has been from elsewhere in the world (877%). Most students are from Botswana, Namibia and Zambia and Lesotho.

There has been a dramatic increase in students from China in 2004, making up 10% of the total foreign student population.

Student Characteristics

The students taking part in the survey represents twenty different nationalities. Majority of respondents are full time enrolled (95%) and are mostly from African countries (65%). An interesting observation is the age category of the students. Most of the respondents are in the age groups of 36-40 (27.5%), and 25-30 (27.5%). A mere 23% are younger than 25. The market segment in this case caters thus mainly for people who left school and probably worked for a number of years saving up money to sponsor their own studies (25% in this survey are self sponsored). Having had working experience and admittedly being more mature than school leavers, foreign students are viewed in a study in the USA to be of a high academic quality, and that they are easily absorbed into research and tutorship positions. Government sponsored students accounted for 30%.

Accommodation is arguably one of the most important components in the tourism industry. It is maintained that the "success of tourism destinations is largely dependant upon the appropriate development of the accommodation sector". In developing countries, national data on the actual economic contribution of tourism accommodation, for example the revenue it earns, number of employment created, expenditure of tourists are unknown, and highly speculative. Accommodation is a broad concept and the categorization of tourist accommodation varies at different scales of investigation.

Considered as part of the tourism hospitality sector, accommodation can be grouped into six types, namely, a paying, rented, static/permanent, serviced, primary purpose, holiday/business establishment. Basically four options of accommodation are evident from the survey where 45% indicated that they reside on campus, 45% live in rental houses, and a minority live in an international hostel, with friends and family.

The University of the Western Cape is a choice destination because of course availability (42%) in a specific field, for example dentistry. Another reason for studying at UWC is the fact that the university fees are affordable in comparison to other universities in the country (this accounted for 18% response rate). To a lesser extent relatives and friends also influenced the choice of the university as a study destination (15%). Apart from these, some students came to UWC as a result of inter-institutional exchange agreements and collaboration (12%).

Most (83%) of the respondents did not have any problem interacting with the local students. This finding is indicative of the nature of educational tourism, namely to learn about new cultural lifestyles. Asked to rank their attitude towards South Africans, the majority indicated that their attitudes were fair (65%) this is followed by those who said that their attitudes were good (12%). Only (5%) of the respondents had a bad/very bad attitude towards South Africans.

Travel Patterns

A number of questions related to travelling patterns focused on the variety of trips undertaken, where tourism information was accessed, where they travel during holidays, and reasons for and not exploring the country. The survey found that 20% of African students do not travel at all. Day trips outside Cape Town are fairly popular (38%), while almost half of the respondents indicated having gone on a weekend trips outside Cape Town at least once during a year. Only 35% indicated having gone on a week trip outside Cape Town. Of this, African students are in the minority.

The reasons why international students travelled outside Cape Town are visiting friends and relatives, adventure, and simply to escape the daily routine of being a student. Of the places visited Durban, Johannesburg and Port Elizabeth were ranked best followed by Pretoria. Majority of the students indicated that they mainly visit places in Cape Town during the vacations however.

Students who do not travel, indicated financial reasons as the biggest obstacle. Other major problems include a lack of personal transport, lack of safety and security, hostility towards foreigners, and to a lesser extent some students indicated that most of the time, they are too busy with studies to have time to travel.

It is apparent that mainly students from Europe, America and Asia make use of tourism information centres whereas students originating from other African countries acquired information mainly from friends and family members in South Africa. Other information sources such as television, internet and newspapers accounted for 9.4 %. Most respondents preferred to organise their trips in groups (52.5 %) and mainly do so due to lack of own transport. Female respondents prefer to travel in groups for safety reasons (47.5 %), and a minority organise theirs individually (4.9%).

Most of the students go home during the end of the year university holiday (55%). Majority of these are married (refer to age categories above) and the one's not committed stay to explore the country further. The likelihood of repeat visits to the tourist spots was determined, and respondents were asked if they would return to these after they have gone home (i.e. once they finished their studies). Majority of the respondents indicated that they would like to return to those tourist spots and more especially would like to come back with their family members (95%). It is evident from the above findings that foreign students are indeed a potential lucrative tourism market.

Economic Impact

The *Sunday Business Times* reported that education is becoming a profitable business for institutions and the country as a whole. According to the article, South African institutions are tapping into a growing market where the total revenue generated from higher education in 2003 amounted to R 21.5 billion. About R 1.4 billion of this was generated by international students. International students are said to spent between R2500-R4000 a month on goods and services. When their relatives also visit they spent between R 5000 and R 12,00028.

Our survey estimated that three quarters of the respondents consider South Africa an affordable (i.t.o cost of living and tuition fees) destination, especially if compared to Europe or America. Those that indicated that South Africa is not affordable stated that foreigners are at a disadvantage in terms of exchange rate to the Dollars from their currencies. A cross tabulation between considering the country affordable and world region of origin showed that all respondents from Europe, America, and Asia indicated that South Africa is affordable. A mere 27% African respondents stated the country is not affordable. Affordability also translates into purchasing patterns. With the exception of major capital expenses such as a motor car, have most Africans spent more money than students from other regions on electrical appliances. Asian and European students mostly invested in a car, primarily to travel and resell again when they return to their country.

African students spent the least on travelling and tourism related activities in comparison to the other students. More Africans however spent more than R3001 per month on living expenses (excluding accommodation) as do American and Asian students. European students spent most money on a monthly basis while Americans on average spent most on travelling. Regional differentiation is of significance to tourism planners especially when identifying new niche markets such as package tours for target groups.

The average amount spent on accommodation per month is R727,00. If the sample is considered representative of the UWC foreign student body then the following amounts spent per year is brought into the Western Cape economy: R19 million per year on living expenses; R24 million per year on travelling and tourism related activities; and R10 million on accommodation. Just over R50 million is therefore estimated to be spent by foreign students at UWC per year. Given the fact that the province is blessed with four major universities (UCT, Univ. of Stellenbosch, UWC, and Pentech and Cape Tech combined) with an estimated 4000 foreign students an annual injection of R200 million can be considered a substantial boost into the economy. (The figure may be higher if other educational institutions such as the language and vocational colleges are also taken into consideration).

Conclusion

A national estimation of a total revenue generated in higher education for 2003 amounted to 21.5 billion Rand, of which 1.4 billion generated by international students. Although it may seem only a fraction of the total capital generated in the tourism industry, are ramifications of foreign students as tourists not given any thought in local debates around tourism development.

With an increasing trend in international students to the country (and to the University of the Western Cape in particular) is there a huge potential to develop this lucrative market segment further. Not only does this market contribute positively to the domestic economy of South Africa, it also contributes to creating a socio-cultural awareness among locals, a so-called 'cosmopolitan feel'. Presence of foreign students is also said to fight against xenophobia and aiding exchange of academic ideas and removing the borders between nations by the establishment of multilateral networks. It facilitates cultural appreciation by other people from different backgrounds.

The following five general recommendations are based on the findings from the survey:

(1) Universities and other higher institutions of learning should increase their marketing efforts to this market segment in order to exploit its potentiality to the fullest.

(2) South African institutions should position themselves in order to increase the number of international students. And, for those who are already having big numbers of international students, they should strive to maintain them.

(3) Tourism marketers should work hand in hand with higher educational institutions in order to exploit this market segment exhaustively. On the same note, they should see to it that they provide a positive image of the country and the institutions of learning.

(4) Tourism marketers should also think of targeting this market segment on a serious note, by maybe, offering some incentives to international students.

(5) University managements should recognise the contribution of this market segment, and take active steps to ensure that foreign students are indeed looked after as visitors, and not simply as a students. Annual surveys among students to identify areas of concern, problems, and so on is a useful method to keep track of the needs and expectations of foreign students as tourists.

Exploring Nature Based and Cultural Educational Tourism

As the new millennium unfolds, we are becoming increasingly aware of the finite, interconnected and precious nature of our planet home. Likewise, tourism is becoming an increasingly popular expression of this awareness. Tourism not only provides an escape from the everyday working life of many, but it also represents the everyday working life of many more. With advances in transportation and information technology, ever more remote areas of the earth are coming within reach of the traveller. In fact, tourism is now the world's largest industry, with nature tourism the fastest growing segment. In response to this increasing appreciation of nature experiences, a new travel ethic has arisen which is now called ecotourism. This term has become increasingly popular in both conservation and travel circles. Most tourism in natural areas today is not ecotourism and is not therefore, sustainable. Ecotourism can be distinguished from nature tourism by its emphasis on conservation, education, traveller responsibility and active community participation. Specifically, ecotourism is not only the act of a foreigner visiting a foreign land, but also the participation of and effects on the local populations of touristed areas. These facilities and programs become part of the local culture, and it is up to the planning of tourism to make sure that they stay within the original framework of the culture.

With the definition of traditional tourism in mind, ecotourism can be discussed as a different entity based on the involvement of local populations in all aspects of tourism. Indigenous populations are the most knowledgeable about the area, and they "possess the practical and ancestral knowledge of the natural features of the area".

Maintaining the important bond between its education and its environment is important to the survival of an ecotourism program. This is especially important now, in a time when ecotourism is part of the development strategy of nearly every developing country.

In the second section, it provides a brief description of how and why ecotourism has evolved and what it means. The broadly accepted definition of ecotourism is presented along with definitions of other terms related to ecotourism. In the third section, we suggested a model of the various players involved in ecotourism management and development.

In the fourth section, we argued naturalist guide of the role and how it could be cultivated to develop ecotourism. Finally, I make an assertion volunteer tourism that could be another form of alternative ecotourism for the theoretical development of EATOF member's countries.

Literature Review

The Definition of Ecotourism

There are various definitions of ecotourism, most of which have to do with combining the travel industry with an ideal that emphasizes conservation and preservation of the wilderness in which people spend their vacations. The Ecotourism Society defines ecotourism as "responsible travel which conserves environments and sustains the well-being of local people,".

Ecotourism is a relatively new concept, and it is still often misunderstood or misused. Some people have abused the term to attract conservation conscious travellers to what, in reality, are simply nature tourism programs which may cause negative environmental and social impacts. While the term was first heard in the 1980s, the first broadly accepted definition, and one which continues to be a valid "nutshell" definition was established by The International Ecotourism Society in 1990: *Responsible travel to natural areas that conserves the environment and improves the well-being of local people.*

As awareness and experience of the activity has grown, so has our need for a more comprehensive and detailed definition. Martha Honey (1999) has proposed an excellent, more detailed version: Ecotourism is travel to fragile, pristine and usually protected areas that strives to be low impact and usually small scale. It helps educate the traveller; provides funds for conservation; directly benefits the economic development and political empowerment of local communities; and fosters respect for different cultures and for human rights.

However, consensus exists among organizations involved with ecotourism including The Nature Conservancy around the definition adopted in 1996 by the World Conservation Union (IUCN) which describes ecotourism as:

Environmentally responsible travel and visitation to natural areas, in order to enjoy and appreciate nature and any accompanying cultural features, both past and present that promote conservation, have a low visitor impact and provide for beneficially active socio-economic involvement of local peoples.

The Nature Conservancy has adopted the concept of ecotourism as the type of tourism that it recommends its partners use in most protected area management, especially for national parks and other areas with fairly strict conservation objectives. For The Nature Conservancy, ecotourism represents an excellent means for benefiting both local people and the protected area in question. It is an ideal component of a sustainable development strategy where natural resources can be utilized as tourism attractions without causing harm to the natural area. An important tool for protected area management and development, ecotourism must be implemented in a flexible manner. However, the following elements are crucial to the ultimate success of an ecotourism initiative. Ecotourism must:

- have a low impact upon a protected area's natural resources;
- involve stakeholders (individuals, communities, ecotourists, tour operators and government institutions) in the planning, development, implementation and monitoring phases;
- respect local cultures and traditions;
- generate sustainable and equitable income for local communities and for as many other stakeholders as possible, including private tour operators;
- generate income for protected area conservation;
- educate all stakeholders about their role in conservation.

Evolution of Ecotourism

Ecotourism is a concept that evolved over the last 20 years as the conservation community, people living in and around protected areas, and the travel industry witnessed a boom in nature tourism and realized their mutual interests in directing its growth. Ecotourism has brought the promise of achieving conservation goals, improving the well-being of local communities and generating new business promising a rare win-win situation. Relations among conservationists, communities and tourism practitioners have not always been smooth and collaborative.

However, the concept and practice of ecotourism brings these different actors together. Ecotourism has emerged as a platform to establish partnerships and to jointly guide the path of tourists seeking to experience and learn about natural areas and diverse cultures.

Conservationists and Ecotourism

Specific circumstances on all sides motivated this new interest in ecotourism. On the conservation side, protected area managers were in the midst of redefining conservation strategies. For practical reasons, they were learning to combine conservation activities with economic development as it became obvious that traditional conservation approaches of strict protectionism were no longer adequate and new ways of accomplishing goals were needed.

For years, conservationists established and managed protected areas through minimal collaboration with the people living in or near these areas. Circumstances in many countries, particularly in developing regions, have changed dramatically in recent years and have affected approaches to conservation.

Local Stakeholders and Ecotourism

Over the past two decades, many developing countries have experienced large population increases with declining or stagnant economic conditions. These countries have frequently been pressured into exploiting their natural resource base in an unsustainable fashion in order to meet immediate economic needs and to pay interest on foreign debt. This combination leads more people to compete for fewer natural resources. Outside protected areas, the natural resources that many people have depended upon for sustenance and many businesses have relied upon for profit making have disappeared. For most countries, protected areas have become the last significant pieces of land that still retain important reserves of plant and animal diversity, water, clean air and other ecological services. Meanwhile, protected areas have become increasingly attractive to farmers, miners, loggers and others trying to make a living. The economic development pressures on these areas have intensified on local, national and global scales. Thus, ecotourism has become very important for potentially reconciling conservation and economic considerations.

Because of this competition for resources, conservationists realized that local people and economic circumstances must be incorporated into conservation strategies. In most cases, local people need financial incentives to use and manage natural resources sustainably. Existing economic and political conditions often limit their options and increase their reliance on natural areas.

Conservation work often means creating alternatives to current economic practices so that multiple-use zones around protected areas can be maintained and threats to protected areas minimized. In looking for alternative economic activities, conservationists have become more creative and are exploring many options. Ecotourism is one such alternative. The rationale behind ecotourism is that local tourism businesses would not destroy natural resources but would instead support their protection. Ecotourism would offer a viable strategy to simultaneously make money and conserve resources. Ecotourism could be considered a "sustainable" activity, one that does not diminish natural resources being used while at the same time generating income.

Related Terms

As a popular word, ecotourism has been used loosely. But if implemented fully, it is a critically important conservation strategy for achieving sustainable development.

There are a variety of related terms that are frequently linked, and sometimes confused with ecotourism, including the following:

- Nature tourism is simply tourism based on visitation to natural areas. Nature tourism is closely related to ecotourism but does not necessarily involve conservation or sustainability. This is the type of tourism that currently exists in most natural areas before a plan is established and conservation measures are in place. As different elements of ecotourism are integrated into a nature tourism program, its effect on the environment may change.
- Sustainable nature tourism is very close to ecotourism but does not meet all the criteria of true ecotourism. For example, a cable car carrying visitors through the rainforest canopy may generate benefits for conservation and educate visitors, but because it represents a high degree of mechanization and consequently creates a barrier between the visitor and the natural environment, it would be inappropriate to describe as an ecotourism initiative. In altered and heavily-visited areas, sustainable nature tourism may be an appropriate activity. For example, larger "eco" resort development would not be considered low impact if it required significant clearing of native vegetation but may contribute to conservation financially and provide conservation education.

The line between sustainable nature tourism and ecotourism is subtle but very important. A project must meet all of the necessary criteria listed above before it can accurately be defined as ecotourism.

Projects that fall short on any of the criteria do not truly benefit conservation or the people involved over the long term.

- Cultural, ethno or cultural heritage tourism concentrates on local traditions and people as the main attractions. This kind of tourism can be divided into two types: The first and conventional type is where tourists experience culture through museums and formalized presentations of music and dance in theatres, hotels or occasionally in communities themselves. In many instances, this has lead to the "commodification" of culture as it becomes adapted for tourist consumption, often resulting in degradation of the hosts" cultural traditions. The second type is more anthropological and contains a strong visitor motivation for learning from indigenous culture rather than simply viewing an isolated manifestation of it. For example, there is growing interest in learning how indigenous people use natural resources. It is important that cultural tourism be managed on terms defined by host communities and that indicators of the cultural impact of tourism be monitored to ensure visitation does not erode the cultural resource.
- Green/Sustainable tourism refers to travel operations that use natural resources judiciously. Green or sustainable tourism can be considered the "greening" of the tourism industry. Examples include the airline industry becoming more energy efficient, the cruise line industry recycling its waste or large hotel chains adopting environmental regulations. Large hotels have discovered that by advising guests to reduce water consumption or recommending that they not expect their towels to be washed every day, the hotels not only gain a "greener" image which is increasingly important to consumers, but they also reduce operating costs. Thus, green tourism is clearly an attractive proposition to the conventional tourism industry. In reality, reducing the hotel's water consumption by 15%, although desirable and relatively easy to achieve at most large hotels, is not enough to convert the hotel into a sustainable operation. Sweeting et al. (1999) review this issue comprehensively and make recommendations for reducing conventional tourism's impact on the environment.

While greening the existing conventional mass tourism industry will produce some benefits, new developments in natural areas, including beaches, need to address energy consumption, waste management and environmental interpretation in the design phase and not as an afterthought if they are to be truly sustainable.

Large hotels washing towels only every other day may not be enough to protect the water table in an arid area. Not building the hotel in the first place in an area where water resources are scarce may be the best option.

Developing a sustainable or green tourism industry in all its dimensions is as worthy a cause as working to maintain protected areas through tourism. In fact, some would argue that promoting sustainability of the broader tourism would be a better conservation mission than focusing on protected areas alone. However, for the present purposes the foçus will be on ecotourism development. It may be easiest to think of ecotourism which works to protect natural areas through tourism and sustainable tourism which works to make the whole tourism industry more environmentally friendly as two valuable, but distinct, missions.

Key Considerations for Successful Ecotourism

These days, most conservationists recognize that working with communities is fundamental to achieving protected area goals and conservation strategies, including ecotourism. There are a number of basic principles that should be considered in planning for community involvement in ecotourism activities. Ecotourism organized at the local community level can rarely be successful without assistance or cooperation from tourism operators. Links to the market, language skills and poor communications are three major aspects which limit communities ability to "go it alone" in ecotourism. Protected area managers must play a role in guiding ecotourism implementation outside of the protected area, but in many cases that role may have to be a "second-hand" one. NGOs are generally perceived as neutral parties and thus more acceptable as providers of technical assistance to local communities. In some cases, the NGOs may be the protected area managers. Training, for example in basic accounting and guiding, is a key need for communities to effectively participate in ecotourism. This is a role that NGOs are best placed to provide.

For ecotourism to promote conservation, local people must clearly benefit and understand that the benefits they receive are linked to the continued existence of the protected area. There must be a close working relationship between the protected area administration and the surrounding communities.

Unfortunately, the limited benefits provided by many tourism projects frequently are not recognized by local residents as connected to the protected area.

A huge range of players with varying interests and goals participates in ecotourism. Some play more prominent roles than others, but almost all are represented in the development and management of ecotourism sites.

A key to the success of ecotourism is the formation of strong partnerships so that the multiple goals of conservation and equitable development can be met. Partnerships may be difficult because of the number of players involved and their different needs, but forging relationships is essential. The key players can be classified as community organizations and individuals, private sector tourism industry members and a variety of government officials and non-governmental organizations. Their effective interaction creates effective ecotourism.

Core Decision Makers

Local Government. Officials

Many government departments should participate in ecotourism planning, development and management. These departments include tourism, natural resources, wildlife and protected areas, education, community development, finances and transportation. Ecotourism involves officials primarily from the national level, although regional and local levels also contribute to the process.

Government officials have several significant functions in ecotourism. They provide leadership. They coordinate and articulate national goals for ecotourism.

As part of their overall tourism plans, they provide vision for this industry. They may even propose a national ecotourism plan; in Australia, the government created a National Ecotourism Strategy and then committed AUS$10 million for its development and implementation.

Government officials at the national level may also establish specific policies for protected areas. For example, government officials decide about visitor use fee systems at protected areas, and their policies outline what systems are established and how revenues will be distributed.

They may also delineate private sector practices, e.g., tour operators may be required to use local tour guides in certain areas or developers" property ownership rights may be regulated. Government policies direct ecotourism activities and may easily advance or hinder their growth.

Additionally, government officials are responsible for most basic infrastructure outside protected areas ranging from airline facilities in big cities to secondary roads leading to remote sites. The government generally takes the lead in all major transportation systems and issues. It may also provide other services important to ecotourism such as health clinics in rural areas.

Finally, government officials promote ecotourism. Sometimes the promotion is part of a national tourism campaign. At other times, advertisements for specific nature sites are created or perhaps a flagship species is identified and promoted. National government participation gives prominence to ecotourism destinations.

Local Communities

People who live in or near protected areas are not a homogeneous group. Indeed, even within one small community there will be a diversity of people with a range of views and experiences.

But we can make a few generalizations about local residents and their relationship to ecotourism. First, some rural communities that once featured quiet living are finding themselves in the middle of an international trend. Nature tourists are invading their homelands, but they are generally just passing through the neighbourhood, not coming to meet residents. Residents have mixed reactions to this intrusion. Some want nothing to do with tourists; they want privacy and do not welcome the changes that tourism brings. Others are intrigued by tourism and are taking steps to develop it. Tourism may be particularly alluring if other employment options are limited or if residents feel tourism may help protect their precious resources.

Many communities in developing countries are hosting visitors and creating ecotourism programs. Sometimes their motivation is to protect their surrounding natural resources. For others, they may see ecotourism in a more economic perspective, as a means to gain income. Many communities have organized their own ecotourism programs.

Whatever their initial reaction to tourism, local residents are often unprepared for its demands. Those who do not want tourism have no means to stop it. They often cannot compete with the powerful tourism industry or the fiercely independent travellers who want to discover new areas. Those who are interested in pursuing tourism may not be familiar with its costs and benefits. Many have little experience in tourism business enterprises and are not connected to international tourism markets. The interests and concerns of local residents regarding tourism development need special attention.

Tourism touches all the other groups involved professionally, in a mostly economic sense. For members of communities, it also touches their personal lives by affecting their lifestyles, traditions and cultures, as well as their livelihood and their long standing ways of organizing themselves socially and politically. In addition, most of the other players enter into tourism voluntarily, whereas in many cases communities must deal with tourism impacts whether or not they choose to. Local residents play an important role in ecotourism for two main reasons.

First, it is their homelands and work places that are attracting nature travellers. Equity and practicality require that they be active decision-makers in ecotourism planning and management.

Second, local residents are key players in conserving natural resources both within and outside of neighbouring protected areas. Their relationship to and uses of natural resources will determine the success of conservation strategies for protected areas. In addition, local or traditional knowledge is often a key component of visitors' experience and education.

Tourism Industry

The tourism industry is massive. It involves a huge variety of people including: tour operators and travel agents who assemble trips; airline and cruise ship employees; minivan drivers; staff of big hotels and small family lodges; handicraft makers; restaurant owners; tour guides; and all the other people who independently offer goods and services to tourists. The complexity of this sector indicates how challenging it can be for protected area staff and local communities to learn about and form partnerships with the tourism industry.

Consumers are in contact with many members of the tourism industry throughout their journeys. For an international trip, the traveller often first contacts a travel agent, tour operator or airline. The agent will generally contact an outbound tour operator based in the tourist's country of origin, who in turn will contact an in bound tour operator based in the destination country. The in bound tour operator is best placed to make local travel arrangements such as transportation, accommodations, and guide services.

Once the traveller is at the destination, many local entrepreneurs will also become part of this scenario. One element that binds all businesses within the tourism industry is the pursuit of financial profit. There may be additional motivations for some businesses, particularly those involved in ecotourism, but tourism companies exist only when they are profitable. Members of the tourism industry are valuable to ecotourism for many reasons.

First, they understand travel trends. They know how consumers act and what they want. Second, the tourism industry can influence travellers by encouraging good behaviour and limiting negative impacts in protected areas. Third, the tourism industry plays a key role in promoting ecotourism. Its members know how to reach travellers through publications, the Internet, the media and other means of promotion, thus providing a link between ecotourism destinations and consumers.

Non-governmental Organizations

Non-governmental organizations are valuable players because they provide a forum for discussion and influence regarding ecotourism. They offer a means of communication with great numbers of interested individuals. These organizations can serve as vehicles for bringing together all the elements of ecotourism. NGOs can play many different roles in ecotourism implementation: directly, as program managers or site administrators; and indirectly, as trainers, advisors, business partners with ecotourism companies or communities and, in exceptional circumstances, as providers of ecotourism services.

There are several different types of non-governmental organizations. Among them are for-profit tourism associations consisting of private tour operators, airlines and hoteliers; ecotourism associations such as those in Belize, Costa Rica, Ecuador, etc., that bring together groups from all the sectors involved; and other trade organizations that handle travel issues.

These NGOs often have members who meet regularly and

communicate industry concerns through publications such as newsletters. Members are often asked to subscribe to certain principles or "codes of ethics." These associations and organizations are effective at keeping the industry informed about current trends and events. Another set of non-governmental organizations involved with ecotourism includes the private, non-profit groups that focus on conservation and development or may be dedicated specifically to ecotourism.

Their focus may be local, national or international. Frequently, these organizations serve as facilitators between protected areas, communities and all the other players in ecotourism, sometimes providing financial and technical assistance or directly managing ecotourism sites. Some of these NGOs have constituencies that enjoy nature and would be interested in ecotourism education and promotion.

NGOs play an important role in advancing ecotourism implementation through their positive interaction with local communities, the private sector tourism industry, government-administered protected areas and others. The particular role adopted by an NGO depends upon the set of circumstances within which it operates, e.g., its mission and purpose, the degree of openness to NGO collaboration and the interest of the tourism industry. Opportunistic situations also arise which affect an NGO"s role, such as donation of a tract of land for ecotourism purposes or development of a friendly relationship with a community leader.

Supporting Players

Funders

Many different groups can fund the development of ecotourism through loans or grants: financial institutions, including investment corporations; bilateral and multilateral donor agencies; private investors; venture capital funds such as the Ecoenterprise Investment Fund; NGOs; and private banks. These contributions are often critical for protected areas that pursue ecotourism. Typically there are studies to carry out, facilities to build, infrastructure to create and people to train. With protected area budgets so limited, outside funding is necessary.

Financial institutions do not generally participate in planning for ecotourism or in decisions about what is appropriate for a particular protected area. In this regard, they may be considered a second-tier player in ecotourism, but they are important nonetheless. For anyone that wants to develop ecotourism, access to funds is often the biggest obstacle confronted.

Academics

Academics at universities is another group that plays a secondary, though valuable, role in the planning and daily functions of ecotourism. It is a group that helps to frame the issues of ecotourism and raise questions to ensure that ecotourism meets its stated goals. Researchers and academics facilitate learning by asking such questions as: Who exactly is benefiting from ecotourism? How do we measure benefits? How does ecotourism contribute to our existing knowledge about conservation? What are the links between ecotourism and tourism? Academics can focus on the big picture and help us understand how ecotourism interacts with other concepts and global trends.

In addition to helping shape the hypotheses, academics conduct research. In coordination with NGOs, governments and local communities, they may:

- Educate and create naturalist guides.;
- produce data about tourism patterns;
- inventory flora and fauna;
- document tourism impacts and share results to develop a good base of information;
- provide material to guide us in our discussions and conclusions about ecotourism;
- facilitate the sharing of this information and conceptual thinking through conferences, publications, the Internet, etc.

Travellers

Travellers have a unique position as players in ecotourism. They are the most vital participants in the industry and provide motivation for everyone else's activities, but few participate in formal meetings about ecotourism. Nevertheless, the choices they make when they select a tourism destination, choose a tour operator or travel agent and, ultimately, the kind of tour in which they wish to participate, have a tremendous impact upon the eventual success or failure of ecotourism projects.

Ecotourism, then, is a multifaceted, multi-disciplinary, multi-actor activity requiring communication and collaboration among a diverse range of actors with different needs and interests. Consequently, achieving ecotourism is a challenging process though ultimately enormously rewarding for all involved.

Creating Naturalist Guides

Naturalist guides play a central role in the implementation of the ecotourism concept. They are the principal providers of the educational element to the ecotourism activity, and their capacity and commitment ensures that the negative impacts of tourism are minimized. At the same time, guiding is an obvious economic opportunity for people from local communities. These and other important benefits underline the importance of a protected area establishing and implementing a naturalist guide training and licensing program.

The use of tour guides in protected areas is not a new phenomenon. Guides have been a part of nature tourism in many places for many years. These tour guides usually were employed by private tour operators and had little or no relationship to the protected area they worked in even though they didn't have any background knowledge about the importance of environment. Over the years, this situation began to change as protected area managers realized the potential for using guides to increase contact with visitors and for accomplishing other ecotourism objectives as well.

The Roles of Naturalist Guides

Naturalist guides truly play a multifaceted role. They have responsibilities to their tour operator employers, to their clients the visitors, and to the protected areas and communities where they work. Tour operators count on guides to provide experience enriching interpretation of natural and cultural attractions to add value to the tourists' itinerary. They also require guides to manage logistical aspects of trips in the field, such as coordinating with accommodation, food and transport service providers. Guides are responsible for the tourists" safety and in general represent their tour operator employer in the field.

Tourists look to the naturalist guide for information, interpretation and insight about the places they are visiting; for help preparing for a visit through formal briefings and informal talks; and generally to be a friendly, knowledgeable intermediary with unfamiliar places and people. Protected area authorities look to the guides as extensions of the park ranger staff, to educate the visitors, to protect the natural and cultural resources of the area visited, to participate in monitoring programs and generally to support the conservation objectives of an area. In addition to these roles, a naturalist guide should seek to inspire visitors to become supporters of conservation.

Nature Interpreters

Environmental interpretation is a subset of communication that focuses on how best to explain environmental and ecological concepts to the general public. One of the central tenets of ecotourism is to educate the visitor. Naturalist guides, who spend a considerable amount of time with visitors, are in a perfect position to educate through skilled interpretation. Many local residents have a detailed knowledge of the plant and animal life as well as of other natural and cultural attractions. They can also relate first-hand experiences with wildlife, medicinal plants and other local phenomena.

Conservationists

As the main contacts that visitors may have with an ecotourism site, guides serve as important role models both to visitors and their own communities. Their attitude and behaviour send an important message to others about the ecotourism concept. Does the guide pick up pieces of trash along the hiking trail? Does the guide actively support and cooperate with site managers by reporting illegal activities? Does the guide adapt ecotourism to his/her own home and community situation? Some tour guides make a point of discussing the importance of conserving the incredible diversity found at a site, what the major threats to it are and what visitors might do to help conserve it.

Park Rangers

Unfortunately, not all visitors to ecotourism sites know how to behave appropriately in sensitive natural and cultural settings. It is the guides' responsibility to ensure that visitors are aware of all applicable rules and regulations as well as other relevant ethical considerations. In a polite but firm manner, they must make sure that visitors comply with whatever restrictions there may be. This is perhaps the most difficult role that guides have because their major responsibility is to help provide visitors with an enjoyable experience. As members of the private sector, it can, in rare situations, create a conflict of interest between the guides' conservation obligations and their obligation to the visitor and, in some cases, their employer. For example, a tour operator might promise clients a close encounter with a whale, but a guide may judge that at a given moment the whales seen in the distance are nursing young and should not be approached. The guide's obligations to an employer and to a park authority might be divergent at this point. Guides need special training in how best to deal with these situations. They also must be vested with the authority to report and deal with infractions of rules and regulations.

Monitors of Tourism Impact

Since guides visit the ecotourism site/protected area on a frequent basis, they are in a unique position to notice certain kinds of impact, such as trail erosion, increasing rareness of a particular bird species, etc. They are also in an excellent position to carry out formal monitoring observations for the site's managers. In many places, guides take the time to carry out observations of the number of nesting birds or of the regeneration of a plant species in a designated quadrant. This can be of valuable assistance to a site's managers when they are short-handed or simply do not have trained personnel to carry out these tasks.

Liaison with Local Communities

When guides are from local communities, they can serve an important role in improving communication between the site's administration and local people. This is particularly important when there may be some misunderstanding between the two different "communities," which there frequently is. Naturalist guides should establish government financed organizations to further conservation objectives.

In order for a naturalist guide system to work well in an ecotourism site situation, several conditions must be met.

Control and Licensing

The site must have effective control over the use of guides and the conditions under which guides will operate within the site. This implies that managers either own the site or that there is legislation or some other legal mandate for exercising this control. Most effective guide systems have a licensing mechanism. The site's administration, or some higher authority acting at the administration's request, will issue a license to guide visitors within the site if the guide complies with relevant rules and regulations. The site's administration reserves the right to suspend or revoke the license if a guide's behaviour is inappropriate. Licenses are usually extended to those individuals who pass a training course or a test. The site's administration reserves the right to set other criteria for attending a training course, such as: being a member of a local community, being of a minimum age, the absence of a police record and having a minimum level of education. It is important to avoid flooding the market with too many licensed guides as this would force down wage levels as many compete for an insufficient number of jobs. However, it is necessary to have a sufficient number of guides to satisfy demand; a rough guide would be to license about 25% more guides than will be working each season.

In spite of the control that the site's administration must exercise over the guides' activities, the relationship between them should be more than one of employer and employee. Both the site administration and the guide have much to offer each other, and they should actively carry out their respective roles in order to benefit from each other's work. Unfortunately, it is not uncommon for one side or the other to lose sight of their mutually supportive roles and for the relationship to become non-productive. Constant and positive feedback is the best way to avoid this situation. Involving tour operators and guides in the ecotourism program planning process from the beginning is also crucial.

Training

Naturalist guides need training in order to fulfil the many roles they are charged with. The primary themes for a training course curriculum are listed below.

- Natural history of the site and surrounding areas. What are the major species, plant and animal communities and ecosystems? How do they interact with one another? What is their conservation status?
- Cultural attractions. What are the historical, archaeological and traditional cultural activities that can be found in the site and surrounding areas? What is the relationship between natural and cultural attractions?
- Site conservation priorities and activities.

Guides should be able to explain to visitors what the site's management is doing to further the conservation of the natural and cultural resources found in the site as well as how the site relates to other protected areas and the surrounding communities.

- Rules and regulations. Guides need to be aware of all the rules and regulations governing public use of the site and its facilities. In particular, they need to be aware of what ecotourism is and how it is applied at this site.

- Group management. All guides need to learn how to best manage a group of visitors that can have widely varying attention spans and reasons for being there. Maintaining everyone's attention and keeping the group together can sometimes be a major chore. Experienced guides are sometimes the best people to teach this part of the course.
- Interpretive/communication techniques. There are very special techniques for communicating ideas to a group of disparate people. Learning the techniques comes easily for some guides; for others, a significant amount of time will need to be spent. Training should not be a one-time event for guides. Good guides should be continually refreshing and updating their knowledge, and the site's administration should consider carrying out periodic courses for this purpose. Courses should be developed with, and at least partly financed by, the tourism industry. In addition to specialists in each of the themes outlined, tour operators should be instructors in courses, as should older, respected members of the local community.

Young men often dominate the competition for places in guide training courses, but it is important to ensure that women participate too. They make good guides, and at least 50% of tourists are women! Rare (formerly the RARE Centre for Tropical Conservation), with the support of The Nature Conservancy, has developed a comprehensive guide training manual that is highly recommended.

Guide Availability

Ecotourism encourages the inclusion of local people in as many circumstances as possible. While it may be useful to utilize local people as naturalist guides, managers should realize that residents may not be "natural" naturalist guides. Their interests or educational levels may be obstacles to reaching the level of expertise required of guides at a site. Significant training may be needed before they can function effectively.

Work Availability

Work availability is a very sensitive issue in many situations. Naturalist guides have the potential to earn significantly more money than other members of their community. For this reason, when a site initiates a naturalist guide system, there are sometimes many more candidates than available work. Managers must be careful not to create high expectations among guide candidates, especially if visitor numbers are not sufficient to guarantee work for everyone. If some candidates for a training course are selected over others who appear to have similar qualifications, conflicts may arise. Site managers may do several things to minimize these problems:

- Ensure that specific criteria are used to select guide candidates and that the criteria are strictly followed. Limit training course size to a specific number of people and accept candidates on a first come, first serve basis.
- Initiate policies that encourage or mandate the use of local guides in the ecotourism site or in specific locations or zones within the site. This may cause conflicts with other, non-local guides.
- Encourage the creation of a naturalist guides association that will help to organize guides and their response to a limited number of guiding opportunities, e.g., a system of rotation. This is also an excellent way to minimize cutthroat competition and to standardize prices. The site could mandate that guides charge only a certain amount for a given service, but the mandate would be better received and complied with if the guides were allowed to determine their own price structure.

Language Skills

Local guides can face a language barrier since most ecotourists are from another country, usually one where a different language is spoken. Local guides can be very ingenious at communicating with visitors whose language they do not speak. However, they cannot express themselves at the level that a high quality naturalist guide would need to communicate effectively, expressing complex ideas and concepts.

It is not uncommon for organized tours to arrive at an ecotourism site with a guide who works with the tour company and comes from the capital city, or even another country. Sometimes these guides are very knowledgeable about the site, but many are not. However, local community members should be given priority for positions as naturalist guides.

In the case of areas that are ancestral lands of local communities, hiring a trained local naturalist guide should be obligatory. If tour operators require higher level scientific interpretation, they may choose to hire a university educated non-local guide to also accompany their clients. Training courses for local guides will likely emphasize different themes than courses for university-educated naturalists. If the situation is developed appropriately, guides from both categories can learn a lot from each other. Regardless, all guides should take and pass the training course and be licensed. It should be mandatory to train and provide licenses to local guides.

Conclusion

The environment is one of the primary concerns of ecotourism, which often involves travel to relatively undisturbed areas. As the tourism product is often dependent upon nature, negative impacts upon that resource should be minimized. As Cater [1994] notes, even the most conscientious tourist will have some degree of impact on the environment and so ecotourism should therefore attempt to minimize that impact. Many studies of tourism attempt to identify an environmental carrying capacity but a major difficulty of this technique is that it "implies the existence of fixed and determinable limits to development and that if one stays below those threshold levels no changes or deterioration will occur".

Great importance is attached to the need for local participation in ecotourism. According to Wallace and Pierce [1996], ecotourism is a type of tourism that "maximizes the early and long-term participation of local people in the decision making process that determines the kind and amount of tourism that should occur". There are important reasons for local involvement other than a moral obligation to incorporate the people tourism will affect. The degree of control the local population has over tourism in their locality is generally perceived as being a significant element of sustainability. As was noted earlier, ecotourism is required to provide direct economic benefits to the local community and minimize negative environmental and socio-cultural impacts. The most likely way these objectives can be achieved is if the local community are actively participating in and empowered through ecotourism.

The final principle to which ecotourism should adhere is that of education. Ecotourism should involve education among all parties –

local communities, government, non-governmental organizations, industry and tourists before, during and after the trip. Guides should therefore have been taught conservation issues and the tourists should be told about local conservation efforts and why they are deemed important. Tourists should be made aware of the damaging potential of their stay and should be properly informed on "ecotourism etiquette" and how to behave to reduce any negative impacts they might have.

A pool of trained and licensed naturalist guides can be a tremendous asset to protected area conservation. Creating a naturalist guide program should be a high priority for all sites with an ecotourism program.

Proposal

The annual "yellow dust" spring storms, which originate in China's Gobi Desert before sweeping south to envelop the Korean peninsula and parts of Japan, are blamed for scores of deaths and billions of dollars in damage every year in South Korea. The dust picks up heavy metals and carcinogens such as dioxin as it passes over Chinese industrial regions, before hitting North and South Korea and Japan.

The state-sponsored Korea Environment Institute said the dust kills up to 165 South Koreans a year, mostly the elderly or those with respiratory ailments, and makes as many as 1.8 million ill so that volunteer tourism could be an another form of alternative ecotourism for the theoretical development of EATOF members countries. Accepting that a person is rarely forced to go on vacation, we can then infer that tourism as an activity is voluntary. An exploration of volunteer tourism consists of the principles it adheres to, its goals, and the characteristics that define eco tourism.

The motivations of volunteer tourism can broadly be stated as volunteer-minded and vacation-minded. Push and pull factors also look at the motivations of participants. One of the example of volunteer tourism is to dispatch a voluntary team consisting of some EATOF youngsters and citizen to plant trees in desert areas in China and Mongolia to reduce damages from desertification and yellow dust. It can provide people of EATOF countries with opportunities to realize the importance of voluntarism and environmental movement. The tourism strengthen partnership of cooperation on combating desertification and yellow dust. In cooperation with the all EATOF member, the Green forest is going to be established a long green belt, namely the Great Green Wall in Kubuqi desert in Inner Mongolia, China to fight desertification and yellow dust storm.

Through various programs such as tree planting, environmental education and cultural exchange, the Green Forest will provide young people and citizen with opportunities to realize the importance of voluntarism and environmental movement.

Goals

The volunteer tourism aims to arouse public awareness on the issues of desertification and yellow dust storms, to promote participation of the young generation in environmental activities, and to contribute to the establishment of ingenuous friendship among youths all over the world.

Vision

1. To combat desertification and yellow dust storms by constructing.
2. Organize Green Corps in cooperation with the all EATOF members.
3. Make a brighter future for the next generation.

Travel Agencies Selling the Nature Versus Sustainable Tourism Development

The growth in alternative forms of tourism has occurred simultaneously with an increased recognition of the need to implement the concept of sustainable development. Ecotourism has been widely assumed to be inherently sustainable, although few attempts have been made to verify this assumption. Ecotourism incorporates environmental and cultural conservation objectives, and emphasizes economic benefits to local communities. Hence, ecotourism would appear to be, and is increasingly presented as, a tool for sustainable development. However, it also has the potential to be more environmentally damaging than mass tourism since it typically occurs in fragile environments and opens up previously undiscovered destinations to the mass market.

By the late 1980s, a shift in the tourism industry's marketing strategy occurred alongside the emergence of the global environmental movement. In the decade of "green consumerism", critical consumers were soon leading the demand for "environmentally sound" holidays. Tour operators and travel companies began to promote themselves and their products as "environmentally friendly", and a number of companies published ethical and environmental codes of conduct and guidelines for travellers as well as guidelines for self-regulation. Tour companies also started to promote ecotourism holidays to all corners of the world, to coincide with the inclusion of the environment on the mainstream political agenda. At the same time the tourist hunting industry has expanded dramatically.

Literature Survey

Sustainable Development

In the 1987 Brundtland Report of the World Commission on Environment and Development, sustainable development is defined as the " development that meets the needs of the present without compromising the ability of future generations to meet their own needs" (World Commission on Environment and Development, 1987:43). To meet the needs of the present, the new development has to provide ground on which the basic necessities of all humans and the opportunities for a better life can be satisfied.

Sustainable development is being discussed for the last two decades, mostly among academicians. The core elements of these discussions are:

- The idea that the needs of present and future generations must be considered;
- The need to ensure that renewable and non-renewable resources are conserved, not exhausted;
- The requirement that access to and use of natural resources must take fair account of the needs of all people;
- A recognition that issue of environment and sustainable development must be treated in an integrated manner.

Sustainable Tourism Development

The tourism and recreation industry is at a crossroads in its development. Now as one of the world's largest industries, it is increasingly confronted with arguments about its sustainability and compatibility with environmental protection and community development. Consideration of tourism, the environment, and concepts of sustainability should consider four key challenges: (1) a better understanding of how tourists value and use natural environments;

(2) enhancement of the communities dependent on tourism as an industry; (3) identification of the social and environmental impact of tourism; and (4) implementation of systems to manage these impacts.

The tourism and recreation industry is confronted with serious and difficult choices about its future. The decisions made now will for decades affect the lifestyles and economic opportunity of residents in tourism destination areas. Many of these decisions are irreversible because once communities lose the character that makes them distinctive and attractive to nonresidents, they have lost their ability to vie for tourist-based income in an increasingly global and competitive market place.

Owen (1993) characterizes sustainable tourism development as:

- Tourism should be one part of a balanced economy.
- The use of tourism environments must allow for long-term preservation and for use of those environments.
- Tourism should respect the character of an area.
- Tourism must provide long-term economic benefits.
- Tourism should be sensitive to the needs of the host population.

Butler suggests the following working definition of sustainable development in the context of tourism: "tourism which is developed and maintained in an area (community, environment) in such a manner and at such a scale that it remains viable over an indefinite period and does not degrade or alter the environment (human and physical) in which it exists to such a degree that it prohibits the successful development and well being of other activities and processes".

The growth in alternative forms of tourism has occurred simultaneously with increased recognition of the need to implement the concept of sustainable development. As with "ecotourism", "sustainable development" is another environmental catch phrase with no single definition. On the face of it, no other economic activity would appear to lend itself to sustainable development better than tourism. Alternative forms of tourism that incorporate environmental and cultural conservation objectives with an emphasis on economic benefits to local communities would appear to be a panacea for sustainable development. Because damage to the environment threatens the resource base on which alternative forms of tourism depend, it would be logical to expect all involved in tourism to ensure the protection of these resources. All forms of tourism consume resources such as land and energy. However, when practiced against the standards of its definition, the small scale and dispersed nature of ecotourism, combined with connotations of sound environmental management, means that it has the potential to consume far less basic resources than other forms of tourism or other developments.

A recent article in the UK Youth Hostel Association's magazine, Triangle, takes up this theme:

> *"Spending your holiday in one of the latest artificial all-weather tropical pleasure domes or in intensely developed but properly managed holiday resorts like Benidorm and Torremolinos can be more environmentally friendly than indulging in trips to remote or fragile areas where tourism is more likely to be environmentally and culturally damaging and puts little or nothing back into managing and protecting the environment".*

Quoted in the same article, the popular conservationist David Bellamy comments "Ecotourism is already a dirty word. Hill walking, jungle trekking and all the rest are just as potentially harmful as conventional resort holidays, if not more so. Most of the tourism industry is simply sponging off clean water, fresh air, the natural and cultural environment and is putting nothing back in. But there are praiseworthy exceptions, which not only do not damage the environment, but also actually help to restore it. This is real ecotourism.".

In addition to the potential damage caused locally to tourist destinations, the air transport of tourists to remote areas of the globe seriously undermines the concept of sustainability of the industry as a whole. For example, air travel contributes 2-3 percent of global emissions of fossil fuel derived carbon dioxide, the principal greenhouse gas, as well as nitrogen oxides, which contribute to low-level ozone formation. Paradoxically, nitrogen oxides released at high altitudes also contribute to the thinning of the protective ozone layer over the earth.

Not all of the impacts of tourism are necessarily negative. If development and change are bound to occur in a particular site from some activity or other, tourism may be a far less damaging alternative than many other more polluting industries. The Overseas Development Association (ODA) Manual of Environment Appraisal (1996) provides a checklist to help develop management strategies to minimize negative impacts and maximize positive benefits. Therefore, alternative or other forms of tourism are not necessarily a panacea for sustainable development, unless well planned and well regulated. In most countries, there usually is no coordination between programs that promote and market tourism and those that manage environment and culture. On the other hand, agencies dealing with the promotion of tourism are not involved with the evaluation of its effects or with advance planning and management of the adverse impacts of tourism through avoidance, mitigation, and compensation strategies.

Ecotourism

The term "ecotourism" is often assumed largely to alternative tourism that involves international travel by people from rich developed countries to developing countries, as a means of providing much needed foreign exchange for hard-pressed national economies, and earnings for poor rural people. The notion of these interrelated conservation and economic benefits has led to much confusion surrounding the variety of terms currently in use that appear to have similar meanings and aims. These include "alternative tourism", "sustainable tourism", "soft tourism", "special interest tourism", "green tourism", and "ecotourism". Some of these terms frequently appear to be used interchangeably, while others may be defined in a variety of ways. In reality, ecotourism has become widely adopted as a generic term to describe tourism that has, as its primary purpose, an interaction with nature, and that incorporates a desire to minimize negative impacts. Implicit in the term is the assumption that local communities should benefit from tourism and will help to conserve nature in the process. In this study, the term "Ecotourism" will be used to generalize all the other terms, and if a specific section of ecotourism like wildlife tourism or alternative tourism is explained, then those terms will be used specifically. The terms "eco-tourists" and "eco-tours" will be used in this study to summarize the group of tourists and the tours created for them in the name of ecotourism.

As with the term "ecotourism", there is similar confusion regarding the term "alternative tourism" that is often used as a generic term encompassing a range of variations such as ecotourism and green tourism, all of which purport to offer a more benign alternative to conventional mass tourism. Indeed, ecotourism has been described as "one of the most widely used and abused phrases of the last decade", which it is argued can mean anything to anyone.

A Few Definitions of "Ecotourism":

"An enlightening nature travel experience that contributes to the conservation of the ecosystem while respecting the integrity of host communities".

"Responsible travel to natural areas, which conserves the environment and improves the welfare of local people".

"Purposeful travel that creates an understanding of cultural and natural history, while safeguarding the integrity of the ecosystem and producing economic benefits that encourage conservation".

Ecotourism can contribute enormously to the management of protected areas. Benefits include foreign exchange revenues, employment opportunities, improving awareness of conservation objectives and stimulation of economic activity. While protected areas are major destinations for eco-tourists, private enterprise is playing an increasing role in the ecotourism sector. In addition, ecotourism is a major vehicle for realizing tangible benefits of conservation for local communities with wildlife populations occurring on their land. However, the benefits accruing to local communities from tourism have so far been overstated. The type and magnitude of the environmental impacts associated with ecotourism vary with the type of tourist activity pursued. Some impacts are obvious and easily identifiable, while others are indirect and difficult to quantify.

Strategies to manage the impacts arising from ecotourism may also be direct or indirect. Direct strategies include limiting the total numbers of visitors to an area; dispersing visitors; zoning; using fixed viewing points; and setting guidelines for minimum viewing distances. Indirect strategies are those that aim to modify the behaviour of tourists. One of the most important ways of achieving this is to educate visitors about the potential disturbance they can cause and to provide advice on how to reduce it.

Ecotourism has the potential to be more damaging than mass tourism since they often occur in fragile or unique environments. Small-scale operations in environmentally sensitive locations may eventually turn into much larger and more destructive operations. Ecotourism may simply represent the early stages of the conventional tourist destination life cycle. The life cycle concept essentially revolves around the premise that, unless intervention occurs, tourist destination areas and resources inevitably will become over-used and, consequently, will decline. The six stages of the cycle are as follows:

- Exploration (few tourists, poor access and facilities, environment unchanged);
- Involvement (local initiatives, some promotion, increasing numbers);
- Development (many tourists, locals lose control, deterioration of environment);
- Consolidation (tourist numbers exceed local residents, all major chains represented);
- Stagnation (numbers peak, destination falls out of fashion, environmental and social problems);
- Decline or Rejuvenation (or intermediaries).

This cycle has a number of obvious implications for sustainability, based on the consideration of factors such as carrying capacity, local participation, ownership, social and environmental impacts.

Mass tourists may have less impact than eco-tourists, because they tend to limit themselves to well known, easily accessible areas and insulate themselves from the local people. In some instances, the zoning of mass tourism (or enclave tourism) is adopted as a deliberate policy by a host country. For example, tourists in the Maldives are confined to self-contained, purpose built resorts on isolated, often formerly uninhabited islands, in order to avoid a culture clash between bikini-clad tourists and the conservative, Islamic islanders. Bhutan limits the annual foreign tourist entrance to their country to 3,000 pax only.

Ecotourism proved to be a very lucrative sector of the industry, and commercial considerations of marketing the latest "undiscovered" paradise quickly overshadowed any concerns for environmental or cultural degradation. Indeed, the marketing of ecotourism may well have accelerated social degradation, because more and more previously unknown destinations were discovered and subsequently opened up to mass tourism.

Turkey & Sustainable Tourism Development

Without giving due regard to the underlying principles of ecotourism, tour operators and even governmental agencies seem to be securing the short-term economic benefits to sell regions or products.

As a developing country, Turkey's choice of pursuing a tou development strategy is to create opportunities for econo improvement, since it suffers from deficit in the balance of paymer Tourism is also a tool for decreasing unemployment, because it is labour-intensive industry. Turkey is trying to secure the short-tern inflow of the foreign currency by increasing its bed capacity and trying to attract more tourists. Although the industry is centralized as being governed by the ministry, there are not any records available of any act for sustainable tourism development. Some accommodation units and travel agencies to a certain extent, as a tool for revenue generation, only use sustainable tourism. Accommodation units try to decrease the operational costs like usage of sun energy. Some demand less usage of towels. Clearly, the aim of these acts is not to maintain sustainable tourism, but to minimize their costs. Indeed, the travel agencies' main concern is to maximize the total number of tourists to increase their profit. Therefore, the carrying capacity is totally ignored.

Like many other developing country governments, Turkish governments have helped the fast development of tourism without taking into account the factors of local culture and environment. All governmental acts have been related to monetary gains, since Turkey have been used to economic crises during the last decade. Even IMF has expected certain tourism income figures in order to give credits.

Research Methodology

The purpose of the research was to explore the perceptions of and the possible commitments of Turkish travel agencies engaged in ecotourism to sustainable tourism development. An exploratory study were undertaken since not much was known about the situation at hand, and there were not any information available on how similar problems or research issues have been solved in the past. In other terms, there were not any previously defined theoretical framework and any hypothesis to test, so this research was to develop related subjects and their groupings by content analysis.

In order to address the quality of information obtained about nature tour operators, substantial attention will be given to survey design and administration. The aim of the research was to examine how travel agencies perceive the impacts of their development and to evaluate their level of response to environmental concerns. In order to satisfy ns, the objective was to obtain rich data. This pointed towards qualitative method involving relatively few people. According nheim (1992) 'the longer, the more difficult and the more open-he questions schedule is, the more we should prefer to use ws.' In the light of this, a decision was made to undertake face-, in-depth interviews.

order to reach desired information, directors or senior personnel TURSAB member agencies who are engaged in ecotourism as it of analysis were interviewed. Having obtained the booklet of SAB listing the agencies as the population frame, the initial intention o undertake systematic random sampling; however, this method mpling proved unsatisfactory due to the high number of companies willing to participate and the fact that only around one-third of the population were in Istanbul, making the rest impossible to reach regarding the time limits. The choice of researcher was, therefore, very much decided on by the respondents' willingness to participate, i.e. the first ten agencies in Istanbul to agree. Given the seniority of all the interviewees, this was effectively 'elite interviewing': the individuals are influential and in a position to report on their organizations policies and future plan. Furthermore, 'elites respond well to... intelligent, provocative, open-ended questions'.

Among the total population of 362, 135 were located in Istanbul and the rest 227 were located especially where ecotourism activities took place. A limitation should be noted that the number of agencies rapidly change and figures of 2000 may not be the exact values of today, yet helped us for a fair idea of the population, since links on TURSAB website of the updated lists of agencies did not work during research process. The research was a cross-sectional study with respect to time horizon, because data were gathered by the interview once, for a period of days. In-depth, face-to-face interviews with managers of travel agencies engaged in ecotourism have been used as the data collection method. Other data sources were used during the literature survey such as publications, manuals, archives, journals and related books.

For qualitative data analysis, systematic coding by content analysis was used to analyze the transcripts of the interviews. In this method, the researcher analyzed interview answers and prepared a list of subjects. The researcher and one independent sorter categorized these subjects independently. After a discussion between the researcher and the independent sorter, who was a manager of one of the visited travel agencies, a common categorization was agreed upon. For reliability testing, two independent graduate students who have studied research methodology also categorized the subjects. According to the reliability test, the results of the content analysis came out to be significant.

Findings and Discussions

Types of Tours

According to the segmentation like mass tourism and ecotourism, travel agencies engaged in ecotourism also sell tours for the mass market. When the respondents were asked to compare the two types of tours with respect to sustainability, there was a clear dichotomy between the two segments. At the first glance, special tours and eco-tours might be considered more sustainable; their volumes are lower, they are more likely to use local accommodation, local guides and services, and attract more environmentally aware clients. However, a differentiated tour for the mass market may attract eco-tourists as well. On the other hand, some specialist markets are evolving into mass markets, because of the increase in volume and the rapidly changing markets. This shows the danger of using broad statements, as eco-tours are more sustainable.

Types of Activities

According to the frequency order derived from the answers of the respondents, the following activities are marketed by the travel agencies: Walking/rambling, alternative water sports, trekking, golf, adventure, cycling, hunting, safari, photographing, mountaineering, rafting, horseback riding, fishing, alternative winter sports, bird watching. Many of the agencies sell more than one type of tours.

Why to Sell Alternative Forms of Tourism?

Travel agencies sell alternative forms of tourism in order to earn more money. Other reasons are to reach the young generation, to increase the variety of products and to enter a new market. Travel agency executives feel that their companies should be considered like markets or small shops in evaluation of any effects of operations, but they forget the fact that they do not sell products of another company like a market, but they produce the eco-tours themselves and sell them. Since those tours selling the nature are their products, they are responsible for the positive or negative effects of their products. These effects may be to the environment, to the local culture or to other aspects related to sustainable tourism. Travel agencies do not seem to accept the fact that some of the activities they make are acting against sustainable tourism by opening new areas to tourism without considering carrying capacity, using the nature as a marketing concept and allowing uncontrolled contact with local culture and tourists.

Sustainable Tourism

Sustainable development is a new subject of concern that many of us are not familiar with. Sustainable tourism development is also new, but it is being discussed in meetings of many international organizations. The first and obviously the main finding was that most of the interviewed senior personnel or managers of travel agencies in Turkey that are engaged in ecotourism do not even know what sustainability is all about. Interesting answers on the definition of sustainability, which were totally unrelated to it, reminded the researcher the fact that many of the employees and managers in the tourism industry are uneducated or did not have their education on tourism. This was proved by the respondents' education levels, which were mostly high-school graduates. The most interesting answer for the researcher was: 'Sustainable tourism,... should be related to renovations of the hotels, planes... it should not be related with travel agencies, we sustain tourism'. No matter the answer is funny or dramatic, but it seemed to be the reality for general knowledge of travel agency executives in Turkey related to sustainability. So, the respondents did not take into consideration the important aspects of sustainability like local culture or environment, since they did not know the term.

Who is More Responsible for Realization of Sustainable Tourism?

Economically, travel agencies feel that any attempt to take steps on sustainable tourism will put them at a commercial disadvantage because of increasing costs. They agree on helping the realization of sustainable tourism only if the tourists accept to pay more. Therefore, they feel that governments are more responsible for imposing restrictions, limiting growth and controlling volumes and so helping sustainable tourism. The result of this study showed that, travel agencies are willing to comply with regulations if governments impose them to the whole sector. Another point that Turkish travel agencies engaged in ecotourism mentioned is their operations are too small with respect to the whole market to make any influence.

Conclusion and Implications

This study has examined the social, environmental and cultural impacts of alternative tourism activities with regard to the travel agencies in Turkey engaged in ecotourism. First conclusion is that it has become harder to segment the market into mass tourism and ecotourism, since the two segments are becoming more integrated into each other and there are products, which cannot be put under a certain category. Second conclusion is that, although these travel agencies sell eco-tours and earn money, they believe that government has the major responsibility to ensure sustainable development. The third general conclusion is the fact that most of the travel agency executives has learned the definition of sustainability after the general explanation of the researcher.

It is easy to make an assumption like because travel agencies are small enterprises; their responsible behaviour may have a very small effect on sustainable tourism. Yet, specialist tours take tourists deeper into nature and sensitive local culture, and import the necessary skills instead using local work force.

Environmental policies and sustainable acts have become nothing more than a marketing ploy and a vehicle or eluding regulation. Environmental departments and affiliations with glossy campaigns have arguably become a PR exercise designed to meet the growing awareness in some markets to appear environmentally sound and to attract higher spending tourists. For sustainable tourism to be a marketable concept, tourists themselves have got to really buy on it.

To conclude, the researcher wants to point out that sustainability is mostly considered as an utopia and will probably never be achieved.

Limitations and Weaknesses of the Study

Since the respondents were not aware of the topic, it was hard to evaluate travel agencies' attitudes towards sustainable tourism. Most of the respondents did not want their company names to be published because of their lack of knowledge on the topic.

Certainly, as far as travel agencies are concerned, it is almost impossible to make generalizations, with each company having a different product, market segment, strategy and philosophy. Another weakness is that the respondents were busy with the new coming hot season. They demanded the time of the interview to be as short as possible. This limited the number of words used and so the frequency numbers.

Adult and Senior's Tourism

This status report summarizes the history of the Florida Library Literacy state grant program and outcomes achieved as a result of the grants. The Florida Library Literacy Grant program has reached over 6,000 adult learners through literacy programs at local public libraries from April 2000 through September 2001. Libraries have documented improvements in 63% of the adult learners attending their programs. Individual outcomes can be seen in the Activities and Accomplishment section of this document. The Florida Library Literacy Grant program was established by the State Legislature in spring 1999. Its purpose is to support the development and implementation of innovative adult literacy programs through Florida public libraries.

Fifty-two grant applications have been received and 41 have been funded. Among those counties receiving funding are 17 of the 33 rural counties, certified as such by the Office of Trade, Tourism and Economic Development (OTTED). Florida Library Literacy Grants provide funding to 11 of the 13 counties and one of the four communities identified as in either the first or second Rural Area of Critical Economic Concern.

Of the 30 counties and two municipalities receiving funds, more than 50% have greater than the state's average of poor persons (15.2%). Nearly two-thirds of the grant recipients have more persons at Level 1 literacy, the lowest level of literacy, than the state average (24%). These individuals are unable to find information in text, such as newspapers; complete forms, such as social security card applications; or interpret graphs and charts, such as a table of employee benefits.

Twelve of the grants addressed English as a Second Language (ESL) instruction, either in whole or in part. Five grants received multiple years of funding. The need for ESL occurs across the board, and is not always known at the beginning of a grant cycle.

For example, Lake County discovered that of the people enrolling in the library's adult literacy classes, 94% are seeking to learn English as a Second Language. To meet this new-found demand, the library redefined their mission during the second year and successfully secured funding for the second and a third year. The accomplishments of ESL participants include learning to write letters to landlords and holding telephone conversations in English.

ESL instruction is also critical in many urban areas in Florida. Hialeah's Level 1 literacy rate is 59% and observational data gathered by staff indicates that many of the parents whose first language is Spanish are unable to help their children with their reading assignments. In counties such as Leon, the libraries have targeted specific neighbourhoods that are in desperate need of literacy services. Working through one of its branches, the Leon County public library has targeted a two-mile area, which includes five low-income housing complexes. While there is not in-depth data on each complex, only 10% of adults in one complex has a high school diploma or GED.

Adult learners are gaining literacy skills that enable them to get jobs or better jobs. For example, one disabled man learned to fill out forms, identify jobs in want ads, and read manuals to receive an Air Conditioning Repair certification. Adult learners are also gaining life skills at their own pace. For example, one of the libraries benefiting from the Florida Library Literacy Grant program wrote, "...our students benefit greatly from the fact that these grant funds are NOT tied directly to Workforce Development. Adult learners, seniors, and disabled adults not entering the workforce are "welcomed" by programs funded with these grant dollars."

Of the forty-one grants funded, forty have successfully leveraged funding with partners and the programs will be sustained. The 41st grant involved the purchase of materials that continue to be available to the adult learners. Twenty-two library systems have received funding.

Program Implementation

The Florida Library Literacy Grant program was established by the State Legislature in spring 1999. Its purpose is to support the development and implementation of innovative adult literacy programs through Florida public libraries. The legislature appropriated $500,000 during the first year of funding and reduced the appropriation to $250,000 for the second and third years of funding.

Secretary of State Katherine Harris appointed members to the Florida Library Literacy Grant Advisory Council who designed the focus of the grant program. The Department of State, Division of

Library and Information Services developed procedures to implement the program. The first projects began in April 2000. Thus, the program has actually been in place for 21 months with the third year starting December 2001. The program has evolved as the Florida library community better identified their needs in the area of adult literacy. In the first year, the grant program focused on the broad literacy needs of the family. The second cycle of grants resulted in programs with the adults as the central beneficiary. For the third year, the application guidelines were revised to support the development and implementation of innovative adult literacy programs through Florida's public libraries.

For the first year, the program had two outcomes, 1) adult learners' literacy skills improved and 2) parents or caregivers read to their children. In the second year, successful applicants were asked to put most of their effort on the outcome of improving adult learners' literacy skills. In the third year, the applicants addressed the outcome of improving adult learners' literacy skills in order to create lifelong learners and library users supporting their role as parents, workers and citizens. This evolution has resulted in a program increasingly targeting the hard to serve adult learner.

An important development in the implementation of this grant program occurred with the third year of funding. The Division revised the grant guidelines and application to incorporate the outcomes-based evaluation methodology originally developed with its Library Services and Technology Act (LSTA) grants. In addition to identifying outcome(s) the grant applicant anticipated achieving, they were also required to identify the indicators of the successful achievement of the outcome(s) and the method of data collection. For example, a grant applicant could identify as an indicator of success, the number and/or percentage of adult learners receiving one-on-one instruction who complete a skill book or attain a personal goal.

Many of the library literacy programs funded through the Florida Library Literacy Grant program use alternative assessment which involves site-developed tools to measure success in achieving life skills goals rather than standardized tests which measure reading level improvement. Literacy professionals view both means of assessment as valid. Standardized tests alone "...are limited in their ability to demonstrate the full range of growth shown by program participants.".

3

Introduction to Youth Programme

Introduction

Recreation is an essential service in establishing and maintaining a healthy, livable community. Availability and accessibility to recreation opportunities contributes to effective crime prevention and reducing health care costs. Opportunities and facilities that promote physical and mental well being, bring citizens together in positive, supportive, and fun atmospheres, and create memorable experiences for families are primary in a positive future for our community. By proactively approaching the future needs of a growing and aging population, recreation programs and facilities contribute to a healthy community. The physical, mental, environmental, and economic contributions are great and far-reaching. Roughly 40% of the public has participated in a recreation or arts program offered by the City of Olympia during the past 12 months. The highest participation in recreation programs is by people in the age groups of 25 to 34 (50%), 55 to 64 (48.6%), and 10 to 14 (47.6%).

The most needed recreation programs, according to survey respondents, are organized sports, swimming activities and cultural arts activities.

Youth Programs

The Youth Programs Division provides a safe, positive environment for Olympia's youth by offering a variety of quality recreational activities and self esteem building experiences. These opportunities include the Middle School After School Program, a free drop-in program offered in cooperation with the Olympia School District, summer and school break day camps that target elementary aged youth, year round outdoor adventure camps and trips, and special events such as Middle School Activity Nights. Recreational opportunities focus on the development of positive, meaningful, nurturing, and supportive relationships between staff, youth, school administrators, teachers, custodial staff, parents, and other youth service agencies. Physical and emotional safety for all staff and participants is highly emphasized.

It is important to offer a diverse array of recreational opportunities that allow youth to explore, learn and develop social, physical and problem solving skills. In the After School Program this is accomplished by conducting the recreational components brought to each activity site by recreation leaders on a rotating schedule. Components include Outdoor Adventure Skills, Sports and Field Games, Fitness and Dance, Arts, Crafts, Cooking and Leadership Development and Community Service.

In addition, field trips and special guests are regularly scheduled. Day camp programs also include similar components with field trips, swimming and tennis lessons available.

Youth between the ages of 6 and 14 years of age make up the primary target population for this program area. Day camp programs are appropriate for 6 to 11 years olds, with a Leader-In-Training option for youth 12 to 14 years old.

Many of the youth participants in the After School program would be considered latchkey youth, having no adult supervision between the hours of 2:30 PM and 6:00 PM. The benefits of these programs are preventative, offering positive recreation options during after school hours. Youth participants also have opportunities to associate with positive adult role models in supervised activities where they learn and practice appropriate behaviour and build supportive relationships. Day camp participants also have many of the same opportunities, interacting in positive social situations. They also explore and experience new recreational activities.

Facilities Needed

It is important to work closely with the Olympia School District and other local agencies to access facilities for the implementation of these programs. The After School program is most effective when operating on site at each of the respective middle schools. Access to gymnasiums, home economics rooms, weight rooms, cafeterias and play fields allow for diverse program activities.

Elementary schools are suitable and offer appropriate facilities for day camp activities. The Olympia Centre is widely used during school break camps with the exception of summer camps. Art rooms, cooking facilities, gymnasiums, and outdoor park areas are important in offering well-rounded program activities.

Staff Needs

Competitive salaries and benefits are vital to recruiting and hiring quality staff. It is also imperative to have funding available for quality staff training opportunities. The public demands responsible, intelligent, resourceful, and caring individuals to supervise their children. To maintain safe and appropriate staffing ratios, 1:8 for day camps, 1:6 for adventure camps, and 1:12 for after school programs, additional staffing positions will be necessary as the youth program grows.

Teen Programs

The Teen Recreation Program offers a wide range of activity choices for teens in the City of Olympia. A year round afternoon program consistently offers activities Monday through Friday. Late Night activities are offered on Fridays in conjunction with the afternoon program. Teens know that five days a week including almost every Friday night, a positive recreation alternative is available.

Teen Recreation Program Participants

Quality staff provides a listening ear and positive role models for teens. They also plan and present a wide menu of recreational activities for teens to choose from. The fun includes field trips for bowling and laser tag, professional sporting events, dances, ceramics, photography and art, kayaking and wind surfing, basketball and hacky sack tournaments, concerts and trips. Educational activities offered by local service agencies are also sponsored regularly. The Teen Recreation Program focuses on providing fun, diverse recreational activities in a safe and supportive environment.

Population Served

The teen program targets any interested teen in the City between the ages of 12-17, unless enrolled in high school. Since January 2000, 1,200 teens have registered for the program. On any given Friday, 150-

200 teens seek safe and positive alternatives to parties and other high-risk activities. Staff work diligently to create an environment that honours, promotes and supports diversity. Olympia teens who need support, activity alternatives, or simply a safe place to spend their free time are welcomed at The Olympia Centre, agreeing to respect themselves, the program, the staff, and other program participants.

Facilities Needed

Currently, the Teen Recreation Program is housed at The Olympia Centre, a comprehensive recreation facility that hosts a wide range of populations and activities. Although the program has integrated well within The Olympia Centre, unique challenges such as sharing space, maintaining a reasonable noise level, and accommodating the increasingly successful growth of the program are ever present.

Staff Needs

Competitive salaries and benefits are vital to recruiting and hiring quality staff. It is also imperative to have funding available for quality staff training opportunities. The public demands responsible, intelligent, resourceful, and caring individuals to supervise their youth and teen participants. With the anticipation of future program growth, additional staffing will be necessary to maintain safe and appropriate supervisory ratio of 1:20.

Athletic Programs

The Athletic Program division provides a safe, organized and challenging environment for Olympia's citizens by offering a variety of quality leagues, tournaments, and classes. These opportunities include adult soccer, volleyball and basketball, martial arts, fitness programs and youth clinics and camps. In addition, athletic field allocations for the City and Olympia School District are managed by the Athletic Program within the Department.

Population Served/Benefits

Adults between the ages of 18 and 50 years of age make up the primary target population for adult leagues. Youth sports camp and clinics are appropriate for 6 to 11 year olds.

Preschool Gymnastics Class

Adult athletics provides opportunities for fitness, competition, social interaction, and wellness. Indirect benefits include decreased long-term health care costs and economic opportunities and expenditures diverted to more leisure activities and sports related equipment. Other economic benefits directly impact the community with revenue resources from tournaments positively impacting local hotels, restaurants, and tourism services. Youth participants also have opportunities to associate with positive adult role models in supervised activities where they learn and practice skills, appropriate behaviour and build supportive relationships.

Athletic field allocation management creates an opportunity for a comprehensive and diverse approach to usage. The by-product is a fair that efficiently utilizes existing facility resources.

Facilities Needed

To meet the needs for future athletic programs, it will be important to work closely with the Olympia School District and other local agencies to provide facilities for these programs. The Adult Basketball and Volleyball leagues use middle school gymnasiums as well as The Olympia Centre gymnasium.

The Adult Soccer programs take advantage of local school fields as well as Yauger Park during the fall, which provides lighted fields.

Staff Needs

Competitive salaries and benefits are vital to recruiting and hiring quality staff. It is also imperative to have funding available for quality staff training opportunities. The public demands responsible, intelligent, resourceful, and caring individuals to supervise and implement quality athletic programs, clinics, and tournaments.

Leisure Recreation Classes

Life long learning and recreational activities are taught through a variety of class offerings. Most of the leisure recreation classes are conducted at The Olympia Centre. The offerings appeal to a population of wide interests, skill level, and talents. Classes are available to youth, adults, and families and include art, dance, landscape design, languages, cooking, preschool, dog obedience, gymnastics, yoga, computer education, and investment. These opportunities introduce participants to new recreational activities as well as promote balance, relaxation and creative outlets for our citizens.

Under the leadership of the Parks, Arts & Recreation Department, the City should develop new programs and events to support the recreation activities that are most accessible to Olympia residents: bicycling and walking. The Department should sponsor leisure and moderate paced bicycle rides to help new riders gain strength and confidence for safe and independent riding. In addition, the City should support recreational walking and bicycling by developing maps that show the location of trails, routes, parks, and important interpretative and educational locations. The City should also consider bicycle safety and education programs for youth and adults in coordination with the Olympia Police Department and Transportation Division.

Population Served/Benefits

All segments of the Olympia population are served through recreation classes and special events. Youth, teens, adults, families, and seniors have many opportunities to choose from. Scholarships are available to families and individuals that demonstrate financial need.

Promoting healthy lifestyles through positive and creative recreational opportunities benefits the entire community. Seniors engage in uplifting social interaction, vital to physical and emotional health, while continuing or learning new recreational skills. Youth and teens have opportunities to try new activities in a positive and supportive atmosphere while learning appropriate social skills. Adults enjoy continuing education opportunities, learning skills that empower them to become more self-sufficient, environmentally conscious, and physically and creatively active.

Facilities Needed

In anticipation of population growth, increased participant interest, and furthering skill development and activity offerings, additional recreation facilities are needed. While most classes are conducted at The Olympia Centre, it does not have the capacity or functionality to host the current demand. Inappropriate flooring, classroom size, lighting and other aspects impair functional space. This impacts the cost effectiveness and quality of classes. Limited classroom space and building scheduling conflicts create waiting lists for popular classes, disappointing many would-be participants.

To meet the current as well as anticipated needs it is vital to work closely with other facilities operators, such as the Olympia School District and other local agencies to access facilities for the implementation of these programs. While The Olympia Centre offers a centrally located activity site, local schools offer more convenient and accessible activity sites for many other residents. Seniors and youth particularly will benefit greatly by establishing identified neighbourhood educational facilities as community schools where recreational classes will be available. This concept also allows for the expansion of program schedules into after school hours during the school year and mornings during the summer. Schools offer complete and comprehensive recreational facilities with gymnasiums, art and music rooms, home economic rooms, computer labs, weight rooms, cafeterias and play fields.

More importantly, there is a need to build and maintain facilities that are dedicated solely to conducting a comprehensive recreation menu for all ages and interests levels.

Staff Needs

Competitive salaries and benefits are vital to recruiting and hiring quality staff, contractors, and instructors. It is imperative to have funding available for quality staff training opportunities. The public demands responsible, intelligent, resourceful, and caring individuals to teach and lead a variety of recreational classes.

Special Events

Community events promote family recreation and activities. Ethnic and cultural diversity is celebrated through dance and entertainment, food, art, crafts, and educational demonstrations. Youth activities include hands on projects, games, bubble gum blowing contests, petting zoos, and sensory and large motor skill activities. Families and adults enjoy a variety of music, dance and entertainment presentations. These events are free to the public and sponsored largely by local businesses and sponsorship funding and in-kind services. For the community, special events is a time for people from all walks of life to come together celebrating, playing, and enjoying the vast recreational opportunities available.

Population Served/Benefits

All segments of the Olympia population are served through special events. Families and individuals have many opportunities to choose from. Families enjoy outings and experience a variety of recreational opportunities that they might otherwise not have access to due to limited finances, transportation or knowledge of resources. A sense of belonging to a vibrant community is a common thread throughout all of the events offered.

Staff Needs

Competitive salaries and benefits are vital to recruiting and hiring quality staff. It is imperative to have funding available for quality staff training opportunities. The public demands responsible, intelligent, resourceful and caring individuals to plan and implement a variety of special events. In addition, support staff are needed to assist with set up, supervision and take down of events.

Outdoor Adventure Programs

Olympia and the surrounding area host a tremendous number of outdoor recreation resources. Opportunities to learn about and enjoy land and water activities only require organization and programming. Muscle-powered recreational activities available include sailing, wind surfing, hiking, mountain biking, skiing, whale watching, snow shoeing, rock climbing, and beach exploring.

Population Served/Benefits

Seniors and adults enjoy mid-week or weekend activities where they get outdoors, experience positive social interactions, and engage in physical activities. A chance to explore and participate in a variety of outdoor settings – city, county, state and national parks, wildlife refuge areas, and rivers, bays, and lakes – all offer pristine natural environments for relaxing and invigorating experiences.

Youth and teens explore a variety of outdoor skill development and educational opportunities through Outdoor Adventure Camps and Adventure Days. Camp activities include theme camps, such as rock climbing, mountain biking, sailing, or beach exploration and play, or a variety of combined activities such as hiking, sea kayaking, and rock climbing. Older youth can develop outdoor leadership skills through Adventure Leadership Challenge camps. Skills and instruction in outdoor trip logistics, map and compass, outdoor cooking, low-impact camping, wilderness first aid and trip planning are the primary focus. Team building and leadership skill development enhances the camp activities.

Families enjoy winter sleigh rides, summer wagon train treks, up close tours to wildlife animal parks, and river raft trips. These offer unique and exciting experiences that strengthen and bind families to each other. These activities offer informal educational opportunities, social interaction, and exploration of the outstanding outdoor resources available. Additional benefits include increased environmental and wildlife habitat awareness. Outdoor recreation enthusiasts that are educated and aware of their impact on wetlands, waterways, and trails contribute a great deal to protection, preservation and enhancement of outdoor resources. Citizens who participate in outdoor activities advocate and protect the very resources they use. This further contributes to an overall healthy community.

Economic benefits extend from local businesses benefiting from the sale of outdoor gear and equipment to local state and national parks. Park and trail user fees bring in revenue from entrance fees, back country permits, snow park permits, and some trail fees.

The physical, social, and emotional benefits participants gain from these activities are life long and far reaching. Mentoring and educating future outdoor stewards guarantees that local resources will be available for generations to come. The outdoor environment offers diverse classroom settings for informal education, appropriate settings for a variety of recreational activities-an exceptional atmosphere for uplifting, refreshing, and invigorating the mind and body.

Facilities Needed

While most outdoor activities are conducted in outdoor settings, there is a need for access to indoor facilities. Rock climbing gyms, swimming pools, and classroom space allows for conducting introductory classes related to rock climbing, kayaking, SCUBA diving, and outdoor cooking. Slide presentations and hands on activities such as knot tying, winter clothing and wilderness first aid classes require indoor facilities as well. Many activities and classes are held at local parks with limited shelter available in the event of inclement weather.

Sailing and wind surfing classes and camps are interrupted due to bad weather. With additional indoor facilities available alternative activities related to the camps or classes would allow for uninterrupted continuation of these programs.

Integrating Function, Aesthetics & Metaphor

The Indian Creek Stormwater Treatment Facility was constructed in 2001 as a result of a unique collaboration between the City of Olympia Public Works Department, the Olympia Arts Commission, artist Elizabeth Conner, local Tribes and the Washington State Dept. of Transportation. Although the primary role of this facility is to clean stormwater runoff from Interstate 5, its unique design also integrates public art with the functional aspects of stormwater treatment and slope stabilization. Walking trails, landscape and views of the stormwater cleansing process transform this facility into a publicly accessible site that support creative solutions, discovery and education.

Staff Needs

Outdoor recreation participant interest and skill level continues to increase, creating a demand for more opportunities for youth, teens, seniors, adults, and families. To meet this demand additional staffing is required. An Outdoor Adventure Recreation Coordinator will allow for the required research, planning, development and implementation of additional outdoor opportunities for the community. Pre-trips to new activity areas including the Cascade Marine trail for kayaking/ camping, Capitol Forest trails for hiking and mountain biking, numerous state and national parks trails for hiking and back packing as well as special tours such as Family Christmas tree cutting outings require additional hours for quality activities.

Trip leaders and staff who specialize in and meet standard certification requirements are needed to maintain safe and quality programs. Staffs who relate well to youth, teens, seniors, and families are necessary to conduct successful activities. Ratios for youth adventure camps are 1:6 while adult and family trips are 1:12. Competitive salaries and benefits are vital to recruiting and hiring quality staff, contractors, and instructors. It is imperative to have funding available for quality staff training opportunities on an on-going basis. The public demands responsible, intelligent, resourceful, safety conscious, and caring individuals to teach and lead outdoor adventure recreation classes, camps, and trips.

Conclusion

Public recreational programming is vital to a healthy community. The mental and physical well being of our citizens ensures vibrant, supportive, and safe neighbourhoods. Nurturing our youth and supporting our family structure is the most cost-effective approach to crime prevention. Individuals – youth, adults, and seniors who feel nurtured gain a sense of belonging, make great contributions, and invest in their communities.

Future Needs/Challenges

Budget Resources

To meet the level of service demand by anticipated increased participation in youth and family activities, additional budget resources are necessary. Adult programs are currently and will continue to remain self-supporting.

Facilities

A shared vision of recreational programming by the Olympia School District with an enhanced or increased level of cooperation is needed to meet the community's needs. Schools that function as satellite or neighbourhood recreation centres after school hours between 3 and 10 p.m. will allow for the expansion, availability, and accessibility of recreation programs to a larger segment of citizens. After school youth recreation programs, classes for seniors, adults, and families, and sports programs all will benefit by this shared vision.Modifications to The Olympia Centre building are also necessary. It is currently identified as a rental facility, senior centre, youth centre, and for recreation classes. However, limits of space, room configuration, flooring, and availability limit its use as a recreation centre.

The lack of a local community aquatic facility greatly inhibits recreational program offerings. Day camps and youth programs have limited access to local YMCA pools or others operated by outside agencies. Swimming lessons, water aerobics, pool sports, competitive swimming and open swim opportunities are in high demand. Outdoor adventure programs also will be enhanced with access to pool facilities for introductory or educational purposes.

Outdoor athletic facility needs include lighted full sized, year round soccer fields. Tournament level soft ball and soccer fields also will allow for additional recreational opportunities as well as increase the quality of participation and improve safe playing conditions.

With population forecasts showing an aging and growing population, the future of recreation in Olympia needs to be addressed. Either specific recreation facilities must be built or future school facilities need to be designed and built with the intent of meeting this future deficit.

Transportation

Limited availability of adequate program transportation negatively impacts program quality. Currently transportation is accessed through renting or leasing state, county, and private vehicles. Not only is the situation cost-prohibitive it also is often unreliable. To better serve program participants and enhance youth programs, camps, outdoor adventures, and classes, reliable transportation is needed.

Costs

The costs to run quality programs include: 1) staffing and training; 2) supplies and materials; 3) photocopies and binding; 4) uniforms and identification; 5) consumable supplies; 6) equipment; 7) transportation and fuel; 8) admission fees; 9) expert services and/or contractors; 10) marketing and promotion; and 11) photography.

Outdoor Adventure Programs

The costs to run quality outdoor adventure programs include: 1) staffing and training; 2) supplies and materials; 3) photocopies and binding; 4) uniforms and identification; 5) consumable supplies; 6) equipment; 7) expert services and/or contractors; 8) marketing and promotion; 9) photography; and 10) and consistent, reliable, and available transportation for camps and trips.

Equipment needs are numerous based upon the initial program purpose of offering introductory outdoor activities. Many participants do not own or have access to the variety of outdoor gear related to selected activities and would not expect to purchase the gear until deciding to more aggressively pursue certain activities. Equipment and gear needs include snow shoes, cross country ski equipment, kayaks, canoes, and related gear, wind surfboards, binoculars, camp stoves, back packs, tents, and mountain bikes. In order to properly maintain quality gear and equipment these items should be scheduled for replacement every 3 to 5 years.

The greatest challenge is in securing appropriate transportation means. Outdoor camps and trips are often limited due to the lack of appropriate transportation. Transportation needs include multiple 15-passenger vans with trailer hitch capacity and racks for storage containers. A kayak/canoe trailer, bicycle trailer, and enclosed gear trailer are also needed to provide quality activities.

Demographic Trends and their Impact on Holiday Tourism Demand

Demographic Trends and their Impact on Holiday Tourism Demand: Demographic change is said to be one of the important drivers for new trends in consumer behaviour in most European countries. Two important demographic trends, often being in focus at conferences as well as in publications are:

a. an older growing society due to rising life expectancy (developed countries taking the lead),
b. a declining number of children due to sinking fertility in many industrial countries combined with the dissolution of traditional family patterns,

These are major demographic changes that are already influencing society today and that are worth a closer look on how they may have an impact on holiday travel behaviour.

Compared to other trends, demographic trends seem quite easy to identify and predict-estimated future development based on these developments therefore appears to be rather reliable. The problem is the next step: How will these demographic changes influence consumer behaviour? Are they of any importance? Will the senior generation of tomorrow behave the same way as the present one or perhaps completely different? Will a growing number of one-child-households, patchwork-families, grandparents travelling with their grand children etc. affect the expectations on family products? (How) should suppliers adjust?

To draw conclusions about a potential future reality of consumer behaviour based on statistical data not only requires a sound basis of demographic data but a reliable knowledge on the links between demographic data and the tourists' behaviour. Tourism consumer surveys can provide data

- on the importance a segment has in tourism (does change really matter in terms of volume?)
- on the specific behaviour patterns of the segment in focus (e.g. does a "new", emerging segment show a different behaviour from "older" segments?)
- on the direction and degree of change in tourist behaviour patterns related to the general trends in society.

We define a trend as a development in time which can be identified in the past and is likely (with good reasons) to continue in the future. Thus, trends describe *possible* developments likely to come. They can be used as information input for marketing or social planning. According to his objectives, the marketing professional will support or fight the trend, his action of course influencing the reality as well.

This paper gives two examples from Germany on how the results of consumer surveys can be used as a tool for trend research. The first example refers to the growing number and share of "seniors", analyses the fundamental patterns of changes in holiday travel behaviour during the life span, and allows for a surprisingly simple way to have a look at the dynamics ahead. The second example focuses on the declining number of children born combined with the dissolution of traditional family patterns. What does this change mean for holiday tourism?

Database: The "Reiseanalyse" (RA) Travel Survey

The *Reiseanalyse* RA survey (travel analysis), which is conducted in Germany every year, was designed to monitor the holiday travel behaviour, opinions and attitudes of Germans and has been carried out since 1970, using the same method and a comparable set of questions in the questionnaire. The survey describes and analyses holiday trips of 5 days and more as well as short trips of 2-4 days.

The survey is organised by the F.U.R, Forschungsgemeinschaft Urlaub und Reisen e.V., Kiel/Hamburg, an independent association of domestic and international users of tourism research in Germany. F.U.R is a non-profit organisation. The users cover a broad spectrum of companies and organisations in the tourist industry such as (special) tour operators, hotel chains, regional, national and international tourism organisations and ministries.

Data are based on face-to-face interviews with a representative sample (German-speaking population aged 14 years and above, living in private households in Germany) of more than 7,500 respondents, the interviews being carried out in January each year. The sample is randomly selected in several steps.

As the survey has been carried out with the same scientific standards for more than 30 years, with a large sample and a very stable set of questions it offers a sound base for long term analyses and a fine tuned segmentation. These features can be quite helpful to examine some of the effects of demographic change on tourism demand.

Holiday Trips of Seniors

Senior Citizens and Tourism

The growing number of senior citizens in the European Union, and other industrialised countries such as the USA and Japan, looks to become one of the major marketing challenges for the tourism industry to grapple with in the new millennium. This demographic shift has already been the focus of some academic tourism research and the topic for several tourism conferences-such as those sponsored by the WTO in Spain (1993), Brazil (1996) and Portugal (1999) as well as for ITB 2000 and 2003 in Berlin.

The idea that elderly need and deserve special attention is not really that recent. In Germany for example this segment has been an issue in the media for more than 40 years.

Even if societies are already experiencing the change and its impacts the fundamental shift still is to come in the next two decades. In looking ahead, United Nations statistics predicts that the share of people being 60 or older will grow dramatically in the coming decades, and is expected to rise from 10 percent of the world population in 2000 to more than 20 percent in 2050. Such demographic shifts will be seen on all continents whereas Europe is the major area of the world where population ageing is most advanced. Looking at the predictions for Germany, the number of persons aged 60 years or older will rise from 18.9 mn (23% of the population) in 2000 to 22.9 mn (28.5%) in 2020 and 25.2 mn (35.8%) in 2050.

Thus, there is no doubt that these changes will happen. But what do they mean for the development of tourism demand, e.g.:

- Do we have to face a change in the structure of tourists as well (which only will occur, if people don't stop to travel when getting older)?
- Will there be fewer trips (due to a lower travel propensity of elderly people)?
- Will the "new" seniors travel differently (compared to their predecessors or to the average tourist)? Will we experience a change in basic holiday behaviour patterns?

Methodological Approach: Survey Results can be Useful and May be Misleading

Of course, these questions can not be answered with population statistics and forecasts alone. Several market research projects have looked to asses future senior citizen travel patterns.

Such projects have attempted to not only determine the actual number of senior citizens who will be travelling, but have also sought to evaluate and specify certain aspects of future senior travel behaviour. However, they have been based on the implicit assumption of that there is a close relationship between the travel behaviour of past, present and future seniors. But, is this a valid assumption?

Lohmann (1989), Lohmann & Merzbach (1997), and Lohmann & Danielsson (2001) have examined the problem with the help of time series data from the German "Reiseanalyse".

Their approach focuses on the development of holiday travel behaviour in the course of life of cohorts, e.g.: How do Germans aged 65 to 75 years travel today, and how did they travel 20 years ago in the age of 45 to 55? As age sure is not the only variable influencing holiday travel behaviour, such an approach has its limits. But we felt it was worth a replication.

Holiday Travel Propensity and Age

Before we try to study the dynamics in the data over time, we examine the holiday participation figures for different age groups in the past and the age structure of German holiday travellers.

Travel propensity, which is defined as the share of persons in the population or a sub-group who made at least one holiday trip lasting five days or longer during a certain year, is one of the general parameters that is necessary to consider.

The travel propensity in different age groups of the German population in 1972 and 2003. As can be seen, older people travel less than younger, today as well as 30 years ago. This may lead to the assumption that people cut down on their holiday activities when getting older. The data reveals as well that today's seniors behave different compared to those 30 years ago, and that their higher travel propensity has been one of the important drivers for the general increase in holiday travel.

Table 1: Change of holiday travel propensity 1972/2003

age group	*Holiday travel propensity* *1972*	*2003*	*Change* *1972/2003*
<29 years	57	80	+ 40%
30-39	53	79	+ 49%
40-59	49	81	+ 65%
60-69	41	76	+ 85%
70+ years	33	63	+91%
All	49	77	+ 57%

Figures for German population aged 14 years or older; in % of age groups
Data source: F.U.R, Reiseanalyse RA 1972-2004

In looking at the demographic situation of travellers in Germany, 2. gives an overview of the change of age structure of travellers since 1972.

As the data shows, the overall age structure of holiday travellers did not vary much in the 70s and 80s. Yet, by 1995 the picture had already begun to change quite dramatically with people aged 50 years or older making up more than 40 percent of all travellers.

Table 2: Age structure of German holiday travellers

	1972 %	*1985* %	*1995* %	*2003* %
14 – 19 years	10.1	13,7	7,6	8,3
20 – 29 years	20.9	17,9	17,9	12,1
30 – 39 years	21.0	16,2	18,0	18,5
40 – 49 years	15.4	19,0	15,5	18,3
50 – 59 years	13.2	13,3	18,2	15,4
60+ years	19,4	20,0	22,6	27,5
Travellers (mn)	23.0	27,6	48,9	49,45

Obviously, there is a parallel development in the age structure of the population and of the travellers. However, the cross-sectional data is not sufficient enough to answer the question about whether any generation or cohort *changed* its travel behaviour during their life. Thus the results are of limited value when it comes to the question of future developments.

Participation in Holiday Travel during the Life-Cycle

In order to fully answer that question in-depth, a carefully prepared longitudinal cohort study (panel) would be necessary. Such a study could monitor its subjects travel patterns throughout their life-cycle.

Obviously, such a research project would have to face a lot of practical problems, be very expensive to conduct, and it would take decades to generate any data. Looking at this issue from a methodological perspective, the development of a longitudinal trend study (with a fresh sample each year) based on a series of independent surveys representing the population in different years is a possible solution. The *Reiseanalyse* RA.

Using the RA surveys of different years it is possible to take a look at the travel propensity of different generations between 1970 and 2003. Referring to this RA-data, we define a 'generation' (or cohort) as a group of interviewees who have a similar age at one time, e.g. persons from 70 to 79 years in January 2004 (= the 75 years old), 60 to 69 years in January 1994 ("65 years"), 50 to 59 years in 1984 etc. The data in a specific year for an age group always refers to the group of respondents which is defined by a ten years' range. So, in discussing the 75-year olds in 2004, the group of people then at the age of 70 to 79 years is described.

Thus, we examine the behaviour of a cohort over time by looking at the results of independent samples each representing this very generation in a given year. This approach allows us to follow these generations through their life-cycle using the RA data. While this methodological approach is not necessarily very sophisticated, it does have the important advantages of being both cost-effective and pragmatic.

The times series Lohmann & Danielsson (2001) have presented suggested that cohorts when becoming older stick to their once established travel behaviour. These findings were in line with previous publications.

To examine if these findings still hold true, we have now used the same approach starting with the most recent data on the holiday behaviour of Germans based on the RA survey carried out in January 2004 and going backwards in time to trace the cohorts being 50-60 years old in the year 2003. Table 3 shows the travel propensity of these two German "generations" (cohorts).

Table 3: Holiday Travel Propensity for two German generations over time

Year	1973	1979	1983	1988	1993	1998	2003
population travel propensity (%)	49	57	54	65	75	76	77
cohort 25 to 55 years age	25	30	35	40	45	50	55
travel propensity	56	66	59	74	81	82	80
cohort 45 to 75 years age	45	50	55	60	65	70	75
travel propensity	52	57	56	60	66	67	65
Figures for West-Germany; % of age groups							

What we see is:

a. for the first cohort an increase of the travel propensity from 25 years (56%) till 45 years (81 %, @ +45%) with a temporary decrease at 35 years and a stabilization at around 81% till 55 years.

b. for the older cohort a lower travel propensity and in total less variability, but still an increase between 45 years and 65 years (@ +27%), after 65 years little variation (travel propensity at about 65-67%).

Previous findings showed, that travel propensity increased throughout life until the age of about 50 years of age and was then kept stable until very late in life. Partly these recent results seem to contradict the previous findings as there is no rise from 45 to 50 in the new data for the younger cohort. The lack of additional growth could possibly be interpreted as a "ceiling-effect" at a travel propensity level of 80%, the 45-year-olds have simply reached the limit;

The most important result is that the travel propensity of a cohort while getting older is not going down between 65 and 75 years. Of course, the overall development of this variable is influenced by a lot of other factors which are responsible for quite a variation over time.

It is now possible to suggest that the general pattern of travel propensity is one of the key indicators for holiday life-cycle travel behaviour, and can be observed going though three stages:

1. Growth – tends to increase from early adulthood until 45 years old or when reaching some 80%.
2. Stabilisation-from the ages of around 50 until 75 years old, starting with a soft transition phase with lower increase.

3. Decrease – a slight decrease occurs once people reach the more advanced age of 75 to 85 years old.

The data indicates that while the travel behaviour of today's seniors is different from that of senior travellers in the past, it is for one simple reason-it is just another generation. Thus the development of the 'new seniors' market has come about largely because each new senior generation has a different behaviour pattern from its predecessor. Furthermore, in looking at this from another perspective, it can be seen that a particular generation's behaviour changes little. In other words, they seem to adopt a quite rigid and conservative set of pattern over a period of time, and it is this rigidity which seems to establish itself during the middle of the life-cycle and to last for about 20 years.

Holiday Destination Choice During the Life-Cycle

Such conservative behaviour is not only true for the general characteristic of travel propensity, but also-within limits-seems to hold true for the choice of holiday destinations. This can be seen in Table 4.

Table 4: Travel destinations of different generations

All travellers in %	1975	1990	2003
Domestic	46	30	28
Abroad	54	70	72
Austria	15	7	5
Italy	9	10	10
Spain	10	13	16
Other foreign countries	20	40	41
Travellers aged 55 to 79	1975 (55 yrs*)	1990 (70 yrs*)	2003 (83 yrs*)
Domestic	52	51	59
Abroad	48	49	41
Austria	18	8	2
Italy	8	10	5
Spain	7	8	10
Other foreign countries	15	23	19

The data shows a considerable change in the destination choice of Germans in general from 1975 to 2003 with domestic trips loosing market shares while outbound travel switched from Austria to the Mediterranean and a lot of destinations which have been of low importance thirty years ago. The generation becoming a senior in the period from 1975 to 1990 as a cohort fairly maintained their destination preferences at least with respect to the distribution between domestic and outgoing trips. In 2003, now in an age between 78 and 88 years, they show a slightly higher preference for domestic destinations. Of course, there are numerous factors influencing the decision of a holiday destination, and the increasing global competition between destinations makes predictions harder than ever. The longitudinal trend-analysis preferences for certain destinations did show some change within the generations, and presumably for other reasons such as price and image. Nevertheless, a certain amount of rigidity is still evident even for the choice of holiday destination. What we see is not the picture of elderly people avoiding far away destinations. Only when reaching the (statistical) end of their life-cycle do the seniors' preferences for domestic holiday destinations increase.

The Future's Senior Holiday Travelling

Based on these empirically founded assumptions, we dare to have a look into the future. What this paper has shown is that the travel characteristics of today's new senior market largely correspond to the same patterns that they themselves exhibited some fifteen years ago. In other words, those who are currently 55-years old, will keep travelling in the way they do today for many years to come. Given such information, it is now possible to have a basis on which to make some more reliable predictions about the future.

Table 5: Travel behaviour of future German senior generations

	75-year-olds in...		
	2003	**2008**	**2018**
Total in the age group mn	6.4	8.35	8.40
Travel propensity in %	65	70	78
Travellers in mn.	4.2	5.8	6.6
Destination of main holiday trip in %:			
Domestic	50	42	31
Abroad	50	58	69

Note: All figures for West-Germany only; 75-year-olds = 70-80 years of age at a certain year. Figures for 2008 and 2018 are estimations based on the rates of the age groups 65-75 and 55-65 today (2003).

The re-analysis of the RA-data has meant that it is possible to get an idea about how future senior generations will behave. Ignoring other possibilities (such as changing external influences), it can be assumed they will behave in a similar manner as they do at present-being today's 'pre-senior' generation. In looking to the future, Table 5. Shows some projected changes in travelling behaviour. In this case, seniors are defined as being in the age group 70-80, and the columns labelled *2008* and *2018* contain the characteristics of today's 65 to 75 and 55-65 year old travellers, and projecting them into the future. The first column shows the characteristics of tourists aged 70 to 80 in 2003. Due to a larger group of seniors in 2008, and a higher holiday travel propensity, the absolute number of travelling seniors will rise considerably, and they will more than likely prefer holiday destinations outside of Germany.

Own Calculations Based on F.U.R, Reiseanalyse RA 2004

The coming up rise in the volume of senior holiday travellers in 2008 is partly due to the changing age structure in the German society and partly the result of the "rigidity", i.e. the cohort's keeping the once acquired behaviour. In 2018 the socio-demographic change impact is neglectable.

Lessons Learned

The analysis of the RA-data shows that people do not change their travel behaviour just because they turn 60 or 65, or because they retire. Looking at this from a tourism suppliers point of view, these 'new' senior citizens already exist. A change in travel behaviour of seniors cannot be put down to a change in the travel behaviour of a specific generation. Just as the travel behaviour of today's current senior citizens is different from that of people belonging to this age group ten years ago, future senior generations will behave differently as well.

The notion of rigidity in behaviour is only related to the generation as a group. Of course, individuals will change their behaviour from time to time. Furthermore, the role of past experiences on future travel participation and tourism behaviour is important, but far from being the only determining factor. Other aspects such as changes to personal circumstances, or changes in the external macro-environment, may also influence behaviour to a broad extent. Nevertheless, what can be seen is that once people have passed the 55-year old mark, their generation tends to maintain a consistent set of travel behaviours. Their travel experiences during their formative years and the established travel patterns as an adult, will become an important influence on the behaviour in the last third of life. The rigidity-hypothesis is supported by the fact that people older than sixty tend to describe their actual travel behaviour in relation to their former travel behaviour, as not having changed much.

The 'new' senior citizens in five or fifteen years time will be different from the present senior citizens when it comes to travel behaviour. While senior travellers are already relatively active, the new senior generations to come are more than likely to surpass them. Such future behaviour can be predicted from the present, because these travellers, if considered as a generation, are unlikely to change their behaviour for the last third of their life. Of course, this may not be the case. It is possible that future senior travellers will be totally different from today's, by showing a complete lack of rigidity and stability in travel behaviour past 55-years of age. Therefore, it is conceivable that they might keep their unstable and less predictable patterns of travel behaviour their whole lives. While this cannot be ruled out, such a dramatic shift in human behaviour is unlikely to occur in the near term.

In conclusion, the approach described here offers an easy-to-do method to reach some rough predictions of how the target group of tomorrow's seniors may behave in the future. It is likely to be useful for marketing and planning purposes in tourism, and offers a starting point for additional future research on this topic.

Holiday Trips with Children

Family Holidays in a Changing Society

The demographic trends which we have been referring to earlier will not only have impacts on the senior segment but as well on other segments in tourism. Our second example focuses on family holiday trips, i.e. holiday trips (of 5 days or longer) of adults accompanied by children aged up to 13 years of age. The development towards an older society with fewer children combined with a growing individualisation and new patterns of living together (or apart) may lead the tourism destinations and industry to wonder, e.g.

- Is there a need to look for new segments to replace the old-fashioned family trip?

- Are offers tailored to the specific needs of single parents a strategy which may be fruitful for a significant part of the tourism industry?
- Shall we put more emphasis on products for one-kid-families?
- Will comfortable holiday trips with a touch of culture for the senior travelling with (grand) children meet a growing demand?

Before we use the tourism consumer data to check whether there really is a development to support such assumptions for holiday travel we have to take a second look at the underlying trends in society. Again we take Germany as an example.

The Demographic Trends Revisited

There is no doubt that the number and the share of elderly people will rise. In Germany the number of persons aged 60 years or older will rise from 18.9 mn (23% of the population) in 2000 to 22.9 mn. Furthermore we can assume that these new seniors will stay healthy and vital for a longer period than their predecessors. According to Opaschowski (2002) family life and being together with grand children has gained much more importance.

The declining number of children seems to be the real challenge for family holidays. For Germany Eurostat expects an 11% decline in the number of children under 15 years in the period 2000 to 2015. The number of children per woman in Europe has been clearly below the replacement level (2,1 children per woman) for years and this curve is still pointing downwards in many European countries such as e.g. Germany (currently 1,3 children per woman). This will result in smaller families on the one hand (with more one-kid-families) but the number of adults living with children will decrease to a lesser extent than the number of children in total.

The forecasting suggests that most of the Germans will live in multi person households even in the future. The way how and how long they will live together will become more colourful. For the tourism industry it is probably of low relevance whether adults travelling with children are married or not and whether these adults are the biological parents or not. The salient aspect is the structure and volume of persons living with children.

The available data for the household structure in Germany shows that within the last 30 years the share of households with children decreased from 45% to 32%. In West Germany the share of single parents with kids up to 17 years has increased from 8% of all families with kids in 1972 to 14% in 2000. Today, out of 100 families (private households with children up to 17 years) in Germany, 78% (7.3 mn) consists of a married couple with kids, 6% (0.6 mn) of unmarried couples with kids, and 15% (1.4 mn) are single parents (one adult living with kids but not with a partner). We estimate the number of single parents with kids up to 13 years to be some 1.15 mn. According to Statistics Austria one can expect a further rise in the number of single parents.

Thus, the major quantitative demographic trends with possible relevance for family holidays are (each with estimation for the degree of change from 2000 to 2010): more seniors (+ 11%), fewer children (-8%), more one-kid families (+ 8 %), more single parents (+ 12%).

Related trends in tourism behaviour – and their meaning for future development

To identify the meaning of a demographic trend for tourists' consumer behaviour one has to take into consideration the volume of the segment, the direction and degree of expected change with respect to this segment, and holiday travel behaviour data. We have used the data of the German "Reiseanalyse" as a data base and tool for segmentation. The segments are:

(1) all holiday trips with children up to 13 years, and the partly overlapping subgroups:
(2) holiday trips of single parents,
(3) holiday trips of respondents aged 50 or older,
(4) holiday trips with exactly one child.

We have looked at these segments in order to determine their actual volume, the change to be expected for the future applying the change rates derived from the demographic trends and to identify segment specific patterns of travel behaviour.

The segment of holiday trips with children (up to 13 years) has proved to be stable in Germany for more than a decade with some 22% of all holiday trips. In 2003 this share resulted in 14.4 mn holiday trips. An 8% decline would lead to a number of 13.2 mn trips, still an important segment. One can expect even a higher number when considering the fact that the decrease of the number of families will be slower as the one of the number of children. Thus, there is no need for a complete re-orientation of the tourism industry towards new target groups replacing the family holiday. But of course given not only the demographic change but also the strong competition between destinations a strong focus on the needs and expectations of this segment is recommended. Among all holiday trips with children those of single parents are only a small group (less than 4%, some 0.5 mn trips). An increase of 12% in a decade would result in 0.6 mn trips, a change which is – given the limits of a survey – barely measurable. A closer look at the travel behaviour of this group reveals that 87% of their trips are in the company of at least one more adult, i.e. the single parents do not travel as single parents. As far as the data can be interpreted there is not much of a difference between single parents' trips and other family holidays. The small volume together with the unspecific behaviour patterns lead to the assumption that the single parent holiday trip will remain a niche segment.

The share of people aged 50 years or older within all German family trips has been 9.4 % in 2002. This is already today a significant segment which could be considered more closely by the tourism industry, especially as a further increase can be expected. In addition, this segment shows a specific behaviour as tourists, e.g. compared to all family holiday trips a lower seasonality, higher spending, longer stays, and other destinations choices. Against expectations they are not very fond of culture trips and prefer holiday homes or apartments to hotels.

Finally, the one-kid-trip seems to be the standard of family holidays. So, this is not a development to come but today's reality. Again, this segment has specific travel behaviour patterns as e.g. more flight trips and more use of tour operators and as it offers further increase. In addition one-kid travellers have special needs which the tourism industry has to take into consideration.

In general, we see that some of the "new" trends have already affected tourism for a long time. The one-child-family has been the standard in recent years. Other trends are of no significant importance, e.g. single parents are of low relevance for tourism (which doesn't mean: for society) due to their small volume and a holiday travel behaviour very close to other families. And some trends require closer attention as there really is a dynamic development ahead. This should have implications for product design.

Conclusion

These two examples have shown that the transfer of socio demographic trends to a future development needs a closer look at the real changes in society (don't over-estimate!) and that consumer survey data can be very useful in determining the trends in tourism. Or, to put it the other way around, without the data from consumer surveys we would be unable to draw realistic conclusions.

In our first example-on how future senior generations will travel- we have used the survey data to examine the patterns of travel behaviour of a generation getting older and applied the findings to draw conclusions on the future. In the second example – on the future of family trips- we have used a fine segmentation which again would have been impossible without the survey data to get a realistic picture on the travel behaviour patterns of these segments.

These findings together with the statistical data on demographic change allowed for a better understanding of the coming trends in family holidays. In this paper we have only dealt with developments in consumer behaviour related to demographic change. To get a holistic picture of what will happen in the future of tourism one has to consider other influences and drivers as well, for example trends on the supply side or in consumer behaviour in general. But that is another story.

Of course, the future is predictable only within close limits, and unexpected events will always cause confusion. Still it is important (and possible) to prepare oneself for the trends that can be identified with some reliability today. This can be the starting point for the next challenge of trend research: It is not enough to know the trends; this knowledge must be transferred into products and strategies for destinations and companies. But without the survey data and a creative way of analyzing it we will never even come to this point.

Ministry for Regional Development of the Czech Republic

- Programming period 2004-2006,
- Operational Program Human Resources Development,
- Funding: 75% from ESF, 25% from the state budget,
- Priority 4,
- Measure 4.2 Specific Education 7 projects.

European Social Fund

Ministry for Regional Development of the Czech Republic;

- Training and education of employees in tourism,
- Vocational training of public administration officials in tourism,
- Tourism information,
- Destination management and creation of products in tourism,
- Event marketing for tourism,
- Training for public territorial administration officials and employees in tourism in the conditions of tourism development in protected landscape areas,
- Improvement of the quality of vocational training and education in tourism.

Projects

Ministry for Regional Development of the Czech Republic (Courses, seminars, training, publications, e-library) Some announced courses:

- Sustainable development,
- Crisis management,
- Heritage care in relation to tourism,
- Tourism statistics,
- Destination promotion,
- Golf as a specific tourism activity.

Project's Activities

Ministry for Regional Development of the Czech Republic; Next announced courses:

- Practical activities of information centres, call centres and help line,
- Event Marketing MICE,
- Work with media in tourism,
- Marketing communication regarding destination,
- Local, national and international destination marketing,
- Strategic development of tourism destination.

Project's Activities

Ministry for Regional Development of the Czech Republic ;

Summary:

- A total of 68 educational programmes were created,
- 12 professional publications/textbooks,
- 1 teaching DVD was published in these 6 projects,
- A total of about 9 000 persons were trained (businessmen, employees, officers of public sector).

Project's Activities

Ministry for Regional Development of the Czech Republic,

Project "Improvement of the quality of vocational training and education in tourism",

- To analyze and to map the current status of tourism education,
- To prepare comprehensive proposals and suggestions for introduction of an educational system in the tourism sector,
- To prepare a realistic proposal for the use of finances provided by Structural Funds for the tourism sector in schools, life-long and further education of employees and employers, including support for labour market development.

Project's Activities

Ministry for Regional Development of the Czech Republic in tourism education:

- Schools providing secondary education with a vocational training,
- Secondary schools and colleges,
- Universities,
- Public administration, regional and local self-administration,
- Life-long education and retraining,
- Tourist guides,
- Employment agencies in tourism,
- Employee unions, professional associations, trade unions in tourism.

Partial Evaluations

Ministry for Regional Development of the Czech Republic;

- 2,301 retraining entries were generated to the tourism category,

- 708 questionnaires were distributed among employers in the sector of hotels and similar facilities, travel bureaus and agencies, sports and other recreational services, cultural services,
- 12 ministries were analyzed; as regards regional, city and municipal authorities, the evaluation covered all 13 regional centres, including Prague, 50 cities with more than 20,000 inhabitants, 20 cities with 5,000 to 20,000 inhabitants, 30 rural municipalities and 11 municipalities that are centres of tourism.

Partial Evaluations

Payment of the Czech Republic;

- Schools providing secondary education with a vocational training (249),
- 121 secondary schools with generate certificate of education focusing on tourism and 18 colleges,
- 15 universities focused on tourism were generated out of the total number of 72 university-type schools in the Czech Republic,

Partial Evaluations

Ministry for Regional Development of the Czech Republic Schools providing secondary education;

- Optimization of number of schools,
- Increasing professional level of teachers and involvement of schools in further education of pedagogues,
- Development of practical training,
- Promotion of cross-border and international cooperation,
- Involvement of employers in further education of employees,
- Ensuring financial participation of employers in initial vocational training,
- Creation of teaching aids for specialized tourism-related subjects Establishment of a system for monitoring of labour market requirements,
- Creation of a life/long learning system,
    - basic education programs,
    - individual education .

Conclusions

Ministry for Regional Development of the Czech Republic Universities;

- Involvement of students in scientific research,
- Supplementing study programmes with compulsory practical training by cooperation with employers,
- Development of distance and combined forms of study,
- Preparation of further education courses for secondary school pedagogues,
- Creating a module-based solution of further education,
- Introduction of regular evaluation of universities by an independent entity.

Conclusions

Ministry for Regional Development of the Czech Republic;

- Network of secondary schools, where courses for,
- teacher will take place,
- Recognition of partial qualifications in tourism,
- Solution for students, who couldn´t finish theirs studies at the secondary schools (hospitality and gastronomic services, and other specializations in tourism) and back to school,

Present and Future

Ministry for Regional Development of the Czech Republic Cooperation with Czech TV:

- Production of 18 episodes of an educational programme cycle,
    - tourism,
    - hotels, other accommodation types,
    - gastronomy,
    - travel bureaus and travel agencies,
    - spa, wellness, rural tourism,
    - guides, congress tourism, events, etc.
- Production and broadcasting of a 10-part TV cycle designated for general public,
- Production and broadcasting of 3 TV spots.

Tourism as Education

Tourism has emerged as an instrument for employment generation, poverty alleviation and sustainable human development. Tourism promotes international understanding and gives support to local handicrafts and cultural activities. It is an important segment of the country's economy, specially in terms of its contribution towards foreign exchange earnings, generation of additional income and creation of employment opportunities. The foreign exchange earnings from tourism during the year 2000 were estimated at about Rs. 14,408 crores with an estimated direct employment of about 15 million, which is about 2.4% of the total labour force of the country. Tourism is the third largest foreign exchange earner for India. The International tourist traffic in the country is estimated to be 2.64 million during the year 2000.

However, according to the World Tourism Organisation (WTO), India's share in world tourism arrivals is only 0.38%, accounting for 0.62% of the world tourist receipts. This indicates that much of the tourist potential is yet to be tapped. With rapid advances in Science & Technology, tourism has acquired the status of an industry in all industrialised countries. The high influx of foreign tourist traffic has accelerated demand for certain economic production and distribution activities. Tourism has emerged as an industry next in importance only to Information Technology industry in the Services sector. By 2005, the contribution of Tourism to the world economy will be doubled. The economic liberalisation in India and consequent foreign investment opportunities, development of tourist facilities including expansion in air-line services, etc. provide an impetus for a spurt in tourist arrivals as in South.

Asian Regions

Domestic tourism plays a vital role in achieving the national objectives of promoting social and cultural cohesion and national integration. Its contribution to generation of employment is very high. With the increase in income levels and emergence of a powerful middle class, the potential for domestic tourism has grown substantially during the last few years. Realising the importance of tourism, the Government of Tamil Nadu has accorded high priority to tourism promotion and has taken initiatives to improve/create infrastructure in tourism potential centres and geared to encourage private sector investment in this regard. The many splendoured State that Tamil Nadu is has been described in the following paragraphs:

Tall palms and taller gopurams, the towering, intricately carved temple towers of a land of temples welcome the traveller to Tamil Nadu. There is no better place to begin one's discovery of the ageless South than in this colourful historic State, an ancient land of proud cultural heritage.

Tamil Nadu is a window to the modern South as much as it is a wide open archive of ancient legacies. Yet amazingly, for all its modern-day progress, Tamil Nadu retains its old-world charm. The harmony of the ancient and the new and the picturesque is truly remarkable here. Giant chimneys, symbols of an industrial upsurge that has put the land of the Tamil people in the fore-front of Indian development; stately palaces and exquisitely hewn temples of by-gone eras; beautiful unspoilt hill resorts and beaches and forest sanctuaries, massive developmental projects and new industries-they all mingle in one marvellous mosaic in Tamil Nadu. Chennai-a tiny fishing village that has mushroomed leisurely into a sprawling metropolis in the 300-odd years since it was founded in 1639-is the capital of Tamil Nadu, a land that has seen the rise and fall of many ancient kingdoms, the Cholas, the Pandyas, the Cheras, the Pallavas and many others, each leaving behind in the sands of time ineradicable cultural treasures.

Chennai a spacious city of distances, a city open to the skies, a city free of most of the ecological problems of the major cities of today, a city of beaches and parks and historic landmarks, is the pleasantest starting point for one who sets out to enjoy the delights of the South.

From Chennai no part of Tamil Nadu is too far. Excellent road and rail and air services speed travellers to any point in this ancient land. None of which is very much more than 24 hours away from the capital, each of which has something delightfully different to offer. The names of the towns are as musical as the ancient language of the people and they roll off the tongue sounding as exquisite as the sights they have to offer the beholder. Here are ancient capitals of once-proud kingdoms.

Like magnificent Madurai, its temple one of the wonders of India, and ancient Thanjavur, its Brahadeeswarar temple, a tribute to the splendour of Chola builders, among the greatest the world has ever known. Here are the ruins of historic Poompuhar, the Chola port and planned city known to Ptolemy and Pliny. Here are the Pallava towns of Kancheepuram and Mamallapuram, the former, one of Hinduism's seven sacred cities and a town of a thousand temples, the latter, famed for its sculpture but now becoming better known as one of India's finest beach-resorts.

Here are Tiruchirappalli and Kanniyakumari where ancient legends live on, in rock and plaster and wood. Here are hill stations that waft the aroma of tea and coffee, eucalyptus and pine. Hill resorts that seem like little bits of England's green ·ountry that are as rugged as India's own. And here, too, are forest anu sanctuaries untouched by man. Mudumalai, Vedanthangal and Point Calimere where the deer and the buffalo roam and the stork and the flamingo and egret nest.

Tamil Nadu has immense potential in tourism. The multitude of choice the State offers from beach resorts to hill stations, adventure holidays to cultural tours, heritage packages to wildlife sanctuaries should be presented to holiday makers.

Ninth Five Year Plan Review

For the Ninth Plan period, a sum of Rs. 30 crores was provided for Tourism sector. Against this the total expenditure during the Ninth Plan period is expected to be around Rs. 24.06 crores. This works out to 80.20 % of the total outlay. For the year 2001-02, the outlay for the Tourism promotion activities was stepped up to Rs. 11.82 crores. A sum of Rs. 2.95 crores was also spent on Tourism promotion projects under the Hill Area Development programme.

The following schemes were taken up during the Ninth Plan:

(i) Establishment of Tourist Information Centres at Tiruvandrum, Bangalore & Hyderabad,

(ii) Conduct of Fairs and Festivals,

(iii) Provision of Infrastructure facilities and important Tourist Centres,

(iv) Identification of heritage towns and their preservation,

(v) Grant of incentives for construction of Hostels, purchase of generators,

(vi) Luxury Coaches,

(vii) Encouragement to joint venture schemes,

(viii) Development of Taragambadi, Marina Beach and Children's Park at Guindy,

(ix) Grants-in-aid to State Institute of Hotel Management and Catering.

Technology, Thuvakkudi

The position in regard to tourist arrivals during the period from 1995-2000 may be seen from the Table below:

The home of Carnatic music and Bharata Natyam, the legacies of temple songs and dances handed down through the centuries. The home of magnificent schools of art and architecture. The home of great cultures and philosophies. This is Tamil Nadu. Gloriously ancient. Proud preserver of its traditions. Now magnificently modern. Everywhere here, there is exciting experience, splendid sights and havens away from it all.

Vision

- To make Tamil Nadu the number one State in India in respect of Tourism sector and place it on the map of International Tourism by marketing it as an important destination with heritage sites.
- Double the tourist arrivals and revenue to the Government by the end of the X Five Year Plan period.
- To address rampant unemployment problem through tourism.
- To make tourism a major economic activity in the coming years.

Goals, Objectives and Strategy

The following elements *inter alia* will influence the policies and programmes of the Tourism Department during the Tenth Five Year Plan period:

Sustainability

Hitherto the maintenance of the assets created was not taken care of adequately. In recognition of this aspect, the State Government has taken recently earnest efforts to improve infrastructure at various destinations. In order to ensure sustainability, proper upkeep and operation and maintenance also would be made part of the projects in future. As a first step in this direction, a project directory containing all relevant details of tourism related projects implemented in the State since 1980 is being prepared. This maiden venture will not only provide an opportunity for review and evaluation of the facilities already available, the facilities required to be created etc., but also help the State plan its future activities.

Tranquillity, Public Order and Tourism

The terrorist attack on world trade centre, U.S.A. on 11-9-2001 was indeed a black day in the history of tourism. The attack had a devastating effect on Tourism as fear gripped all over and, in its aftermath, several nations issued negative advisories regarding travel. The situation has, however, quickly returned to normalcy.

The ethnic strife in Sri Lanka, the ongoing warlike situation in West Asia, the cross border terrorism from western borders of the country have all had a contributory role and share in affecting tourism. Tourism can thrive and prosper only if there is peace and tranquillity. Tamil Nadu offers from this angle a very safe destination. However, the issues concerning safety and security of tourists and their belongings should be kept in mind.

Private Sector Participation

Recognition of the fact that tourism is essentially a private sector activity and the Government has to play only a catalytic role and that of a facilitator and to provide the platform for accelerated growth of tourism in the State. And the realisation that the Government need no longer be a service provider.

Institutional Arrangement

More effective coordination among various organisations and sectors of Government such as civic administration and adequate road, rail and air connectivity, communication, general administration etc. would be ensured.

'Product – Identification' and 'Product Development'

Keeping the clientele in view, products such as cultural and architectural heritage, pilgrims and religious destinations, eco–tourism destinations such as hill stations, beaches, rural and village tourism, arts and performing arts, crafts, and handicrafts, music, dance, the whole life-style yoga, health, Ayurveda, Siddha etc and provision of world class infrastructure/support systems etc., would have to be on the top of agenda.

Paradigm Shift

To recognise that tourism is an economic activity and is a major engine of economic growth; for it has very extensive forward and backward economic linkages that builds upon and has impact on overall income, employment etc., especially for the vulnerable sections such as women, children, disabled etc.

Tamil Nadu as a Complete Tourist Destination

To position Tamil Nadu as a complete tourist destination for all seasons and for all.

Information Technology and Tourism

At the working level, therefore, evolve a new work culture taking note of the requirement of an environment of co-operative federation, diversification and technological advancement.

Goals/Objectives

1. To increase the Tourist inflow to Tamil Nadu to 10-12 % per annum from the present level of 7-9 % (special focus will be on tourists from abroad as also up country domestic tourists).
2. To increase the period of stay of domestic tourists in Tamil Nadu from 7-9 to 10-12 days and in respect of foreign tourists from 4-7 days to 6-8 days; and restore the prime position Tamil Nadu had in the tourism sector in the past.
3. To evolve a Government led, private sector driven and community oriented framework at the organizational level, since tourism essentially is a private sector activity where Government has to play only a catalytic role.
4. To fully exploit tourism potentials and convert these as employment generation and poverty alleviation programmes.
5. To recognise the deep rooted innate relationship between Tourism and Culture and promote as such.
6. To promote ecotourism.
7. To tap the tourism potential in the coastal belt.
8. To expand the product base to have more effective coordination with other States in India in general and immediate neighbours in particular.
9. To make extensive use of information technology and other technological advancements.

10. To make tourism a CORE competency sector.

The thrust areas, keeping the above goals/objectives in view, therefore, during the Tenth five year plan period would be:

(1) Clear product identification, development and expansion, such as destination, circuits, services etc.;

(2) Creation and upgradation of required infrastructure, basic amenities etc., following an integrated and holistic approach;

(3) Human resource development and skills upgradation; and

(4) Promotion and marketing these aggressively and holistically.

Strategies

At strategy level also there would be a paradigm shift; instead of looking at various destinations & activities in isolation, attempt would be to look at Tamil Nadu and various tourism products holistically and in integrated manner.

Long Term Measures

For Increasing the Tourist Inflow

Aggressive marketing strategies will be adopted to publicise the tourist potential of Tamil Nadu both nationally and internationally. Some of the main features of this strategy are as follows:

(a) Opening of Tourist Information Centres in other States.

(b) Appointment of marketing agents throughout the country and also abroad.

(c) Advertisement *blitzkrieg* in print and electronic media.

(d) Publishing of high quality literature in Indian and foreign languages, and

(e) Screening of documentaries in theatres, railway stations, airports, bus termini etc.

World Class infrastructure will be provided at all important tourist destinations. Mega tourism projects pertaining to the products/ infrastructure and destination development, of tourist circuits, large revenue generating projects like rope ways, sound and light shows, cruises etc., and capacity building (training of personnel engaged in the hospitality and related skills) will be launched. Setting up of natural therapy centres, developing village tourism, construction of jungle lodges, promotion of adventure tourism, Yoga/transcendental meditation centres, constructing star hotels at important pilgrim centres, eradication of beggar menace, deployment of tourism police together with good civic governance would be some of the important aspects of the strategy.

For Promoting Private Participation

The Government will gradually assume the role of a catalyst/ facilitator and involve the private sector in restoring the prime position occupied by the State in tourism earlier. Besides facilitating clearances to attract the private entrepreneurs, it is proposed to adopt a multi-pronged strategy, viz.,

(a) A land bank will be opened where available government and private lands throughout Tamil Nadu will be identified and pooled. Land from this bank will be made available to the private entrepreneurs on long term lease basis on concessional terms;

(b) The Project proposals submitted by the private entrepreneurs will be cleared instantaneously through single window clearance system; and

(c) Attractive incentives will be offered; and

(d) Required technical assistance would be made available.

It is a well known fact that tourism industry is capable of generating huge employment (both direct and indirect) opportunities. It is estimated that world wide tourism industry enjoys a 10 % share in generation of employment opportunities.

Therefore, steps will be taken to train educated un-employed youth in the tourism related fields. i.e., Hotels, Guide, Recreation activities, Studio services, Theatres, Communication net work, Bar, Beauty parlour etc. The unskilled rural folk will be trained in the fields of Driving, Hospitality, Costumes, Traditional arts, Handicrafts etc. Proposals are also there to include Tourism studies in the Schools and College curriculum to create awareness among youth so as to fully prepare and sensitise the coming generations.

For Promoting Tourism in the Coastal Belt

Tamil Nadu has been bestowed with a spectacular thousands kms. long coastline. With respect to tourism related activities, the Government of India also have granted certain relaxations as to the ' coastal regulation zone rules'. These would be fully utilised to establish recreational and entertainment provision by roping in the private sector in a big way.

Short Term Measures

For Promotion of Cultural Tourism

The rich culture and heritage of Tamil Nadu is renowned the world over. Foreign tourists especially from ethnic countries and non-resident Indians are specially attracted by this unique feature of Tamil Nadu. To fully exploit this potential it is proposed to conduct fairs/festivals at more centres and also expand the product range by introducing new festivals, which will highlight the salient features of Tamil culture and heritage.

For Promotion of Eco-Tourism

Rapid advancements in science and technology are threatening to turn the world into a concrete jungle. Hence the tourists nowadays yearn to visit ecotourism centres like hill resorts, water falls, mangrove forests etc. Therefore, in the Tenth Five Year Plan period, the endeavour will be to exploit the natural resources maintaining complete harmony with nature and without endangering the otherwise extremely fragile ecology and to introduce trekking, boating, water sports, hang gliding etc. in a big way both by refining and repackaging the available products as also by enlarging the product base.

For Co-ordination with other States

Recognizing the need for developing suitable inter-regional circuits and products as also with a view to properly packaging and marketing these, emphasis would be laid on establishing more effective coordination with other States. The first step in this direction was the signing of memorandum of understanding with Andhra Pradesh, Karnataka, India Tourism Development Corporation, Uttar Pradesh, Uttaranchal, Rajasthan, Delhi and Orissa Tourism Development Corporations. Tie-up arrangements with West Bengal, Kerala, Maharashtra, Andaman and Nicobar Islands tourism departments as also with other States are also on anvil.

To explore and Develop new Global Markets for Tamil Nadu Tourism Products

Communication scenario has witnessed a sea change, thanks to the advent of computers. Tourism Department has already established Email, Web site, Touch Screen and C.D. Rom facilities. Computerisation of the various units under the control of Commissionerate of Tourism and Tamil Nadu Tourism Development Corporation are underway. Once this process is completed, online booking facilities for the tours and accommodation in Hotels by TTDC will be possible by just a click on the mouse from anywhere in the world. In this scenario besides US, European and African Countries, it would also be the endeavour to make full use of good relations with the countries in the South Asia/ South East Asia regions to attract more regional tourists.

Programmes/Schemes for the Tenth Five Year Plan Product Identification

The tourists visiting Tamil Nadu can be broadly classified into three main groups viz., international, national and local.

International Tourists

The international tourists form a considerable chunk of tourist inflow into Tamil Nadu. In the year 2000, the number of foreign tourists who visited Tamil Nadu stood at 7-9 lakhs. An analysis of the international tourist traffic shows that foreign tourists usually arrive in Tamil Nadu between October and March. U.K. is by far the single largest source of tourists to India. East and South East Asia are the most important tourist generating markets for South India. Americans and Japanese also prefer to stay far longer periods in India. Europe is the biggest tourist market globally. The strategy in respect of overseas market will be tailored to suit the above pattern. The products which can be sold to the foreign tourists mainly comprise cultural and architectural heritage, temples and historical monuments, arts, performing arts, handicrafts, festivals, wild life etc. The availability of good infrastructure at the tourist spots is critical, particularly as far as foreign tourists are concerned. Hence during 2001-2003, the Government of Tamil Nadu made a budget allocation of Rs.17 crores to update/create infrastructure facilities. This will be sustained and stepped up in the years to come. The products, both destinations and circuits, identified for the International Tourism are:

Thanjavur, Dharasuram, Gangaikondacholapuram, Chidambaram, Pichavaram-Madurai, Thiruvannamalai, Gingee, Tranquebar, Trichy, Ooty, Kodaikanal, Yercaud, Mudumalai, Top Slip etc. In addition to the above, Velankanni in Nagapattinam district and St.Thomas Mount in

Chennai could be two other important destinations, that could be developed and marketted.

Similarly the classical Bharathanatyam, folk dances, classical music both vocal and instrumental, handloom, Thanjavur painting, Swamimalai crafts etc. also form part of attractive products/services.

National Tourists

The national tourists arrive in Tamil Nadu from all the States of India. The number of domestic tourists to Tamil Nadu in a year is around 25 crores. These tourists visit mainly hill stations, pilgrim centres, beach-resorts, dam sites, cultural & heritage destinations etc. To attract such tourists, it is proposed to fully develop and equip with required facilities all the pilgrim centres, develop trekking routes in hills and blend the product with adventure water sports, boating, fairs/festivals etc. For the national tourism, the products (destinations and circuits) identified are: Kanniyakumari Rameswaram, Madurai, Tiruchirappalli, Thanjavur, Tranquebar, Thiruvannamalai, Chidambaram, Pichavaram, Kancheepuram, Mamallapuram, Ooty, Kodaikanal, Yercaud, beaches along the nearly 1000 kms long coastline, wild life sanctuaries etc.

Local (Domestic) Tourists

Besides the above, marketable products (destinations and circuits) for the benefit of local tourists identified for development in the first phase are Palani, Gingee, Tiruchendur, Elagiri Hills, Courtallam, Tiruthani, Point Calimere, wild life sanctuaries, local circuits and destinations in the districts of the State.

Product Development

Development of Infrastructure Facilities at Tourist Destinations

To increase the number of tourists visiting Tamil Nadu, it is proposed to create infrastructure facilities of international standards. Under this scheme, development of Dam sites and minor water falls, like Thirparappu, Papanasam, Jalagambarai, will be taken up. It is also proposed to identify centres in the Districts with tourism potential and declare them as District Tourist Centres/Circuits. These centres would include the places of worship, water falls, minor wild life sanctuaries and other lesser known tourist places.

The District Tourism Centres will be provided with infrastructure facilities like hotels, approach roads, toilets, street lights, drinking water, etc., of high standard. Each district may have small towns, which may not have any amusement centres. In such places, City Entertainment Centres will be set up.

The attractions would include cinema halls, videogames, virtual reality games, simulators, cyber cafes, food courts, multi-purpose cultural centres, shopping mall etc. These are some of the areas and activities where large scale private investment is also expected. Initially, it is proposed that City Entertainment Centres may be put up in Tirunelveli, Kanniyakumari, Tiruchirappalli, Salem and Thanjavur Districts. More towns can be covered in the subsequent phases. During the Tenth Five Year Plan, 80 Tourist Centres are proposed for which an amount of Rs.25 crores will be provided.

Further, an amount of Rs.10 crores is proposed for the development of infrastructure facilities for tourists in important tourist attraction centres under the Coastal Area Development Programme (CADP).

Provision of Basic Amenities at Tourist Destinations

The object of this scheme is to develop and improve basic amenities such as drinking water supply, sewerage and sanitation systems, in particular "Pay and Use toilets", provision of Cloak room facilities, hygienic eateries etc. at the Tourist Centres.

Initially 20 Tourism centres will be selected for this purpose during the Tenth Plan period in coordination with other Departments like Public Works Department, TWAD Board, Department of Rural Development, Town and Country Planning and a sum of Rs.10 crores would be earmarked for these. Similarly 38 towns have been identified as heritage towns and Rs. 50 lakhs has been earmarked for provision of basic infrastructural facilities in each of these towns. This amount would come from the Local Administration budget.

Sound & Light Programme

Sound & Light shows will be set up at Mamallapuram, Thanjavur Big temple and Kancheepuram to attract more tourists. Sound and Light shows at Thirumalai Mannar Palace, Madurai will be upgraded using the services of professionals and using advanced techniques in Audio visual communications and Acoustics. The cost has been estimated at Rs. 1.50 crores for each of the above three places and Rs. 0.50 crore for restoring and upgrading the programme at Madurai.

Cultural Festivals and Fairs

Tamil Nadu's ancient and rich cultural legacies and heritage and a variety of living traditions and cultures spread over throughout the State have high marketability. Therefore, for promoting cultural tourism, festivals such as Cape Festival at Kanniyakumari, Dance Festival at Mamallapuram, Tea and Tourism Festival at Coonoor, Mango Festival at Krishnagiri, Chithirai Festival at Madurai besides Pongal Festival in all tourist centres, Summer Festival in important hill stations and celebration of World Tourism Day in all tourist centres, Natyanjali Festival at Chidambaram, Indira Vizha at Poompuhar, Saral Thiruvizha at Courtallam and Kattabomman Vizha at Panchalankurichi are some of the events for which cultural package tours would be organised by travel agencies. Presently, Summer Festivals are being organised in the months of May and June every year at:

(1) Udhagamandalam,
(2) Kodaikanal,
(3) Surili Falls,
(4) Sirumalai,
(5) Elagiri,
(6) Kolli Hills,
(7) Yercaud,
(8) Nagappattinam Beach,
(9) Valparai,
(10) Javvadhu Hills,
(11) Pachamaiai,
(12) Silver Beach and
(13) Panchalankurichi.

September 8th Festival at Velankanni in Nagapattinam District could be another important Festival to be marketted effectively. A new Festival at Rameswaram could also be thought of, since it could enhance its holding and retaining capacity. It is proposed to identify new festivals and showcase them throughout the country and also abroad. A calendar of the above programmes prepared and distributed well in advance to all concerned through departmental offices across the country and also the Government of India tourist offices abroad will enable dissemination of the required information to the prospective tourists. A sum of Rs.5 crores would be provided for this purpose.

Product Expansion

Setting up of New Boat Houses/Upgradation of Existing Boat Houses

Apart from backwaters on the East Coast stretch, there are lakes, corals etc., where boating is feasible. One of the objectives in the 10th Five Year Plan is to increase the influx of tourists to Tamil Nadu by at least 10% per annum. Secondly, tourists should stay for a longer period. To achieve these objectives setting up of new boat houses and upgradation of the existing ones will be taken up for these are likely to increase the holding capacity of the place: (1) Opening of new boat houses at Adyar (Chennai), Pulicat, Nainarkulam (Tirunelveli), Alambarai, Muttukadu-II, Iddaikazhinadu @ Rs.50 lakhs per centre, and (2) Upgradation of the boat houses at Kodaikanal, Muttukadu, Udhagamandalam and Yercaud @ Rs. 50 lakhs per centre. Besides Introduction of Row boats, motorboats etc. upgradation will also include improvements to boat-jetty, purchase of new traditional boats & water-sports equipments @ Rs. 15.55 lakhs per centre. Similarly, such centres would be identified throughout the State and developed for local tourists.

Development of Hill Stations & Natural Falls

The Yercaud Hills: The Boating Centre and other Tourist spots will be renovated. The lake will be cleaned up for a better boat ride.

Hogenakkal Falls: Boating will be developed.

Javaddu Hills: During the Plan better boarding/lodging facilities will be provided.

The Elagiri hills: It is proposed to develop a bird sanctuary and improve all tourist attractions in particular, the lake.

Arapalleeswarar Falls at Kolli Hills: It is proposed to improve the Hotel and Transport facilities.

Surli Falls at Kambam Valley: Basic amenities like road, restaurant, hotels (with boarding & lodging) and public toilets, park etc. will be provided during the Tenth Five Year Plan. An amount of Rs. 5 crores would be earmarked for this purpose.

Subsidy

Tourism has been declared as an Industry and realizing the importance of private sector participation in the Tourism Industry, it is proposed to continue the scheme of capital and generator subsidy for the construction of hotels, amusement parks, golf courses etc.

The Tourism Department of Government of India extends financial assistance to Tourism projects. However, the State Government is to bear the cost of land, external amenities like approach road, parking lot etc. Hence, it is proposed to provide Rs.10 crores as the State's share for tourism projects during the Tenth five year plan on the assumption that the Government of India's allocation may be Rs.100 crores.

Tourism Police

The Safety and Security of tourists is extremely important and is a critical factor for the promotion of tourism. Tourists-foreign and domestic, have nightmarish experience at times at some of the tourist centres. Some of the tourists lose their travel documents, some encounter local anti-social elements while they visit places or during the stay in hotels. In some places they meet hostile youngsters.

The local people forget that they are expected to be tourist-friendly and to extend all possible help to make their visit and stay pleasant so that the influx of tourists increases. Therefore, the Government has proposed to introduce Tourism Police facilities in all important tourists centres like Mamallapuram, Rameswaram, Kanniyakumari, Madurai, Kancheepuram etc., as also at places like airports, railway stations, monuments etc., in a phased manner.

Other Product Expansion Programmes

Village (Rural) Tourism-The new concept of Rural and Village tourism as envisaged by the Government of India aims at providing adequate infrastructural facilities while maintaining the rural ambience. The villages for promotion of village tourism are identified by the District Tourism Advisory Committees. The tourists may meet and mingle with the village community, halt overnight and observe the life-style of the rural folk before resuming their journey to their further destinations. Many foreign tourists like the experience of visiting and having further sojourn in a simple Indian village. As this will generate rural employment and advance development of these areas, bring out the rich and un-adulterated culture, tradition, fine arts, martial arts, games, worship forms, handicrafts, herbal cures etc. which are preserved, protected and maintained only in the villages, it is aimed to bring out these inbuilt talents and expose some of the salient features of rich tradition to the outside world.

Adventure Tourism-Though, there is tremendous potential in the State to promote adventure tourism, very little has been done so far. Hence a fillip would be given to adventure tourism activities in the Tenth Plan. Trekking, hang gliding, para gliding, para sailing, balloon expeditions and water sports will be promoted with active participation from the private sector.

The trekking routes identified in Kodaikanal, Ooty and other hill stations will be developed and expeditions will be conducted regularly during the seasons.

Alamparai on the East Coast Road 120 kms., from Chennai has been identified as a ideal centre for development of adventure water sports. Water sports will also be developed at Muttukadu. The private sector will be encouraged to invest in adventure tourism projects for which speedy clearance will be ensured through the Single Window Machinery.

Eco-Tourism-Eco-Tourism is a form of "tourism that involves travelling to relatively undisturbed natural areas with the specified object of studying, admiring and enjoying the natural sceneries, wild plants, animals, as well as any existing unique aspects found in these areas " according to the World Tourism Organisation. Natural environment is the primary attraction in Ecotourism.

Tourists especially from other countries are keen to enjoy visiting Eco-friendly environs. They never fail to include eco-friendly tourist spots in their itinerary while visiting Tamil Nadu. Out of the total number of tourists more than 25 percent visit natural surroundings in Tamil Nadu every year.

Among the biosphere reserves in India, two (*the Nilgiris and the Gulf of Mannar*) are located in Tamil Nadu. In order to explore eco-friendly tourism potential in the Kurusadai group of islands near Rameswaram, Glass Bottom Boats will be introduced and Eco-friendly adventure tourism activities could be encouraged at Kolavai lake, Muttukadu, Pichavaram etc.

Jungle Lodges-Tamil Nadu has been bestowed with dense deciduous forests in which there are abundant wildlife, rare species of birds and landscapes full of greenery. Tourists love to visit places which abound with natural wealth, e.g., jungles. As the jungles fall under the "Reserved" forest areas, where taking up any major construction activity will endanger

the extremely fragile ecology of the region, it is proposed to construct jungle lodges with minimum human intervention, which will be operated and maintained by the Forest Department. The expertise and financial resources of the private sector will also be utilised in these ventures. The jungle lodges will enable the tourists to watch the wildlife, flora and fauna etc. and offer to them the luxury of a star hotel in a natural elegant setting. There are numerous places where it may be worthwhile to take up construction of jungle lodges, e.g., Mudumalai, Anaimalai, Kalakkad, Mundanthurai, etc.

Convention Centre (NRI/Private Sector)-It is proposed to construct a massive Convention Centre with NRI/private sector support with 1500 capacity in between Chennai and Mamallapuram. This Convention Centre will have World class facilities for conducting National and International Conferences. This project will be taken up as a joint-venture in an area of around 500 acres and will contain a Five Star Hotel with 1000 rooms, Mini Conference Halls, shopping arcade, Disney land, ethnic village, handicraft emporium, children park, textile museum, swimming pool, bar, theatre, all modern communication links, wide car parking area, huge exhibition mansion, art gallery, etc. The total cost will be worked out at the time of implementation since it is to be fully entrusted to NRI/Private Sector.

Perspective Plan

Tourism is a field of human activity known to mankind from time immemorial. The State Government officially stepped into this sector nearly three decades ago by creating a Tourism Department in the Secretariat. Right from the first year of its inception, the Tourism industry in Tamil Nadu has received a big fillip. The main tasks assigned to the department were to attract more tourists to Tamil Nadu and provide the very basic requirements like transport facilities for sight seeing & Hotels for food/accommodation etc.

To provide these facilities, the Government of Tamil Nadu and Government of India have pumped in crores of rupees. A major portion of this expenditure has gone into creation of assets like Hotels, Parks etc. th State Government has made a big allocation of Rs. 17 crores for improving the infrastructure at tourist centres]. It is necessary to ensure that the funds are spent judiciously & purposefully. This is possible only if a critical analysis is made of the facilities already available, the gaps and the maintenance of the facilities. Such a scientific

study could be undertaken only by professional agencies. The Government of India has selected a private firm, M/s. Consulting Engineering Services.

The firm has also prepared its report, which has generally identified the following bottlenecks:-

- Lack of accommodation facilities.
- Poor water supply & sanitation.
- Poor connectivity.
- Inadequate power supply.
- Piling up of garbage near tourist centres.
- Lack of travel booking facilities.
- Insecurity.

The report has also suggested to introduce a number of facilities; some of the important ones being as follows:

- Kiosks at Beach.
- Haat at Chennai & few other places.
- Development of lesser known Tourist Centres.
- Airport at Kanniyakumari.
- Improvement to Roads leading to important tourist spots.
- Heli-taxi.
- Folders in foreign languages.
- New Boat Houses and
- Sound & Light shows.

According to them, the factors affecting the Tourism Industry in Tamil Nadu are:

1. High luxury tax.
2. High camera entry ticket & regulations.
3. Presence of Health Centres in Kerala, which may divert tourists from Tamil Nadu to Kerala.
4. The report has suggested augmentation of infrastructure at National Tourist Centres of Kanniyakumari, Courtallam.

Kodaikanal & Rameswaram

During the Tenth Five Year Plan Period, the new initiatives will therefore focus on the above mentioned lines. The Consultant has also opined that to implement short term schemes, it will be ideal to prepare a master plan, which would be operational for a limited period of 4-5 years. Master plans will, therefore, have to be prepared for development of destinations, circuits, product etc.

Technical Assistance/Outsourcing

Tourism Department, since its inception has been executing several projects in and around tourist spots throughout Tamil Nadu. These projects relatively small in nature were mainly in the nature of providing basic amenities required by tourists, viz., drinking water, toilet, roads, lights, restaurant, rest shed etc. Such projects do not require much technical know-how. But in the coming years, as mentioned in earlier paragraphs since the Government would be implementing Mega Tourism Projects and the cost of such projects will run into crores and the state of the art technology will have to be employed, outsourcing of technical assistance is envisaged. As each project would require a detailed techno-economic feasibility study before the work is commenced on the project to begin with, a technical consultancy wing has been created in the TTDC. This wing will comprise of technical staff drawn from TTDC and elsewhere. This will help not only in preparation of techno-economic feasibility study for major projects like ropeways, sound and light shows etc., by outsourcing professional consultants, but would also help in management of the projects. This wing will also offer technical support to private entrepreneurs, who are likely to invest in tourism projects thereby considerably increasing the private sector participation. To facilitate this, therefore, an outlay of Rs. 2 crores has been suggested.

Tourism Circuits

Tamil Nadu is the "complete destination" for all reasons and seasons. To facilitate tourists visiting their desired destinations without any hardship as also to properly package and market the products holistically in an integrated manner, it is proposed to identify and develop 'Tourism Circuits'. The infrastructure in these circuits would be created and up-dated keeping the twin objectives of attracting more tourists and extending their stay in Tamil Nadu in view. Accordingly, the following tourism circuits have been identified:

For International Tourists

Most of the international tourists visiting India are from U.K., U.S, Japan, Australia, South Asian, Africans regions etc. These countries abound in hill and beach resorts, water falls, forests etc. Hence, such products cannot be marketed to the international tourists beyond a point. The foreign tourists however show keen interest in historical, architectural and cultural heritage, monuments and temples of Tamil Nadu. They enjoy the exquisite, unique, inspiring, extravagantly sculpted carvings in the temples. The carvings are not only delicate and distinct and at the same time integrally linked with each other but also display the ingenuity and artistic skills of the sculptors. Hence circuits linking Mamallapuram, Kancheepuram, Thanjavur, Gangaikondacholapuram, Poompuhar, Madurai Rameswaram, Thiruvannamalai etc., destinations will be the most ideal itinerary for the foreign tourists. These, however, would have to be packaged along with other products and presented in such a way so as to offer attractions for the foreign tourists of all the age groups. The tourist circuits identified for the purpose, therefore, are:-

(a) Chennai-Mamallapuram-Kancheepuram,
(b) Chennai-Mamallapuram-Pondicherry-Gingee-Thiruvannamalai-Kancheepuram,
(c) Six abodes of Lord Muruga (particularly for NRI Tamils),
(d) Chennai-Pondichery-Chidambaram-Pichavaram-Gangaikondacholapuram-Thanjavur-Tiruchirappalli-Rameswaram-Kanniyakumari-Madurai-Chennai-(Tamil Nadu Tour),
(e) Navagraha Sannidhi (for NRIs),
(f) Thekkadi-Kodaikanal-Madurai-Rameswaram-Kanniyakumari.

National Tourists

Tourists from all the Indian states visit Tamil Nadu. The top six States which account for generating the maximum number of tourists to Tamil Nadu are U.P. Andhra Pradesh, Maharashtra, Gujarat, Karnataka and West Bengal. These tourists usually visit the religious destinations, hill resorts, which are a beautiful mix of mountain ranges and plains, bays and sun drenched beaches, wild life sanctuaries, meandering rivers, water falls which provide an awesome spectacle of colossal cascade of water and pilgrim centres. The circuits most suited and popular among these tourists are:

(a) Chennai-Tirupathi-Kancheepuram-Mamallapuram-Chennai,
(b) Mumbai-Chennai-Tamil Nadu-Tirupathi-Mumbai,

(c) Kolkatta-Chennai-Tamil Nadu-Tirupathi-Kolkatta-,
(d) Chennai-Trichy-Thanjavur-Kumbakonam-Dharasuram-Gangai-kondacholapuram-Chidambaram-Pichavaram,
(e) Kodaikanal-Madurai-Rameswaram-Kanniyakumari,
(f) Six abodes of Lord Muruga and Navagraha Sannidhi,
(g) Chennai-Yercaud-Ooty-Kodaikannal-Chennai,
(h) Chennai-Velankanni-Chennai,
(i) Chennai-Nagore-Chennai,
(j) Chennai-Andaman and Nicobar-Chennai,
(k) Buddhist and Jain Circuits-Showcasing Tamil Nadu.

Local Tourists

The local tourists would have visited all the important tourist centres in the State. Some of them may have visited the tourist spots even more than once. However, many of them may not have visited the lesser known tourist places like small water falls, dam sites, heritage towns etc. With this target group in mind, the State Government has declared 38 towns as cultural and historical centres. Similarly 41 centres have been declared as District Excursion Centres (DECs). Intensive publicity and marketing will have to be undertaken to popularise these centres among the local tourists. The circuits will cover all the districts in which the cultural/historical towns and D.E.C. are located. Some of the popular circuits so identified are:

(a) Chennai-Coimbatore-Sabarimalai.
(b) Chennai-Melmaruvathoor-Sathanur-Thiruvannamalai-Hogenakkal-Chennai.
(c) Chennai-Vellore-Elagiri Hills-Chennai.
(d) One day Chennai-Tourist covering temples in and around Chennai.
(e) Chennai-Puttaparthi-Bangalore-Chennai.
(f) Chennai-Vellankanni, Nagore-Chennai.
(g) Chennai-Coimbatore-Ooty-Mysore-Bangalore.
(h) Chennai-Palani-Madurai and around-Palani-Coimbatore.
(i) Madurai City Tour.
(j) Trichy and Thanjavur.
(k) Buddhist/Jain Circuits-showcasing Tamil Nadu.

Human Resources Development

Human Resources Development is vital for promoting tourism. This may be considered under the following three heads:

Hospitality

Hotels are places visited by almost all the tourists, either to have food or for accommodation. The hotels require qualified personnel to understand the specific requirements of tourists & fulfil them according to the taste/spending capacity of the tourists. Ill-behaviour or discourtesy by the hotel staff will create an adverse image of the hotel, the people and the State.

To train qualified youth in hospitality, there are two Institutions in Tamil Nadu, one functioning under the aegis of Government of India, i.e., Institute of Catering Technology & Applied Nutrition, Taramani, Chennai and the other one, the State Institute of Hotel Management & Catering Technology, Tiruchi, sponsored by the Govt. of Tamil Nadu. Both the above institutions turn out graduates, young and well equipped to attend on the tourists. During the Tenth Five Year Plan, it is proposed to improve the curriculum, increase the intake & create and upgrade the facilities. Efforts will also be taken to open more such institutions, preferably with private participation.

Guides

Another area where the human factor is important pertains to Guides. Today, tourists have multifarious means like Telephones, E-mail, CD Rom, documentary film, folders, touch screen, website, press etc to apprise and upgrade themselves with information on tourist products. But inspite of all these facilities, the Guides present at the tourist spots have a very important role. They, therefore, have to be well informed, courteous and should possess good communication ability and knowledge of language and of history, art and culture of the State. Since they interact directly with the tourists, efforts would be made to bring out an elite group of guides, for which well equipped youngsters will be selected & they will be given intensive training. Such guides will be deployed in important tourist spots in a phased manner.

Skilled Workers

Un-employed youth will be trained as drivers, travel agents, beauty parlour attendants, costume designers etc., and their skills upgraded.

Promotion of Marketing

Publicity & Direct Marketing

Tourism is one of the 3 leading "socio-economic and service businesses" of the new century and "Promotion, Publicity & Marketing" play a vital role in promotion of Tourism. For an aggressive, powerful and effective marketing, dissemination of tourist information through various media is absolutely essential to motivate the potential tourists. Publication of good quality brochures, posters, picture post-cards etc., and their distribution through various outlets of the Tourism Department including Government of India Tourist offices and other means is equally important.

Airlines, travel agents, release of advertisements in leading journals within the country and abroad, production of short films and screening at important locations, conduct of press meets and familiarisation tours for leading domestic and foreign travel writers, Road shows at important centres, participation in tourist marts within the country and abroad would be strategically used to market various tourist destinations, circuits and other products. A focused, integrated & holistic publicity and marketing campaign during the Tenth Five Year Plan period would, therefore, be an important element of the strategy for promoting tourism. An amount of Rs.10 crores will be provided for the following measures during the Plan to attract tourists:

(1) Creating a 'Tamil Nadu Brand ' position.

(2) Differentiate from the competitive destinations and develop a unique market position image.

(a) Printing of brochures of high quality for free distribution at Airports, Railway Stations, Hotels, Bus terminals and at all destinations.

(b) Production of 30mm short films for screening at Theatres, Railway Station, Exhibition, Airports, Flights, TVs.

(c) Production of CD Rom for free distribution. CD will contain information on accommodation, tourist centres, transport facilities etc.

(d) Advertisements in India and Abroad.

(e) Participation in National & International Tourist Marts.

(f) Erection of Glow Sign Boards and self-luminous sign boards in and around Tourist Spots.

(g) Establish an effective and ongoing presence in each source market.

(h) Establish an internet portal in various languages for global consumption.

Opening of New Tourist Offices/Renovation of existing Tourist Offices in other State Headquarters

Tourist Offices are at present functioning at Mumbai, New Delhi, Kolkatta, Panaji, Jaipur, Agra and Tourist Information Centres at Bangalore, Thiruvananthapuram and Hyderabad. During the Tenth Five Year Plan it is proposed to open Tamil Nadu State Tourist Offices/ Information Centres in all the State Headquarters and at important Airports/Rail junctions in a phased programme and to upgrade the existing Tourist Offices/Tourist Information Centres. The details are as follows:

(a) Opening of new Tourist Offices/Information Centres in 17 State Capitals of India, all important Airports etc.

(b) Renovation and upgradation of the existing Tourist Offices/ Tourist Information Centres (7 Nos.) and

(c) Utilising these Tourists Offices/Information Centres as marketing agents for tourist facilities in Tamil Nadu.

Institutionalised Marketing

To attract foreign tourists, marketing agents have been appointed in London & Malaysia. It is proposed to appoint marketing agents in all potential markets like Thailand, Mauritius, South Africa, France, Italy and other South/South East Asian Countries. So also, marketing agents are being appointed at least in important cities & towns within India.

Strengthening Communication Network

The Department of Tourism has under its control 20 Tourist Offices and 19 Tourist Information Centres for dissemination of information to tourists. Out of this, six Tourist Offices and three Tourist Information Centres are functioning outside Tamil Nadu. In the first phase of computerisation, 9 Tourist Offices have been computerised. It is now proposed to computerise the remaining Tourist Offices/Tourist Information Centres, hotels of TTDC, bookings of accommodation and tour packages etc., besides total computerisation of the Head Office. All the above units will have STD, ISD, Fax/

E-mail/Internet facilities. By employing state of the art technology, all the units will be inter-linked through Wide Area Network (WAN). As Internet is becoming an increasingly powerful vehicle for travel information, marketing & sales, to keep pace with this latest trends in communication, the Tourism Department has created an exclusive website, which contains full details of Tamil Nadu's Tourism potential & related information. The proposed Computerisation and connectivity will enable potential tourists in any part of the globe to obtain information and facilitate online booking.

Role of Tamil Nadu Tourism Development Corporation (TTDC)

Tamil Nadu Tourism Development Corporation (TTDC) was started in the year 1971 on a modest note with 2 coaches and 5 hotels. It has made rapid strides since then and has earned the distinction of owning the largest chain of hotels in South India numbering 54. The hotels are spread throughout Tamil Nadu. TTDC offers the following facilities to tourists:

(1)	Hotels and Youth Hostels	34
(2)	Boat Houses	10
(3)	Restaurants	3
(4)	Canteens	4
(5)	Telescope Houses	4
(6)	Parks	3
(7)	Tourist Service Centre	1

Petrol Bunk, Mamallapuram Out of the 54 hotels, 12 Hotels at Tirunelveli, Mettupalayam, Mandapam, Sriperumpudur, Coonoor, Ranipet, Kotagiri, Namakkal, Mettur Dam, Sathanur Dam, Virudhunagar and Vaigai Dam have been franchised to private sector. Action is being taken to franchise the remaining hotels to private sector. Youth Hostels have been constructed to cater to the budget tourists at all the major tourist destinations, wherein dormitory type of accommodation is provided at economic tariff. Package Tours ranging from ½ day to 14 days covering several States like Bihar, Uttar Pradesh, Madhya Pradesh, Maharashtra besides covering all Southern States like Andhra Pradesh, Karnataka, Goa, Pondicherry and Kerala are being conducted. New package tours would be evolved. Necessary steps will be taken to organise new Air Package Tours.

In the changing scenario as above, TTDC would be required to act mainly as an institutionalized vehicle of the State to attract, organise, lead, support, direct and facilitate private investment in the field of destination and other product developments. It would also provide technical support and assistance in the areas of Human Resources Development, project preparation, evaluation, market survey, research and related subjects and would serve mainly as a facilitator.

New Schemes for Tenth Plan for Development of Infrastructure

During the Seventh, Eighth and Ninth Plans, the Ministry of Tourism was assisting the State Governments/UT Administrations to undertake a large number of small, isolated projects spread through out the length and breath of the country resulting in the resources being spread very thinly. The Central financial assistance had, therefore, not been able to create any major impact on the development of tourism infrastructure in the country. In order to provide a quick and substantial impact to tourism growth in the Tenth Plan, the following new schemes for the development and promotion of tourism in the country have been proposed:

(1) Integrated Development of Tourism Circuits.

(2) Product/infrastructure and Destination Development.

(3) Assistance for Large Revenue Generating Projects.

Whereas the GOI would meet the entire expenditure towards the development of tourism circuits, in the case of Tourist destinations, the share of the Department of Tourism, Government of India would be 90% of the project cost and 10% would have to be met by the State Government. The GOI has identified initially the following two circuits in Tamil Nadu:

(1) Chennai – Mammallapuram – Pondicherry-Gingee-Thiruvannamalai – Kancheepuram-Chennai; and

(2) Thekkadi – Madurai-Rameswaram-Kanniyakumari.

In respect of tourist destinations besides Mamallapuram, it is proposed to develop Kanniyakumari in the first phase. The maximum amount for the development of a tourist destination would be around Rs. 5 crores. Keeping these in view, therefore, it is proposed to earmark Rs. 10 crores as State Government's share towards Government of India assisted Schemes assuming the total share of Government of India during the entire plan period to be Rs. 100 crores.

Hill Area Development Programme

Funds are also allotted to the Nilgiris District for tourism schemes under the Hill Area Development Programme to create infrastructure facilities/basic amenities etc.

Tenth Five Year Plan Outlay

While a major part of the investment is going to come from the private sector, there are certain promotional activities that have to be undertaken, and certain infrastructure that has to be established by the State only. In view of this position and considering that efforts are being made to make Tamil Nadu the number one State in India and position it firmly on the global tourism map, programmes/schemes for a total cost of Rs. 1202 crores would be taken up.

4

Educational Tours of Railroad Trains and Motor Vehicles

Introductory

The tour of the peddler with a pack or cart stocked with goods for sale and a budget of news for free distribution, and that of the patent medicine man with his illustrated lecture of misinformation that sells his dubious wares are forms of travelling publicity campaigns long familiar in rural districts.

Of recent years many peddlers, carrying new ideas and useful information but no goods for sale, have been going about the country representing national and state government bureaus and private organizations. Their varies are helps to better crops, better houses, better health. Their mode of travelling has progressed from wagons to trains and from trains to motor trucks. The size of the enterprise has varied from a single wagon or automobile with a speaker and a batch of leaf-lets to a train of railroad cars or trucks that carry a travelling exhibit rivaling the "Greatest Show on Earth." The tours extend from a jaunt through the county or the districts of a city to a trans-continental journey. Whatever its form, if the purpose of the enterprise is to spread information or ideas, or to promote a community program, it is of interest from an educational and publicity standpoint.

Although travelling campaigns have been many and varied and the method has been in use for a number of years, to our knowledge there has been no attempt up to this time to set down' the methods and experiences, the successes, failures, and difficulties of the various campaigners.

Believing that this method of promoting social programs will continue to be employed, whatever the type of vehicle used to convey travellers and their outfits, we have gathered information about a number of campaigns and offer it here, together with comments and suggestions for the benefit of those who may be considering the method for the first time or who have tried it and wish to compare their experiences with those of others. The descriptions and suggestions are drawn from accounts of about seventy-five tours of trains, trucks, trolley cars, and other vehicles, obtained from printed reports, articles, letters, replies to questionnaires and interviews, as well as from the observations and experience of the writer.

Purposes and Advantages of Travelling Campaigns

THE popular educational tour on wheels is a method of carrying news and facts from town to town, instead of distributing this information in wholesale manner to many towns at the same time through newspapers, letters, posters, and other familiar avenues for disseminating information quickly and widely. This use of a method resembling more or less the old-time place-to-place spreading of the news but in a modern, up-to-the-minute dress, even under the most favourable conditions involves a considerable outlay in money, a great deal of hard work, careful and detailed planning, and equally careful oversight throughout the journey and the follow-up period. Therefore the person or group con-templating such an undertaking will naturally wish to consider carefully its efficiency as a method of publicity before embarking on it.

In some instances the reason for using the truck or train is that it may be routed to remote rural districts not well served by the more modem methods of news distribution. Wherever it goes, however, the train or truck has two chief advantages as a publicity method; first, it is an economical way of bringing before scattered audiences well-equipped speakers or graphic and otherwise attractive illustrative material—economical be cause a single group of speakers or unit of exhibits may in this way be made to serve a large territory; and, second, its visit to each town may be made an important event, something which creates news and which may appeal to the imagination of people generally.

The tours that are described in the following pages suggest just a few of the unusual and graphic features that may be assembled in a travelling show to attract attention and to make facts and ideas more easily understood and remembered. The train or truck in addition, as already suggested, to bringing into town especially talented or well-informed speakers and demonstrators, brings also equipment for demonstrations that may be bulky, expensive, or for other reasons difficult to duplicate and distribute for display; also rare objects such as the people in the communities visited would not be likely to see at all, except as they are brought in for this brief visit.

The Train as an Event The visit of the train, like the revival meeting, the fair, or the Fourth of July celebration, may be made sucft a striking event in each community that its program gets and holds the attention of many people who would not read a newspaper article or go to an ordinary meeting to learn about the same topic. Such an event may be especially timely if a new movement or plan is about to be launched within the territory to be covered. The brief demonstration presented before a representative group of citizens gathered to meet the truck or train often pav the way for the organization of a permanent activity in the community. This is true because the method often allows for a more concentrated educational effort than can be effected in the same time through other types of campaigns.

For example, the occasional visit of the agricultural special, demonstrating improved methods has, in many instances, preceded the forming of a county organization of farmers to devote themselves continuously to studying and experimenting in better farming.

A train or truck campaign, well handled, will help to give freshness to ideas which may become stale if they continue to reach the people in the same familiar forms. Whatever the subject matter or purpose of a local movement for community education or welfare, both the workers or leaders and the people who form the audiences are re-freshed by variations from familiar methods of presenting the ideas that need to be gone over time and again in order to get the greater numbers to listen, to understand, and to assimilate them. The local effectiveness of the work of the county agricultural agent, or the tuberculosis committee, or the movement for better rural schools may sometimes be stimulated through the visit of travelling campaigners bringing reinforcements in the way of enthusiasm, news gathered along the route, or old ideas illustrated in new and striking ways.

A Tour as a Campaign "Feature"

One occasion when a train tour may be desir able is when the need is felt for a unique feature or "stunt" in a campaign that employs a great variety of methods. The Liberty Loan trains were expected to add "punch" to local campaigns and to make bond selling easier. When a vigorous effort is being concentrated on an issue or an idea, a tour of prominent speakers, or striking exhibits, or both, may add a spectacular element and secure much publicity; first, by getting direct attention for the idea, and second, by providing material for "news" both in the press and in the everyday talk of the people.

Novelty and the Danger of its Wearing Off

As a novel device for attracting attention both train and truck have a real though possibly a short-lived value. In many sections of the country the exhibit train has long ago become familiar, and already those who are seeking some new form in which to get their story over are equipping and operating motor trucks. In a few years these, too, may lose their power to arouse curiosity. However, the fact that the novelty of a device wears off does not necessarily destroy its value. While the novelty of the method itself may wear off, the contents of the train and the program of the itinerant campaigners leave no end of possibilities in the way of fresh attractions.

In the use of graphic methods there have been great advances within quite recent years. So far, only a few of the newer forms of expressing information in picturesque and dramatic forms have been used in truck and train projects. There is no reason why trains and trucks should not continue indefinitely to draw expectant visitors looking for the new features that may be added this year, just as a circus, a fair, or exposition is repeated successfully year after year. The exhibitor who uses an attention-getting device for the first time in any locality is to some extent responsible for the future success of any similar travelling shows in the places visited. People who went to see the first train or truck are likely to visit the second or stay away, according to the impression made by the first. This responsibility can be met through careful preparation and good management.

Not a Quick Method

A point sometimes urged in favour of the educational tour is its rapid method of carrying information over a wide area. It is undoubtedly the quickest way of displaying the same objects to a number of communities. But if you wish the people throughout your territory to have the same information as nearly as possible at the same time, any method in which the material is duplicated and sent out to all points at once from a central place is obviously more suitable than conveying the message from place to place.

Travelling Campaigns and Results

One objection frequently raised by those who have conducted educational tours is that they are quickly forgotten and bring no lasting results. This is probably a valid objection to the incompleteness of a particular campaign rather than to the method itself. If the follow-up work is not planned just as carefully and carried out as conscientiously as the tour itself, there is no reason to expect that people will remember it or that action will follow. Every form of publicity, whether a newspaper article, leaflet, lecture or motion picture would be just as quickly forgotten if it were an isolated effort and not part of a well-rounded educational campaign. In the section on follow-up work, page io, methods are discussed of fixing the impressions made on the minds of visitors to the train and of inducing them to apply the instructions given.

Cost of Tours

What it costs usually plays a larger part in the choice of a publicity method than any other single factor. Analysis of the whole plan of the tour is needed in order to decide regarding the wisdom of spending money on it. An advance estimate ought to indicate whether a given expenditure on a travelling campaign appears likely to bring larger returns than the same amount spent on some other method.

The cost and the scale of different enterprises vary so greatly and prices are so different from year to year, that it is impossible to estimate, on the basis of one project, what another one is likely to cost.* By writing to the sources of information listed in the appendix, beginning on page 117, the reader will probably be able to obtain detailed information about the cost of any enterprise of a type that may interest him. Several directors of tours have reported that they consider the method too expensive. It was found too expensive in one northern state because the initial outlay was so great in comparison with the relatively short season during which the truck could be operated. In one southern state the expenses of an automobile tour were found to be out of proportion to the following records of tours may prove at least suggestive: A three-car train, which travelled through Pennsylvania Tor five months in 1918^ had running expenses of approximately $32 5 a week. This included travelling, living expenses, and salaries of three staff members, the initial cost of exhibits and printed matter, and repairs. It did not include the salaries of three additional demonstrators, or the initial cost of rebuilding the interiors of the cars, or any expenses for hauling of the cars.

A motion picture tour with an automobile truck, travelled for twenty-eight weeks in 19 17 in Maryland at an expense of 24 a week. This included the fuel and repairs for the car, expenses of the field staff, rentals of films, and various miscellaneous expenses connected with the operation of the tour. Total budget of the organization. A number have reported the method inexpensive, but they may not have charged against their budget items that others have been obted to include. Cars and hauling may have been provided by a railroad company; the truck may have been a gift; the specialists and demonstrators may have been regular members of the staff of the organization and their salaries not charged against the budget of the tour. In some cases the truck drivers have been volunteers. All of these things need to be taken into account in making any decision on the basis of the amount a tour has cost someone else.

It is safe to say that, under the most favourable circumstances, a well-conducted travelling campaign is not a cheap method of publicity, and the organization considering it should be very sure that the enterprise is timely and especially suited to their purpose before embarking on the venture.

As Between Trains and Trucks

The most serious drawbacks to a train are that it must stay on a railway siding, is frequently inconvenient to reach, and its location hot and dusty in summer, lacking in open space where crowds can gather comfortably, and, worst of all, is noisy. Still another drawback is that the shape of a car is not adapted to the effective display of exhibits and it is difficult also to handle large numbers of visitors. Even with these awkward handicaps, however, the railroad car has the advantage of greater size as a setting for exhibits and demonstrations. Exhibits and equipment for demonstrating, moreover, may be permanently set up in a train of cars, so that everything is in readiness for visitors at the time when the train reaches its stopping place. But the truck is a place for storing rather than displaying exhibits, which means that each time a program is given, material must be un-packed and set up in tents, in a hall, or out of doors.

Good points for the truck are that, roads and weather permitting, the truck campaigner may go wherever and whenever he pleases and stay as long as he likes, independent of the rails and schedules that limit the freedom of a train tour. Even bad roads have not prevented some campaigners from reaching what had seemed to be inaccessible districts.

While the trucks have in certain ways greater adaptability to varied conditions than trains, the latter will undoubtedly continue to be employed where its own special uses are of paramount importance and particularly in cases where the rail-roads may find it possible, as in many instances in the past, to provide transportation free or at a nominal price. The truck, on the other hand, is probably only at the beginning of its usefulness in educational and publicity work. There are still untried possibilities of contriving methods for the carrying of materials especially adapted to a quick a number of years, with the cooperation of the railroads, state agricultural colleges, departments of health, and private state organizations have carried on educational and organization work through demonstration trains. The war propaganda which utilized practically every known form of publicity did not overlook train, truck or trolley. One or more of these was used in the campaigns for Liberty Loans, food conservation, and child welfare.

Descriptions of a few of these trains will illustrate the varied types of campaigns in which they have been employed.

Agricultural Trains

A Peach Demonstration Train started on a tour in November, 19 for the purpose of encouraging and stimulating the peach industry in the East Texas Fruit Relt. The train consisted of two baggage cars containing exhibits of insect pests that menace the peach industry, life-sized models of diseased and perfect fruit, and actual branches of affected peach trees, and a box car containing a tractor, orchard plows, and various other kinds of farm machinery needed by an up-to-date orchardist.

Regarding this train Mr. P. T. Cole, Agricultural Commissioner, St. Louis Southwestern Rail-road of Texas, writes as follows:

The cars were moved on local freight trains nearly all the time, although on a few occasions we were moved by a through freight. The cars were opened to the public at 9 a.m., and the farmers were taken through in groups of about fifteen and a thorough lecture given them with explanations in detail regarding the various exhibits. We usually let the school children go through, but did not allow them to interfere with the work we were giving the farmers. In the afternoon, at about one o'clock, we accompanied the farmers to a nearby orchard taking with us pruning tools, the power sprayer, and the tractor. In the orchard we gave lectures on pruning, and then pruned about a dozen trees, or sometimes as many as fifty, after which we gave them a thorough spraying. This demonstration usually consumed the greater part of the afternoon, but we would return to the cars and discuss the different problems of orcharding with the growers and in many cases they remained with us until dark.

The ´growers in most cases were very enthusiastic over this work, and we had some excellent demonstrations. Some of the very best were given in orchards where we had done the same work last year, and where it was an easy matter to point out the beneficial results of proper spraying and pruning. We have a number of fine demonstrations to go back to next year to show the results of the work we have just done.

The Hessian Fly Special, as described below, is an example of a highly specialized effort toward accomplishing a very definite purpose:

Since its first appearance in Kansas as an important factor in wheat production, the Hessian fly has alternately disappeared and reappeared. During the forty-four years of its known presence in the state it has\ produced seven different Out-breaks, the last and the greatest of which destroyed not less than fifteen million bushels of wheat of the 191 5 crop. Believing that not only the attention of the farmers could best be called to the seriousness of the infestation, but also that more interest could be created in the control methods and that a larger number of wheat growers could be reached within a short time, the Kansas Agricultural College decided to request the Santa F6 Railway Company, which had a large mileage in the infested districts, to run a Hessian fly train.... A chart of the infested districts was furnished the dean of the Extension Division who met with the officials of the Santa F6 and prepared a schedule consisting of sixty-two stops. It was left entirely with the college to decide as to the best time-to run the train and it was felt that, inasmuch as the methods of control of the fly should begin as soon as possible after harvest, the best and most opportune time for the train would be the week just before the beginning of harvest.

The train consisted of a baggage car, two modern steel day coaches, each with a seating capacity of eighty-eight persons, which were used for lecture cars, and a private car, consisting of parlour and observation, dining and sleeping compartments.

It was understood at the beginning that the train was to be an exclusive Hessian fly train and thus it was advertised as the Hessian Fly Special, operated by the Kansas State Agricultural College in cooperation with the Santa F6. The speakers consisted of three entomologists^ of the Agricultural College, one entoniologist of the United States Department of Agriculture, the head of the Department of Agronomy, the superintendent of Farmers' Institutes of the college, and one county demonstration agent. In addition to the lecturers, the company consisted of the agricultural agent of the Santa F6, the publicity agent of the Santa F6, the publicity agent of the college, and representatives of some of the principal newspapers and farm publications. The divisional superintendents and roadmasters accompanied the train over their respective divisions of the road.

Addresses were made at all of the sixty-two places scheduled. In fact, at nearly all the places the attendance was such as to require two speakers and, on several occasions, it required a third speaker to accommodate the large crowd. If the attendance did not exceed two hundred, the two speakers took care of them in the lecture cars, but where the crowd was over two hundred the overflow was taken in the waiting room of the depot, where a speaker was provided. Where there was not an opportunity for the insect train to stop, a lecturer was dropped off to hold a meeting at the depot or an up-town place. Later, the man would be picked up by one of the regular trains and left at a station where the Hessian Fly Special was scheduled to stop. Or a man would be sent ahead on a regular train to hold a meeting and would later be picked up when the Special came through.

In a few cases speakers were taken to neighbouring towns in automobiles. During the entire trip every speaker on the train gave practically the same Hessian fly talk. The entomologists and the agronomist of the college prepared the speech, copies of which were furnished not only to the speakers but also to all the railroad officials and publicity men who accompanied the train. The publicity men prepared beforehand all the articles to be used by the newspapers in the places where addresses were made. In other words, every address given and every newspaper article published had just one message and that was the seriousness of the infestation and what should be done to protect the crop of the next year. It is the opinion of the writer that much of the success of the Hessian !fly train and the good accomplished were due to the fact that all departments and all persons concerned were together, and that nothing was said or done but what met with the approval and recommendation of every one. The fact that the very methods advocated for the control of the fly were in keeping with the very methods recommended by the Agronomy Department and which the progressive and successful wheat growers knew should be practiced for maximum yields, appealed to the better judgment of even the most skeptical ones. The time allowed for each stop was about forty minutes. The speakers usually arranged for a few minutes' discussion before closing the meeting. Specimen cases, charts, and illustrated material were used in nearly all lectures. As the men left the lecture cars or the waiting room they were given circulars on the Hessian fly and the preparation of the seed bed for wheat. The Hessian fly circular was printed primarily for the occasion. It was simply a timely article emphasizing the methods of control and closing with a brief life history of the fly.

In nearly all cases large crowds met the Hessian Fly Special and the total attendance for the week was approximately seven thousand.

Health Trains

In the early days of the tuberculosis movement cars were extensively used in travelling health campaigns. A pioneer in carrying the message of health over a state on exhibit trains was Dr. Oscar Dowling, President of the Louisiana State Board of Health. His health train made its initial trip in 19 lo and with many changes since that time has continued in service. After the first tours, made with cars loaned by the railroad, had demonstrated the popularity of the train, the State Board of Health purchased two coaches. One was fitted up as an inspection car with a part of it given over to living and office quarters, and the other as an educational exhibit car, containing displays of models, charts, and laboratory specimens. Later, two more cars were purchased for living quarters and the inspection car was turned into a laboratory car.

A practical application of the lessons taught on the tour was made by inspectors who accompanied the train. In each place visited they inspected and scored buildings in which the sanitary conditions imperilled public health, the reports of their Journal of Economic Entomology, Vol. 9, No. i, 1916, George A. Dean, Entomologist, Kansas State Agricultural Experiment Station.

The Board of Health of Kansas has used a Pull-man car to carry exhibits on child welfare, tuberculosis, and other health topics. A woman physician and public health nurses travelled with the car and gave health talks and explained exhibits. Sixty-nine cities and towns were visited, the stops varying from one to four days. The purpose was chiefly educational, but an attempt was made to discuss their health problems with individuals.

Another example of the Health Special was a car sent out by the West Virginia Board of Health during 19 and described in letters sent, in advance to the newspapers as:

A fine, yestibuled coach, equipped with electrically driven models, health posters, exhibits of living bacteria, exhibits of Red Cross work, a moving picture machine, and a small but complete chemical and bacteriological laboratory in one end.

War Propaganda

During the war, trains were used in several states to carry the message of food conservation and more especially to encourage home canning by simple methods. The Pennsylvania Food Administration, in cooperation with the Pennsylvania State College of Agriculture and the Penn-sylvania Railroad, ran a train of three cars during the first and second summer of the war. The train included an exhibit car containing posters and graphic devices showing why food conservation was necessary; and two cars where skilled demonstrators illustrated methods of baking with wheat substitutes and the canning and drying of fruits and vegetables. A Save the Surplus Special of two cars toured New York State encouraging home canning and helping practically to increase it.

During the Fourth Liberty Loan campaign exhibit trains were used in some districts for displaying war trophies, and during the Fifth Liberty Loan several shiploads of war equipment and trophies were distributed over the whole country for display on trains which were sent into the rural districts and cities. Each train included several flat cars and a baggage car loaded with captured cannon, German aeroplanes, machine guns, trench mortars, gas warfare apparatus and gas masks, and thousands of other interesting trophies. One of our own tanks, dressed up in its fighting clothes, was an interesting feature of the exhibits. Each train was accompanied by an armed guard of returned soldiers, sailors, and marines.

In Missouri a Women's Patriotic Special made a two weeks' trip carrying women speakers who gave talks on the Red Cross, food conservation, and other war topics.

A Government Safety First Train Probably the most elaborate exhibit train that has yet been sent out was the Safety First Train of the Department of the Interior, which toured sixteen states during a period of four months and was visited by over a half million people. This train, which was furnished by the Baltimore and Ohio Railroad, consisted of twelve steel cars, including a sleeper and diner, and was hauled by two powerful passenger locomotives. Six governmental departments and the American Red Cross had exhibits relating to safety work, the purpose of the tour being "to acquaint the people with the work that the Federal Government is doing every day to protect its citizens against injury and death, and with the measures it takes to promote the health and comfort of the people."

Trolley Tours Campaigns have been conducted on interurban lines in several states. For about three months the Woman's Committee of the State Council of Defence ran a Children's Year Special over much of the interurban trackage of Michigan, in the interests of better babies everywhere, and as a help in saving Michigan's quota of the one hundred thousand babies the Children's Year was to save.

The car was divided into' three sections — the first part contained an exhibit, the second a compartment in which babies and children brought for tests were undressed and dressed, and the third a model examination room where tests and examinations were made by skilled physicians and trained nurses.

The Woman's Committee of the State Council of Defence in Massachusetts also ran a children's welfare car. The interior of the car was given over to exhibits of literature and posters on food conservation and child welfare. The front and back platforms were enlarged and surrounded by arm railings. On one platform a kitchen was arranged, where a lecturer gave actual demonstrations of the various food substitutes; on the other a trained nurse instructed mothers upon the care and feeding of children in wartime. motion picture shows, dealing with health and other subjects, travelling dispensaries and tours demonstrating uses of trucks and thus advertising trucks themselves, are the chief educational uses of motor vehicles reported in response to an inquiry widely sent out. Motion Picture Tours Of these, the travelling motion picture show seems to have been longest in the field. Many state health departments and state tuberculosis associations have been and still are conducting a part of their educational work by this means. Recently the Red Cross has carried the story of its overseas work into remote rural districts in a certain section of the country by means of a truck equipped with pictures and machine. A returned overseas worker travels with the truck and gives talks about past achievements and future plans. An organization interested in promoting the use of commercial and industrial films has a number of well equipped trucks which are sent to city parks as well as country districts to give open-air entertainments.

Travelling Publicity Campaigns

A Typical Motion Picture Motor Tour The North Carolina State Board of Health has used a health car equipped with electric lighting plant, motion picture machine and accessories, together with a large selection of health and comic films, all in charge of a lecturer and machinist.

This car was sent out in response to invitations to give health entertainments in cooperation with local committees, the latter sharing the expense. The plan was to give substantially the same program in a different place in the county each day during one week. Each of these places then received a return visit during each of two succeeding weeks with a complete change of program. A single program usually consisted of five or six reels of motion pictures, including three health films and scenic and comedy films. A victrola was carried with the car to provide a preliminary musical program and a musical accompaniment with the comic films. While the health films were being shown, the lecturer made running comments. Free health literature was on display at a convenient place to be given out in response to requests. The programs were given in the school house, church, hall or outdoors. Where special illumination was needed strings of incandescent lights were provided.

The staff carried with them a complete camping, cooking, and sleeping outfit.^ Their schedule Not ail of the touring campaigners have considered it an advantage to carry camping outfits. Some of them say that the work is usually included two prograhis a day and 12 visits to as many places during a week.

Travelling Dispensaries The use of motor trucks for dispensaries or clinics seems to be increasing rapidly. A number of travelling tuberculosis, dental, child welfare, and baby clinics are reported from many parts of the country, not only for rural districts but for large cities. Some of these dispensaries on wheels are intended chiefly to provide service, that is, to examine people, rather than for the purpose of publicity or education. In this case the truck is simply a convenient method of extending clinical work to districts that have no dispensaries, or to the homes of patients who cannot or will not go to the dispensary. But even where service is the main purpose, these trucks are of value educationally, particularly in this early stage of their use when their novelty attracts attention to the clinics. Other travelling dispensaries are intended chiefly to demonstrate to the community the need of establishing, permanently, some such service as the dispensary gives during its brief stop-over. Cleveland Children's Year Special A travelling truck dispensary was adopted as a feature of the Children's Year by the Children's so strenuous that they should have good beds at night and no responsibility for providing for their own comfort. On the other hand, in some districts camping may provide more comforts than rural hotels would.

Year Committee of the Cleveland Council of Defence. Mr. J. Dean Holiday, Director of the Bureau of Health Education of the Cleveland Department of Health, who planned the construction of the truck and directed its use later, had charge of a similar campaign for the American Red Cross Tuberculosis Commission in Italy.

The type used both in Cleveland and in Italy* as shown in several illustrations has side tents, which, when set up, provide fair-sized rooms. The tent on the left was used as a waiting and dressing room for the mothers who brought babies for examination; that on the right as lecture and exhibit room.

Here posters and model outfits for the baby were displayed and literature was given away. The body proper built on the carriage of a large army truck was fitted out as a model dispensary with examining tables, scales, measuring stands, desk, cabinet for supplies, electric lights, and hot and cold water. The equipment included a Screen and motion picture machine which could be set up on top of the truck for evening programs. In Cleveland the truck was driven by members of a volunteer women's motor corps organization, uniformed for the purpose and carried a physician, a nurse, and a sanitary patrolman, all assigned from the Health Department. After making a study of the Cleveland trucks sent to Italy.

The tour included sections of the city known as "death places" because of their high infant mortality rates. As the crowd gathered the physician in charge gave a short talk on the object of Children's Year. While he was thus engaged the district nurse circulated through the crowd and, picking out a likely mother and child, persuaded her to step forward with her child when the physician called for babies to be examined. It was found necessary to do. This in order to get the remainder of the mothers to fall in line quickly.

The physician examined the child and, if normal, it was quickly weighed and measured and the regular Children's Year forms filled out, one for the committee's record and a duplicate for the mother. The mother was advised to report at regular intervals to the city's nearest prophylactic dispensary where she would receive instructions as to how to keep her baby well. For the sake of its effect, she was given a card signed by the mayor, stating that she was entitled to this service and urging her to avail herself of it. She then passed on to the tent containing exhibits where child hygiene and other posters were displayed and educational pamphlets distributed.

The exhibits and literature were usually presided over by the uniformed motor corps driver, although on some occasions an extra nurse was carried for the purpose. In an average afternoon, from twenty-five to thirty babies would be examined.

Although city nurses were constantly carrying on routine work in the districts visited, many cases of contagion and sore eyes were found by the travelling outfit which had been missed entirely by the regular nurses. After the truck had visited a given section the nurses in charge of the district dispensary were instructed to make a note of attendance. Records showed a considerable increase in visitors, a number of whom brought with them the cards received at the travelling dispensary or they said that they had been referred to the dispensary after a preliminary examination on the truck.

Motor Truck Clinics in Italy

In Italy seven trucks were used with practically the same equipment as in Cleveland, and three more were equipped for dental work. They were operated from certain centres in the region where the American Red Cross Tuberculosis Commission worked in cooperation with Italian tuberculosis organizations. From these centres the trucks radiated on one-day trips to neighbouring villages and towns carrying posters, printed matter, and a crew consisting of an Italian physician, lecturer, nurse, and driver. A Government Child Welfare Special A big, gray automobile truck, known as the "Child Welfare Special," has recently been put into the field by the Children's Bureau of the United States Department of Labour to test the usefulness of the autcxnobile in carrying the message of better babies into rural communities.

The Children's Bureau has provided the following description of the truck and its tour: The truck is modelled very closely upon the dispensary truck used by the Chicago Tuberculosis Institute. The body of the car is constructed of wood, painted white on the inside and battleship gray on the outside. The words, "Child Welfare Special" are lettered in blue and white on each side of the car. The truck is roomy enough for a conference room and two dressing rooms. The conference room is nine and a half feet king, six feet wide, and six feet four inches high in the centre. This room has four windows on each side, high enough to be out of reach of praying eyes, yet admitting sufficient light for daytime examinations. The driver's cab, which is entirely enclosed in glass, can be reached from the conference room by a sliding door; with the shades drawn it forms one dressing room. The open-end gates of the car, provided with double folding doors and heavy curtains that fit into grooves, form a second dressing room. When a mother enters one of the rooms, she has the exclusive use of it until the child has been undressed, examined, and dressed again.

Most of the equipment of the truck is built in. A 15-gallon water tank, tucked away over the driver's cab, is connected by faucet with a stationary washstand in the conference room, which in turn is connected with a drain to the outside.

The examining table and the linen lockers are built over the wheel housing, an arrangement that ably convenient in spite of its small space. There are features that would be changed, however, if another truck were to be built. A more powerful engine is desirable. In spite of efforts to keep its weight down, the car when completely loaded tips the scale at 8,000 pounds. It does not seem advisable to reduce materially this weight as the body must be made to withstand the jar of travel and uncertain weather. The thirty-five horse power engine, supplemented by the extra pulling power provided by pneumatic tires, is adequate for most road conditions, but sandy, steep hills are negotiated with some difficulty. A heavier engine, one and a half or two-ton unit, would easily care for this load and at the same time carry enough reserve for any bad spots that are encountered.

Mechanical adjustments made recently, however, have given greater power Because of its size the Special does not travel well over muddy roads. The height of the car could be reduced by five or six inches and still permit easy walking within the car. This would very considerably reduce the sway and the danger of skidding.

The Special has the distinct advantage of at once gripping public interest. This may seem spectacular from the professional standpoint, but it gets results. It is believed that the ground can be covered better by the Special than in any other way, that its improved equipment will make for more satisfactory results than any method tried to date, and that its usefulness is directly in proportion to the ability of the physician in charge to make the public realize that she is merely demonstrating the need of periodic examinations and a method of providing opportunity for such examinations. She must bear in mind that the examinations she gives are merely an incident and not the object of the Special — that her most important function is to stimulate and aid in the organization of permanent follow-up work by the community.

Speaking Tours by Automobile or Motorcycle

One of the simplest and frequently a very effective form of travelling campaign is the speaking tour of which examples are numerous and familiar. Suffrage, prohibition, and many other causes have been promoted by travelling speakers in conspicuously painted or decorated automobiles. The speakers may carry with them all sorts of attention-getting devices, from a supply of leaflets to distribute, to a set of properties that would rival the stock of the old-time patent medicine man.

A Motorcycle Knight of Health

The following picturesque description of "A Modern Knight Errant, Carrying Health Gospel at Fifty Miles an Hour on A Motor Cycle," is taken from an article by Samuel Hopkins Adams, about the work of the Wisconsin Anti-Tuberculosis Associations: The " Flying Squadron of Health" Seven o'clock of a June evening in the lake country to the north. Supper is over. The mail Health to Sell, Samuel Hopkins Adams, La Follette's Magazine, December, 1914, has come jolting down by stage from the nearest railroad point, fourteen miles distant, and has been distributed from the post office which is also the general store and the council-house of the locality. The population, gathered in from a considerable radius, is talking a little politics, chewing a little tobacco, speculating a bit on the likelihood of rain, and yawning itself into readiness for home and bed. Far up the dusty road there is an approaching commotion, perceptible both to ear and eye. Presently the centre of it materializes in the form of a motorcycle bearing a man and a pack. The cycle pop-pops itself into a stationary phase. The man dismounts, gives a pleasant "good evening" to the gossiping group, appraises the immediate lay of the land with a practiced eye, unstraps a pack or two, and in an incredibly short time has a light silk tent up in a chosen spot by the roadway, a cooking kit laid out, a Dutch oven set, and the "makings" of a fire gathered near it.

Now, here is romance for the young of the hamlet, Gypsying a la mode! Knight-errantry at fifty miles an hour! The news runs amuck in the locality and in no time there is a growing gathering. Questions begin to fly; to each the new comer has his brief but courteous answer, all the time busy with his preparations for spending the night in the open. Presently he unfolds carefully a case containing placards, setting them up one by one against the stone fence. Conjecture, by this time, IS at the point of explosion.

"What are you sellin'. Mister?" comes the direct question. "Nothing," answers the stranger, setting up still another placard, and stepping back to estimate the effect. "Got a show?" "Why, yes! in a way." Giving' out samples?" Not exactly." Patent medicine feller, I guess," surmises one.

Seen a couple of 'em over to Humphrey's last fall." "Naw," controverts another, "He's sellin' pictures, can't ye see?" "Ain't goin' to preach, be ye, young man?" queries a third. "That too, in a way," says the motorist. Curiosity is now at its height. The crowd couldn't be driven away by a thunder shower.

The newcomer has nursed the situation until he has an absorbed attentiveness when he addresses the people in direct and simple words, explains why he is there, and talks to them about the peril of consumption and the ready-to-hand methods of guarding against it, using the charts which he has set up to fortify his telling points. It is done with a very conversational, homely and personal touch, so that the audience is encouraged to ask questions about the individual symptoms, the danger of "catching" the disease, the chances of cure for this or that friend, what hospital will take old Mrs. Tinkley, bedridden now for six weeks, and so on through the roster of health and sickness topics which make up so large a part of the immediate interests of countryfolk.

When the talk is over the visitor asks for the telephone, calls up a town perhaps fifty or sixty miles away, and those who are near enough to cock an ear hopefully (which includes as many as can crowd into the store) hear something like this: "Siddallville? Hello! That you, Mr. Conway? Yes. Werle.... I'll be there tomorrow night to speak.... No; I've got everything.... What's that? No; cost. All you have to provide is the hall and the audience. I'll furnish the rest.... Yes; seven-thirty tomorrow. Good-bye!" In the morning all that remains at the cross-roads to tell of the visitation is a little heap of ashes, some queer marks in the dust where the heavy-studded tires have passed — and a germinating seed of education. The gospel has come to Shucktown.

Wisconsin has since tried something believed to be even better than the "modern knight." Finding that the motion pictures were a much greater attraction than stereopticon slides, and having a four-reel health film to show, the Wisconsin Anti-Tuberculosis Association gave up its motorcycle and substituted a motion picture truck which is better fitted to transport the necessary machinery for its travelling campaign work.

Carrying the Canning Kitchen to the Food Supply

An ingenious use of a truck as a first aid to canners is illustrated in the photograph opposite page 38. This canning truck, chiefly intended for service to those coming to see it, but also carrying its message of war service to many neighbourhoods, was sent out by the Women's Committee on Food Conservation of the Pittsburgh Food Administration. The purpose of the truck is well described in a dodger, as follows:

How — With our canning truck.

When — At any time you can use us.

Where — At your own home or any other convenient place for you.

Why — To save home products for home use and leave for the Government the output from commercial canneries for our soldiers. It is a sin today to waste surplus vegetables if they can be canned.

We Furnish — Canning equipment, a teacher, and five or six helpers, who carry their lunches with them to avoid extra work for you. They work from' 9 to 4 o'clock.

You Furnish — Stove room, a wash boiler, the vegetables or fruits to be canned, and the jars. Cost — It will cost you no money, but we will expect some fresh vegetables or one-fifth of the jars canned during the day. We furnish the jars for this share, which will later be used for some patriotic purpose.

Canning Squad and Portable Kitchen Canning squad of the Allegheny County Council of National fense, and their portable kitchen ready to help the farmers' ' save their food products.

State and to the chief official of each town, village and city and to heads of civil and commercial organizations along the route, requesting their cooperation in making the trip a success.

A recruiting officer with proper equipment accompanied the train and often went ahead to placard towns and arrange for meetings at which Motor Transport moving pictures were shown and the newly planned system of vocational training to be given in the Motor Transport Corps schools was explained. All the cargo trucks in the train carried signs describing the various phases of the Motor Transport Corps activities. The Associated Press and the Knights of Columbus had representatives with the train and there were also several free lance writers representing newspaper syndicates.

All the war activity organizations, especially the War Camp Community Service, were advised of the passage of the train and did everything possible to make the men comfortable and to entertain them. As a result of all this publicity the passage of the train was marked by a continual succession of hearty greetings and hospitable entertainments. Each community, large or small, passed through did something to show its appreciation of the visit and its interest in the purposes of the trip. In many instances the entertainment program and street decorations were most elaborate.

Importance of Good Advance Work

The methods used in preparing the communities to receive the train are as important a feature of the project as the visit of the train itself. On the effectiveness with which the advance work is done depends its opportunity to reach as many people as can be accommodated and to have the audiences made up of the most hopeful "prospects," those most likely to !act on the suggestions offered. Advance information that arouses interest will bring visitors to the train in a receptive frame of mind that makes it easier to present the message quickly.

One or all of the following kinds of advance work will need to be done in each place to be visited, according to the nature and scope of the campaign:

1. General publicity and advertising.
2. Specialized appeals directed to selected groups and individuals.
3. Arrangements for distributing attendance over the full period of the visit.
4. Arrangements for local cooperation in the above work, in taking care of visitors to the train, and in organizing or carrying out follow-up work later.

For convenience, the discussion of these matters is given in terms of trains, although most of it applies equally to motor tours as well.

General Advertising

The appeal to the general public in a community may be made through news items in the papers, posters, window cards, window displays, advertisements and inserts in advertisements, and slides in motion picture theatres. Of the wide variety of methods to advertise an event, these are probably the ones best adapted to advance preparation for both large and small cities and towns. It is not the purpose here to discuss the technique of preparing any of this material. Unless they have ability and training in this field, those responsible for getting work out should call in specialists to do it, or at least to advise about it.

The purpose of advertising is more than merely to get a crowd. If there is very little competition from other events, as is often the case in small towns, it may be fairly easy to secure a large attendance. It is the business of your advertising to attract the attention of persons not yet interested in the subject matter and to arouse intelligent interest in what the train or truck will show. To design posters and prepare copy that will bring these results requires skill and practise which may sometimes be obtained as a gift but is worth paying for.

Specialized Appeal

The special groups to whom your message is chiefly directed may be singled out from the general public and definite methods used to insure their attendance. While most of the trains are of general interest to the communities visited, the message of the exhibits or demonstrations is probably addressed primarily to one or a few groups, classified according to occupation, standing in the community, race, age, condition of health, or particular interests. Special efforts to reach these groups may take the form of letters, announcements, or brief talks addressed to schools, churches, clubs, lodges, or employees of factories and places of business. Committees on cooperation may be formed within the groups and delegations appointed to come to the train. A personal canvass may be made by letters, postcards, personal visits, or telephone messages to leaders of groups or members of special bodies.

Arrangements for Distributing the Attendance

The tendency of the majority of the people is to select the same period in the day as the most convenient or desirable time for coming to the train. When the program is to be repeated a number of times, it is necessary to plan special methods for distributing the attendance over the Peach Growers of EmI Trxa. are Bebg Robbed by the liuects and DUeases that-attack Peaches.

Specialists With Exhibit Cars

Poster Advertising the Coming of an Exhibit Train

This is the type of poster that is frequently sent out in advance of agricultural trains. The posters are usually on white paper or card with black letters. The news value of the material on the poster doubtless secures readers who would not be inclined to give attention to so much reading matter if it conveyed only educational information.

The car is a vestibuled railway coach entirely remodeled and contains a chemical and bacteriological laboratory, a health exhibit of posters and electrically driven models and a picture machine. These, with the explanation given by a Health Instructor on the car, serve to impress on the minds of the people the principles of the promotion of health and prevention of disease.

May we count on you to secure the interest and cooperation of the medical, dental and nursing professions in your community, for a public meeting at an hour which you, in consultation with the Superintendent of Schools and a president of an influential woman's organization, may decide? We are also very desirous of securing the attendance of the Mayor and Town Council and any other citizens who do, or should, feel responsibility for community welfare and the conservation of child life. We have also written the Superin-tendent of Schools and your newspapers, realizing that the medical profession, the educational people and the press are the agencies our Government is counting upon for cooperation in constructive, peace-time work.

The Health Car Corps will communicate with you immediately upon arrival in your city to learn of your plans for the utilization of their time and effort while with you. We are anxious to make their stay in each community count for the highest possible things in the interest of the public health and welfare.

The car is supplied with a number of good Health Films which we will be glad to show, free of charge, to the public if arrangements can be made with some one \who has a full-sized picture machine and a hall at his disposal.

The following report from the director of the Texas Peach Demonstration Train, described on page 1 3, is fairly typical of advance work done in local communities without a personal representative:

Articles announcing the tour of this train have been sent to all the large newspapers in the east Texas territory, also to the county newspapers. Individual letters have also been sent to the large peach growers, urging them to attend these meetings. In counties where there is a county demonstration agent, a great deal is being done to bring the matter to the attention of the farmers. Large posters have been put up a couple of weeks in advance of the train all through the different towns at which stops are to be made. The chambers of commerce and business organizations have been called upon several weeks in advance and furnished with full data, and they are doing all they can to make the meetings a success. The county judge in each county has given his cooperation by declaring the week in which the work is being conducted in his particular county as Horticultural Week. The chambers of commerce have, in many in Stances, made arrangements for special features in connection with the visit of our train.

Qualifications of the Advance Agent

The personality and previous experience of the person needed to carry out advance work form an important factor in the success of the whole undertaking. The agent should be able to work successfully with local committees, since much valuable publicity will be secured through their efforts. That to say, he should be adaptable, clear, definite, and orderly in his statements and in handling a meeting, and be able to inspire enthusiastic interest in carrying out the plans he outlines.

His training and experience at best should include knowledge of publicity or advertising methods, experience in working with volunteer committees, and general information of the subject matter of the campaign. Of these three, given an alert; and intelligent worker who has a moderate amount of what may be called "publicity sense," an understanding of how to organize volunteer workers is probably the most necessary element in his or her equipment. For he may acquire in a comparatively short time a working knowledge of the subject, and may call in outside assistance in preparing the news stories and advertising plans that he carries with him. But every local committee presents new and unexpected problems, and no amount of coaching can provide what is gained by experience in adapting plans and methods to the peculiarities of a local situation, winning over a local chairman who has prejudices or skepticisms, or simplifying or expanding plans of work to fit the resources of the town as the agent may estimate them in the brief time that he remains.

The Job of the Advance Agent

The first advance work is done by the committee or individual who directs the whole enterprise from some central point, notifying local persons of the purpose and the date of the agent's visit. If there is already a local representative of the movement in the community, arrangements may be made which will save the agent much time in seeing the editor, minister, school superintendent, and others on his list whose cooperation he must secure. If there is no local representative, letters should be sent directly to the persons upon whom he expects to call.

The agent's visit should be timed long enough in advance of the coming of the train to allow for carrying out the publicity plans, and near enough so that there will be no chance for interest to wane in the interval. A ten-day start has been found satisfactory, especially when the way has been paved for his visit and publicity and advertising materials are ready for use. If an agent travels in an automobile, he is better able to adapt his time to local needs and still keep ahead of the train, than if he is dependent upon railroad schedules.

The Child Welfare Special of the Children's Bureau was preceded by an advance agent and the method is described in the bureau's report of the tour as follows:

The advance agent, who travels two weeks in advance of the car arranges the itinerary, attends to the publicity, and organizes local communities to take charge of the work. Her first step is to call together a county child welfare committee.

With their aid an itinerary is mapped out, and then local committees are organized in the communities to be visited. So far as possible, the agents work through the local child welfare committees formed during Children's Year.

These committees are asked to provide a suitable location for the parking of the Special — spot that is centrally located, well shaded, and near a public room that can be used both as an exhibit and waiting room. They are also asked to make a canvass of their districts before the Special arrives, so that everyone may understand the purpose of the conference. Each committee member has her field of work clearly defined. A number of women are asked to serve as hostesses during the conference, receiving mothers and babies, giving them numbers for examination, and explaining the exhibit material.

The agent then distributes her cuts and other publicity material for the newspapers, printed instructions for the child welfare committee, copies of announcements that ministers are asked to make from their pulpits, and posters advertising the coming of the Special. She visits city and county officials, social agencies, editors, physicians, clergymen, farm advisers, county demonstrators, business men, and other representative citizens to explain the purpose of the visit of the car.

As a result of this work of the advance agent, the staff finds everything is in readiness on the arrival of the Special.

The Land Clearing Special of Georgia, a recent enterprise of the State College of Agriculture, was preceded by an advertising campaign designed to make the Land Clearing Demonstration the big event of the season in each stopping place. In addition to the usual methods of newspaper publicity, posters, and letters, twenty automobiles carrying signs announcing the demonstration, visited the rural districts for a week preceding the event. Telephone owners were called up on the telephone and invited, and arrangements were made to have factory and train whistles blow when the demonstrations were about to start. Information about this plan was widely spread.

Assignments of Advance Work for Local Committees

With time for only a day or part of a day's stop in a town the advance agent has little opportunity to explain fully to the co-operating committee all the details of advance preparation expected of its members. To meet this situation, the directors of the Pennsylvania Food Conservation Train with the cooperation of the present writer prepared and multigraphed a set of instructions for local committees. The agent distributed copies of these instructions to the members of the executive committee in each town during the meeting that was held on the day of his visit. Not all of these directions were suited to every community visited, and frequently suggestions from the local committee were added or substituted. This set of assignments is quoted in full below. The features of the assignments especially worth noting are:

1. That written instructions or suggestions in addition to the agent's personal explanation leave less to chance in getting the plans carried out.
2. That the directions are exceedingly simple and flexible.
3. That each separate assignment was printed on a separate sheet so that it could be placed in the hands, of the person who was to carry it out.

You know the old saying, "If you want to get a thing done, do it yourself." But there is a new one that is much more appropriate in wartime when we should all be working together to win: "If you want to get people interested, give them something to do to help." There is something for everybody to do to make the Food Conservation Train a success.

Dividing the Work. The following list of assignments should be divided among as many dependable people as you can find. Try some new people who have not had a chance to help before.

Each assignment is described on a separate sheet, a copy of which may be given to the person taking the assignment. If necessary, one person may take several assignments.

Assignments Name of Committee Chainman

1. Reception committee.
2. Newspapers.
3. Advertising.
4. Attendance of special groups.
5. Churches.
6. Schools.
7. Attendance of foreign born.
8. Speaking.
9. Personal canvass.
10. Motor service.
11. Miscellaneous.

A reception committee usually of from six to ten members should receive the visitors at the train. It is desirable to have four members on hand, usually from ten to twelve o'clock, and six members from two to five o'clock to welcome delegations, distribute literature, give information, and explain exhibits. The committee will be given a list of expected delegations so that their leaders may be known and introduced to the train staff. The committee will find that the train offers an excellent opportunity to tell visitors of local activities for food conservation and to invite their cooperation. It will be well to have the whole reception committee at the train a few minutes before its first opening at ten o'clock so that they may become familiar with exhibits and have time for a brief conference with members of the staff.

The advance agent will bring with him material for the local paper, to which will be added the names of committee members and of persons who are helping the committee.

Other material that should be of interest to the local papers includes:

1. A list of special delegations from lodges, churches, business groups, and others that will visit the train.
2. Accounts of talks given by Four Minute Men and others about the food train and food conservation.
3. An account of the work that is being done for food conservation by the local committee.

Editorials. Editors may be glad to take advantage of the presence of the train as an occasion for an editorial on some local aspect of the food situation, as encouraging the use of home products, regarding the food hoarders, and so forth.

Out-of-Town Papers. The newspapers in the territory adjacent to your town will carry some news of its coming. In addition to news sent to those editors from state headquarters they will be interested in your local plans and the names of your workers. One of these assignments could be given to each of several members of a committee. The more workers there are the more enthusiasm there will be. Posters. There are probably several persons who would gladly make posters announcing the train if they were asked. Give them the facts and let them work out their own ideas. Have these posters shown in store windows and in public buildings. See that all posters sent from the Philadelphia office are placed where they will do the most good.

Window Displays. Invite merchants to have window displays on food conservation and help them with ideas. The sheets issued by the Retail Store Section of the Food Administration contain pictures of windows that are easy to copy. Be sure that the window display contains an announcement of the food train.

Ask every merchant who has a sign writer or who makes his own window cards to make up in his best style a card or sign announcing the coming of the train. Slides in Moving Picture Theatres. See that slides are displayed in the moving picture theatres announcing the coming of the train. The following makes a satisfactory slide:

Mention in Advertisements of Local Merchants. Local food dealers, especially those selling substitutes, should be interested in getting their customers to see the exhibits and demonstrations. Ask them to mention the train in their newspaper advertisements preceding its arrival. In addition to the usual advertising space of food dealers your newspaper may be able to have a special page of food advertisements with a large announcement of the train in the centre. Other advertisers may also be willing to mention the food train and may find a way to work it into their advertisement as follows: On your way to the Food Conservation Train on Tuesday, don't fail to drop in and see our new assortment of men's neckwear, etc.

Since only a certain number of the people can see the train during its brief stay and ALL the people should receive its message, it is important that special delegations be arranged for, with the understanding that the delegates will pass on the message brought by the train to members of their organizations. Morning attendance is lightest. As many as possible of these special groups should be arranged for during the morning.

The director of the train and the chairman of the reception committee should each receive a list of delegations that expect to attend, also the hour when they will arrive. If any special group promises to come at a given hour, have a committee member meet them and introduce them at the train. People will be more likely to come if they feel some special attention is being shown them. The following groups are suggested; others may be added or substituted as the committee may decide:

Officials. An official delegation made up of members of council of defence, city officials, chamber of commerce, trades assembly. Red Cross and other war agencies, newspaper editors, and others. This delegation should be the first to come in the morning after the reception committee arrives.

Schools. Special arrangements for the attendance of school children in the morning are suggested on a separate assignment sheet, with the heading "Schools." Churches. See the assignment on Cooperation of Churches for a suggestion for having delegations from church societies. Restaurants and Hotels. Managers and cooks of hotels and restaurants should come in a body at a special hour so that information and answers to questions of special interest to them can be arranged. Food Sellers. There are exhibits of special interest to food sellers, and these persons can be very helpful in passing on information to their customers. All should be asked to attend in a body if possible. Can you arrange for the stores to be closed at a certain hour? Employees. Employers might be willing to excuse some of their workers in stores and factories, especially if they are near the train, for a brief visit. If a factory delegation can be arranged for at the noon hour a special session may be arranged for them. Clubs. All fraternal orders, civic, social clubs, and labour unions, should be especially urged to be represented. The men's organizations will be especially interested in the war relics and in the maps showing important facts about food distribution. The Food Conservation Train aims to teach the message of brotherhood — of sharing our food with those whose need is greater than ours. All the churches will be glad to help make it a success if you tell them what to do. Announcements. Ask ministers to have announcement of the train given at all services during the week before it arrives. Announcement forms are supplied.

Delegations. Invite church societies to send delegations to the train. Be sure that the women who plan church suppers, bazaars, and food sales are appointed among delegates. They will receive valuable suggestions. It is important that men's classes and societies send delegates. Sermons. Ask ministers to preach sermons on the Sunday before the train arrives on our obligation to feed the world from our generous stores of food. They may obtain helpful information from (insert name of a food administration bulletin giving general information about the food situation), of which copies may be had from. School children can be of great assistance in spreading the news of the train. Invitations to Parents. The teachers may be asked to have the children write invitations to their parents to visit the train as an exercise in composition Attendance of School Children. Groups of older school children (attending high school) should come with their teachers in squads of about thirty or forty at fifteen-minute intervals during the morning. Domestic science classes should come in a body. Drawing and manual training classes may be asked to study the exhibits with a view to reproducing them at a later date for the benefit of parents and friends.

Committee on Attendance of Foreign Language Groups

Remember those who do not speak English. We particularly wish to reach them. The following steps are necessary: The Leaders. The committee should see and actively interest the clergymen. If they approve, they can do much to interest the members of their congregations. In the same manner, interest the chief foreign business men. Find out what leaders among them have been revealed by the Liberty Loan and other campaigns, and reach them. Workers. Let every employer having foreign workers and every woman employing foreign domestics advertise to and through them.

Arrange special hours for groups by languages and be sure to have an interpreter or a speaker in their own language. Be Democratic I Above all else be democratic in your dealings with these foreign-born workers. Make them feel that they are asked to take a part in a common experience, not that the native born are "unloading" something upon the foreigners. Keep yourselves in the attitude of being willing to learn as well as to teach.

Use the Four Minute Men in advertising the train. Call upon others who can speak. Tell them what the Pennsylvania Food Administration is trying to do with the train and ask them to speak for you.

The director and staff of the train are willing to address noon meetings with the object of urging attendance at the afternoon session. Factory employees can be reached in this way. Arrange with the manager of 'any local corporation, particularly one employing girls, to have such a meeting. Try to have a speaker at any gathering that is held during the week or ten days before the train arrives.

Personal Canvass

The Men. If your men are not as eager to conserve as the women, get them to come to the train and we can help you to interest them. The exhibit car especially contains war relics, pictures, and maps of interest to men. Invite as many men as you can reach personally or by telephone.

The Fanners* Wives. The best publicity to farmers' wives is personal. Let the committee take the telephone book, divide up the names of the farmers, and see that each farm woman is 'phoned to at least three days before our coming. Have letters sent to farmers' wives several days before train arrives. (Forms supplied.) If you know of interested women who are lame, or otherwise shut in, send someone for them in an automobile. Last Minute Calls. Personal telephone calls on a day before the train arrives are an indispensable means of insuring attendance. Get some of the older high school girls to divide up the telephone directory among them and call up the numbers systematically from their own homes. They should simply announce that the Food Conservation Train is going to be in town tomorrow and give the time and place where it may be found. If the train has been generally advertised a large attendance can be insured by this method. It reminds people.

Motor Service. In order to reach the people of outlying districts, it is possible to organize a girls' motor service. Have the automobiles go to an advertised point where they will pick up all who desire to go to the train. They can make several trips in morning and afternoon. It would be well to have automobiles doing this work carry banners advertising the train and its special work.

The message of the campaign includes the ideas, facts, and plans to be presented to the audiences. The choice of a topic or its scope, what to say about it, and how much, are questions deserving more thoughtful consideration and real work than is usually given to them. The most important and the most difficult thing in preparing the message is to have constantly in mind a picture of the way in which it is to be delivered.

If, for example, the project takes the form of an exhibit and lecture train in which visitors will spend part of their time listening to a talk and the remainder passing through several cars to examine displays, we should, as we plan the message, try to picture the train on the siding at, let us say, Jonesville. We should also visualize the numbers and types of people likely to come, how they will divide their time between the talks and the exhibits, how long they will stay, or how long we will wish them to stay, what they know bout the subject already, and what they will want to know, what they could do with this or that kind of information, and how much and what part of the message they are likely to remember.

If the campaign is carried on with a truck and its program includes a demonstration which only a few people can see, and a motion picture and lecture program for much larger numbers, there are two problems; first, visualizing the small groups for the demonstration, and second, the larger audience for the more popular program.

Reports of topics and methods of presenting them that have come in from many and varied travelling campaigns indicate that much more attention could be given to this question of preparing the message, and that frequently topics have been selected and the form of presentation worked out with only a very hazy visualization of the conditions and the people to be encountered at Jones-ville and 'other points along the route.

Choice of a Topic

Experience leads most directors, sooner or later, to choose a single topic that is definite and concrete, rather than a group of topics or one that is broad in scope. This limiting of the topic is all the more likely to be important where the subject of the campaign is unfamiliar to the prospective audience. The titles given to many of the agricultural trains indicate that their directors have found the concrete and single topic satisfactory. Trains have been called the "Stump Pulling Special," "Wheat Special," "Better Seed Car,", and "Dairy Train."

In the health field the topics have often been very general, as "Child Welfare" or merely "Public Health/' One public health car, which seemed to be fairly typical, carried exhibits on the prevention and cure of tuberculosis, care of babies, the duties of the school nurse, food adulteration, communicable diseases, playgrounds, venereal diseases, and a description of the functions of the State Health Department. The more inclusive and thus less specific the topic the more vague and general will be the talk about it afterward by those who visited the train.

A reason sometimes given for presenting varied and general topics is that the purpose is not so much to give definite information which will be remembered and acted on, as to impress people with the scope and importance of the subject. For example, the visitors to a public health car in which many phases of the subject are touched upon may carry away a conviction that public health work is important to the community and should be supported although their ideas of it were very vague.

This result may satisfy the purpose of some campaigns, but more often directors who present a variety of topics hope that some thing about each will be remembered; and there is reason for believing that their hope will not come as near to realization, or at least that the information will not be of as great utility, as it might if the subjects were fewer and more specifically treated.

Another argument frequently brought forward in favour of including several topics is that all sorts of people will visit the train or truck, and while one will be interested in one subject others will be more interested in something else. When those in charge of the program are meeting only a few people at a time, they can talk separately to each visitor about special problems, but the brief stops made on most tours require the message to be presented to a large group at one time or at least in quick succession, so that in practice it usually happens that all the visitors see and hear the same things. In this case the more closely a single and concrete topic is adhered to, the more hopeful campaigners may be that what is said or displayed will be remembered.

An equally important reason for limiting the number of topics is the desirability of having your whole audience get the same message. In connection with the Wheat Specials, for example, not alone should the farmer and the farmer's wife and the farmer's children be informed about the wheat problems of the locality, but the local banker and business man stand in need of much the same information. The preacher and the doctor will help to spread the doctrine, and the school teacher can make good use of what he learns. The more nearly the entire community, young and old, understands and is interested in the same message, the more likely that the desired results will follow. Occasionally two or three topics may be presented on the same train by having separate cars for each topic and a separate audience for each.

Thus, on one train a car containing household labour-saving devices was designed to interest the wives of farmers, and a pure-seed car the farmers. Or several topics may be combined in such a way that they are made parts of one large idea. Health topics might be brought together under "The Health of the Family," and divided into instruction about the care of the baby, the child at school, the teaching of social hygiene to older boys and girls, and the sanitation of the household. But even when thus closely related to the family interests of the visitors, this group of topics is still too varied to permit any one to make a strong and lasting impression.

Having chosen a topic, there is sure to be so much to tell about it that careful selection again becomes necessary. The best guide in preparing the subject matter of the program is the visualization of expected audiences already referred to. It cannot be too strongly emphasized that the relation of the subject matter to their interests, circumstances, and habits will largely determine their response to the suggestions given. Often this relationship exists, but is not explained clearly enough to be readily understood. The fact that the travelling campaigners come from a distance, bringing new ideas expressed in an unfamiliar way, leads an audience to look upon the whole project as something which is no doubt very interesting to see and hear about, but of no immediate concern to themselves. It is worth while to make a very special effort to overcome this attitude of aloofness and to make the audiences see that what you are bringing is something that they have been wanting all the time, without their fully realizing it.

Making up the Program

The term program is used here to include the combined activities and displays that make up what is presented to visitors at each stopping point. It may consist of music, talks, demonstrations, motion pictures, or displays of posters and objects, or several of these features combined, with varying emphasis on one or the other form. It may be held inside of railroad cars or in an open space, using for a stage a flat car, the rear platform of a passenger car, or a temporary structure. Or it may be given in a hall in the town. Sometimes the program includes both indoor and outdoor features.

It is usually a good idea to arrange what might be called a "unit " program that will include everything that it is desirable for a given visitor or group of visitors to do, see, and hear in order to fully understand and enjoy the message. This unit program has an important place in the arrangement of itinerary, schedule, and the arrangements made for the attendance. For example, if the unit program lasts an hour we have a means different forms, in talks, demonstrations, exhibits, and printed matter. If the visitor is obliged to stand during all or the greater part of the time he is not likely to give more than an hour of interested attention to talks and displays. Many will give much less.

The actual period that the average visitors will remain under certain conditions is soon learned by experimenting, and each feature should be timed 'so that a satisfactory presentation of the subject can be assured for the majority of them. However attractively the subject is presented through motion pictures or other displays, a good talker is about the most important element in getting the idea across to the visitors. Whether the speaker accompanies his talk with slides or objects, conducts a demonstration, explains exhibits, or makes running comments on motion pictures, his ability to be heard, to hold interest, and to express himself simply, briefly, and concretely will often be the chief factor in the success of the program. Lecturers for travelling campaigns should be chosen as much for their ability as speakers as for their knowledge of the subject matter.

Programs of Exhibit Trains

The following plan for a program was announced for one of the Liberty Loan trains:

Aerial bombs will be sent off as train reaches stop. Liberty Loan representatives in charge of train will make brief address and ask local committee of three to come onto the platform. Five-minute address by the local chairman or someone selected by him. Talk by returned soldier. Address by experienced speaker with principal object of urging necessity of subscribing to Loan. Invitation by Liberty Loan representative to inspect exhibition. The trains for which this program was planned made short stops and the talks were given from a platform or from one of the flat cars. A large crowd could be reached by a single speaking program. In this case the speaking was the important feature, and the exhibits of war material were an "attraction" rather than an educational feature. It satisfied the purpose of the tour to have most of the time devoted to speeches, followed by a rapid view of exhibits. The extension division of the Texas State College of Agriculture reports the following program method:

Immediately upon going into a town, the people were loaded into the lecture cars and three lecturers would alternate for a twenty-minute talk on different subjects in each car. Where outdoor meetings were held the exhibit cars were closed upon coming into town and general lectures were first had from the platform car," then the live stock were led onto the platform car where special demonstrations were given. As soon as this formal program was completed the specialists were stationed back through the exhibition cars and the crowds were allowed to enter the front of the train and pass gradually through the entire train, making such enquiries of the specialists as they cared to while going through the exhibition car.

Here again the speaking and the outdoor demonstrations are evidently regarded as the important features. Such a plan should not be considered if the exhibits are of real importance. The audience that has been standing during the program of perhaps half an hour or more, and has then waited in line to go through the train, is a tired audience and not nearly so responsive as though its members came fresh to the exhibits.

It is also true that when the program is so arranged that the whole crowd is ready at one time to start through the train, there is much more difficulty in managing the people and much more dissatisfaction on the part of those at the rear end of the line.

It is difficult to get careful attention for exhibits from people who are being moved ahead to make way for an impatient crowd standing in long lines behind them. The managers of trains will do well to decide in advance whether the speaking or the exhibits constitute the really important feature of the program. If it is the exhibits, then the speaking should be made incidental, perhaps, by having a ten-minute talk given from the platform at regular intervals as a new group is to be started through the train.

A Program Combining Demonstrations and Exhibits

A method of dividing the time between demonstrations in two cars and an exhibit car Was worked out satisfactorily on the Pennsylvania Food Conservation Train. All the audience passed through the train in the same direction, starting at the same point, except that at the beginning of the session all the cars were filled at once to avoid delays. When the first car was filled a talk on canning started. No attempt was made to demonstrate a complete process, but different vegetables or fruits were in various stages of preparation continuously, so that a fifteen-minute illustrated talk brought out the points that required emphasis.

After about five minutes of questions and looking at displays of equipment and canned articles, this crowd moved on to the next car, while the first car was filled again with the next group of arrivals. In the second car a similar program was given on uses of wheat substitutes. In the third car two explainers met the audience and explained the exhibits found there. As the topics in all three cars were closely related (the demonstrations showing how to save food and the exhibits showing why food saving was necessary), an hour spent in three cars gave variety enough to keep interest awake and still kept closely to the one big idea — "Save Food."

Outdoor Speaking at Trains

If speaking to a general audience is the important thing, a talk from the outside of the train would seem better than crowding people into the cars; but even outside speeches from the platform or a flat car, or an especially built platform at the train present many difficulties.

The location of the train frequently does not provide good standing room for the crowds; there is frequently distraction from the noise of other trains and persistent rainy weather must be reckoned with also. It is very important to have speakers with good outdoor voices, for the effect on the audience of straining to hear a speaker is irritating and leaves behind a bad impression given on flat cars. On the Liberty Loan trains flat cars were employed to show cannon, machine guns, tanks, and other large equipment. In the photograph opposite page 80 a flat car is shown fitted with a framework for a tarpaulin for protection against weather. This is a necessary precaution in using flat cars.

An experienced director of exhibit trains writes: "An especially built and designed car for the purpose is well worth its additional cost. Such cars as I have seen provided by the railroads for temporary service in exhibit lines have all been old, small, and often broken-down baggage or passenger cars, in every way unsuitable for a purpose where the most extreme dimensions available still leave the exhibit and circulation space contracted. Cars should be built on the largest frames and the most extreme dimensions that the railroads, as governed by their tracks, bridges, and tunnels can handle.

Windows should be set high in the car walls, giving a high source of light and maximum wall space for exhibits, and should be larger than those in the ordinary coach to secure better ventilation. The doors should be built wider than the usual car door." The plan calls for small and compact living and office quarters at one end. The director also adds that the installation of an engine to furnish lights and power for working models is an important item of equipment. One engine is sufficient to run lights, fans, and models for several cars. In these days of portable electrical outfits, this item is' practicable and fairly inexpensive.

Travelling Accommodations for Staff Members

The kind of living. Arrangements provided for the lecturers and assistants will depend, to some extent, upon the frequency of the stops and the number of persons travelling with the train. Several of the more elaborately equipped trains have carried a Pullman sleeping coach and a diner for the staff members. If there are frequent stops, it would seem that at least sleeping quarters on the train are necessary. Meals are sometimes arranged for at stopping places, and in this case the advance agent is responsible for seeing that good meals are assured. When stops of a full day or more are made, the staff members sometimes find rooms and meals in hotels en route. Whatever the arrangements, as is stated elsewhere, they should insure the greatest possible degree of comfort to the staff, in order to offset the severe strain that this kind of campaigning inevitably involves.

Treatment of Car Interiors

The two chief difficulties with exhibits on trains are keeping them clean and so securing them in place as to withstand the jarring motion. Washable surfaces on floors, shelves, and walls are essential. Exhibits should be either of the kind that are easily kept clean or else placed under cover or frequently replaced. No decorations.

There is little opportunity to get attention for detailed or complex displays, no matter how attractive and interesting they may be. The following is taken from a description of a mechanical device shown on a train through which visitors were always moving rapidly because there was a long waiting line: "A model block-signal system about 25 feet in length, illustrating the protection provided by a clock-signal system was in full operation. This model had two sidings and was designed particularly to show single-track operation. Intermediate signals were shown between the clock signals by means of lights." The information that this model conveyed illustrates very well the kind that is too complicated to be understood without a careful examination and some explanation by an attendant.

You must, therefore, in planning the form as in planning the content of your exhibit, keep your eye steadily on the picture of the Smiths and Browns at the train as it stands on the side track in Jonesville with many people moving through the cars. You can test the practicability of your devices and other displays by asking yourself these questions concerning the probable reaction of Brown and Smith:

* Will it attract their attention?
* Will it arouse their interest?
* Will they remember it?

* Will it bring a response from them?

These are generally recognized aims of advertising, and they apply equally to exhibits which are, after all, a form of advertising.

Use of the Space for Display

For displaying exhibits to moving audiences, the use of the shape should be so planned that it is easy to keep visitors moving in a given direction and at the same time make it possible for them to grasp quickly the meaning of what they see. The majority of those who have reported on their experience with trains agree that it is very important that visitors should move in a single direction. This is beyond question desirable unless small audiences are expected; but as is stated elsewhere, capacity audiences are the aim of most enterprises.

Having agreed on a one-way movement, there is, however, still considerable disagreement as to the best arrangement of material — whether on two sides of the centre aisle, or along the centre of the car with an aisle on either side, or finally, with exhibits displayed on one side only with a single aisle.

The first method, that of displaying exhibits on two sides of the centre aisle, makes the progress of the visitor very slow and awkward, for he must continually turn from one side to the other as he goes unless, of course, he violates the rule of moving in one direction only and in so doing comes back along the same aisle. Not only is it awkward to turn continually from side to side in viewing that exhibits should be arranged in some logical sequence. Visitors are sometimes called upon to perform amazing feats in mental acrobatics, leaping from one topic to another with breathless speed. For example, in the exhibit pictured opposite page 84, we see a poster about baby deaths resting on a model of a school building with a placard nearby urging the use of schools as community centres. Across the narrow aisle is a model obviously unrelated either to community centres or baby deaths. The sequence of ideas should be such that each new thought is made easier to understand and more interesting because of what went before it, or each separate exhibit should be clearly related to one central idea. Thus, in the first exhibit of the Pennsylvania Food Conservation Train the series of topics was developed as follows:

* Why we must save,
* Small savings,

* Saving wheat ,
* Saving sugar,
* Saving fats,
* Using all the milk,
* Using home products.

Not only the sequence of ideas but the separation between two topics is important. This can be accomplished by a visible separation, allowing a distance of at least six inches between exhibits relating to different topics; better still, by putting up actual barriers between the exhibits, as is done in the exhibit opposite page 70. The barrier has the advantage of holding the eye at one spot, so that there is no temptation to desert on^ exhibit for the lure of a bright colour or a curious device farther on.

Another consideration in arranging material is that groups relating to one subject should' be so placed that their relation to one another and to the whole be quickly recognized. Sometimes exhibits that belong together are separated because variety of size and shape makes it inconvenient to work out a suitable arrangement. It is worth while to plan carefully in advance the kinds of exhibit material that will harmoniously illustrate a given topic; also to have the sizes and shapes conform to the dimensions of the space reserved for them.

Some Observations From Practical Experience

In a letter describing the exhibit car of the Canadian Forestry Association, Mr. J. R. Dickson, who was in charge of the car, makes some interesting observations regarding the arrangement of exhibits based on his experiences. He writes in part as follows:

> The people, especially at crowded hours, all tend to travel through an exhibit car in one direction and this is very desirable inasmuch as the man in charge of the car can regularly escort through it group after group of eager sightseers or inquirers after knowledge and keep up a cross between a lecture and a conversation with them, answering their questions and drawing their attention to all the pertinent points in the exhibit which they might otherwise overlook.
>
> To accomplish this plan of car lecturing most effectually, the entire exhibit should be arranged so far as possible in a natural sequence, beginning at one end of the car and ending at the other.

This of course is where a single aisle is provided down one side of the car. Such a scheme makes one's talk logical and so helps to impress the lessons of the exhibit in such a way that they are remembered easily and intelligently.... On entering the car the first object to attract the visitor's eye was a large map of Canada, showing the forestry belt of 400,000,000 acres, over 90 per cent of this timber land being publicly owned. When told that each citizen of Canada, man, woman and child, owned on the average fifty acres of this national resource, the imagination and the pocket-nerve of the visitor were at once stimulated and he or she was thereafter taking a personal interest in the whole exhibit.

The visitor next turned to a nursery of small pine and spruce illustrating the essential beginning of all our forest wealth and also suggesting the basic importance of land classification in order that every acre may be put to its best use. Then our modem methods of protecting both such young growth and the resulting mature timber were examined and explained, and the great need for good laws and the generous expenditure of public money in order to safeguard their forests, was readily seen and agreed to.... Before leaving, the visitor... was handed a copy of the last Canadian Forestry Association Journal, and given a brief description of the nation-building work of this society, together with an addressed card inviting him to join. Finally he inspected a cabinet filled with highly finished samples of Canadian woods, and the last thing his eye rested upon and which impressed itself on his memory as he left the car, was this bold fire warning: "A tree will make a million matches; a match will bum a million trees."

Arrangement of Car for Demonstrations

When an audience is to be gathered in a car to witness a demonstration or hear an illustrated talk, the first requirement is that the speaker can be easily heard and each process plainly seen by everyone in the car. The second is that the audience shall be comfortably seated if the demonstration is to last longer than fifteen or twenty minutes. This is about the limit of time that an audience will stand without becoming restless. The illustration on the opposite page shows an interior especially constructed for cooking demonstrations, or rather for brief object lessons, as a feature of the Pennsylvania Food Conservation Train. The demonstrator stands on a platform raised a foot higher than the floor. A counter extending the length of the car curves out at the centre to leave a space for the platform and small kitchen. The maximum space for a standing audience is provided, and all are within easy range of the speaker's voice and near enough there is no room for the definite immediate purpose to stand out boldly where it can been. Don't attempt to crowd into this brief tour the information or activities that belongs in the follow-up program. The same advice extends down to the handling of audiences and every other feature.

The Places to Be Visited

In considering the type of places to be visited, the two main considerations are the size of the place and whether it contains the kinds of people who may be expected to take an interest in the subject matter. Many of those who have conducted trains report that they create more interest in communities of ten thousand or less than in larger places. The larger the town the more varied and numerous are the rival attractions. In the cities the train yards are often busier than elsewhere and, therefore, the noise and confusion as well as the difficulty of handling crowds at the train is greater unless the train be stationed away from the busy yards. The towns should be selected with reference to the relation of the community to the subject, matter. To take an obvious example, it would hardly be appropriate to send an agricultural train into a mining town. The whole plan of campaign may have been made in relation to one type of population, either rural or industrial, and it is rather a waste of time to try to make it serve a population of a kind that it has not been prepared for. In planning the itinerary of a tour that must be completed in a given length of time, it is usually necessary to decide between the importance of visiting a small number of towns and of making a long stop in each, or of visiting a larger number for fewer hours or days.

A stop may be limited to an hour or so because it is thought more important to cover a given amount of territory within certain time limits than it is to stay long enough in a place to reach a large share of the population or give much information. Or the purpose of the tour may be accomplished by presenting to an audience, all of whose members arrive at the same time, a single program lasting an hour and dealing with easily understood facts or ideas. The Liberty Loan trains furnish good illustrations of a purpose of this sort. If your campaigners are not in a hurry to get over the ground by a certain date they will probably find it more satisfactory to spend a full day and sometimes longer with the people of each community visited. The program may then be repeated for a number of audiences and the travelling specialists will have an opportunity to promote closer relationships with local leaders. However, conditions that govern a decision regarding the length of time to spend at a place differ so widely for individual enterprises that general suggestions have not much value.

The stops of a truck tour are more easily arranged than those of a train since the latter is dependent upon the convenience of the railroad. One gain through this greater flexibility is the possibility of return visits to the same place. In this way the truck helps in its own advance publicity work by making a brief stay which attracts attention and spreads the news of its return for a longer stay a little later. In its work in the congested districts of the city, the Cleveland Children's Year Special followed what its director called a "skip stop" system, visiting a neighbourhood long enough to leave a number of people sufficiently well informed to talk about it, and coming back two or three days later to find an appreciative audience ready for the program.

Receiving the Visitors

Visitors are the real reason for the enterprise which is undertaken solely for their instruction or benefit if results are hoped for, and they should not be forgotten at any stage of the planning. We have already considered them in the choice of subject matter, the form and quantity of the discussion in this section is handled in terms of trains for the sake of clearness and convenience, but generally the application is to single cars as well as to trains, and to automobiles or motor trucks or caravans of the same. The paragraphs not applicable to trucks are fairly obvious. However, it is urged that maximum results from a truck tour call for much the same carefully detailed preparation and management as a tour with a train material, and its arrangement. Now, having equipment and plans ready, what shall be done with the visitors when they arrive at the train?

Obviously, their comfort and convenience should be prepared for and every possible help provided for them to understand and enjoy what is displayed. Plans for doing these things should be based on the expectation of as large an attendance as can be handled satisfactorily, arid even on some overcrowding, unless small groups are deliberately sought. As is explained in the section on advance work, local committees should be appointed whose members will cooperate with the regular staff of the train.

A reception committee may welcome special delegations and introduce them to the members of the train staff. If there is a formal program, local leaders are usually asked to take part in it, and as it is important in relation to the follow-up work that they have the opportunity to familiarize themselves with the subject matter and the methods demonstrated on the train, their presence throughout the day should be secured by advance arrangements. An added value in having them at the train is that in the eyes of visitors they will become identified with the movement and thus be in a better position to lead in the local follow-up work.

Helpers are needed to look after the safety of the visitors, to form any waiting crowds into lines, direct people to the entrance, keep them moving in a single direction, prevent unnecessary congestion at any given point, and note questions and suggestions that should be passed on to members of the staff. If local volunteers are well prepared to perform these services the saving of strain on the hard-worked staff will be very great.

The Rate of Progress in Exhibit Cars

Reports show that managers of trains have been satisfied with both extremes in the rate of progress of visitors in moving through the train. One train director reported with pride that by his system he was able to "run 5,000 through in an hour." At the other extreme are the directors who during their stay in a town give a single demonstration in a car that holds only about one hundred people. The method of "running people through" very rapidly is useful only if the exhibits are simply curiosities or objects of interest that may be quickly noted, and that we may risk having soon forgotten without loss to the cause that is being served. For example, the Liberty Loan trains depended chiefly on their program of talks, music, and the appearance of the returned soldiers to arouse interest. The large guns displayed on flat cars were visible while the talking was going on. It did not particularly matter after that whether visitors were passed through the trophy car so rapidly that they had only a glimpse of the various objects.

On the other hand, the attendance in one place, of so small a number as one hundred would hardly justify the work of planning and carrying out a tour unless either the small group are carefully selected as leaders capable of passing on the information to others, or the community is so small that this number is as many as might be expected. It ought to be possible to estimate in advance, or at least after the first week of the tour, the length of time required for the average person to see all that is important for him to see and understand. With this period in mind it is possible to estimate the number of people who can be handled in a given length of time. For example, we may assume the following conditions: A train of three cars. Number that can be accommodated comfortably in each car at one time, 60. Twenty minutes, required time to see the exhibits or hear and see demonstrations in each car, or one hour for the train. Train on view six hours. Maximum attendance practicable during the stop, 1,080 people.

The attendance is, of course, never distributed so evenly as this over the day, and all the visitors do not stay exactly the same length of time. Probably with a fairly even distribution a train with a maximum capacity of one thousand will handle satisfactorily about eight hundred people. An estimate of the rate at which visitors may be passed along will be found exceedingly useful in deciding many questions, such as the arrangement and content of the exhibits, the length of time to continue a demonstration, the number of times to repeat it, the length of the stay, and the quota of attendance to work for in the advance publicity. For example, would you rather have fewer people and have those who come stay longer, would you prefer having a larger attendance with those who compose it spending less time with you?

The selection of exhibits and the program should be arranged according to your decision on these points. If you are giving a few people detailed information which it would serve your purpose better to give to a larger number, you are throwing away your opportunity for want of a little careful calculation. The mistake most frequently made is to plan exhibits and programs on the expectation of having each visitor spend a long time at the train carefully examining each display, and then when the people arrive, to pass crowds through quickly without giving them a chance to see what has been prepared for them.

Distributing the Attendance

Apparently not many of those who have conducted trains have attempted through their advance work to prepare for arbitrary distribution of attendance over the entire period that the exhibit is open. The period from two to five o'clock in the afternoon seems to have been found the most popular by the largest number of those reporting on attendance, with some falling off reported after four o'clock. The period before ten in the morning is agreed upon unanimously as the poorest time to get people out. The experiences reported as to the hourly attendance between ten and four o'clock varies so widely that it would seem to indicate that under the right conditions it should be possible to get people to come throughout this period.

Good advance work can fill up many idle hours. A description of methods of advance work to accomplish this is contained in another chapter, but while we are considering the visitors it may be well to look over the groups that could most easily come at the least attractive hours. On a number of trains arrangements were made to have school children attend with their teachers according to a prearranged schedule, usually during the morning hours. This is an especially good plan when the train is on view all day, because the children tell their experiences when they go home at noon and thus help to get their parents to attend in the afternoon. If there are a larger number of school children than can be handled conveniently it is a good idea to limit attendance to the older children, basing the lower age limit on the estimated number of children that can be accommodated. If they do not fill up the train completely during the morning, it is possible to arrange for the attendance of delegations of leading citizens and other representative groups who come in a body to welcome the train when it is opened to the public, or to be personally escorted through it at a given time. This, of course, has news value as well as the advantage of using the morning hours. The Safety First Train of the government at each stop arranged to have such a morning delegation.

In some places the noon hour may be used for the attendance of factory workers and other employed people who are not far from the train. This is successful if advance preparations are made and if the subject matter is of interest to the workers. It is often possible to adapt the program and some part of the displays to their interests. Using the noon hour depends, of course, on having a large enough staff to allow each member an hour for lunch. The period from five to eight o'clock in the afternoon is probably of the least value. Usually the staff members themselves need relaxation during this time if there is to be an evening session. If there is no session the train may pull out late in the afternoon. If, however, it is desirable to make use of this period, it may be possible to arrange for personal conferences or group conferences at the train or in town with persons especially interested in the subject who wish to have information that is not of interest to the general public or to talk over plans for the future.

Reports as to the success of evening sessions vary greatly. Many have used the evening successfully for outdoor motion pictures or for meetings in town. The fact that many who could not leave their work during the day can come then seems to argue that it is possible to have a good attendance if the advance work has been thorough — provided also that the location of the car or train is satisfactory and that the time schedule will permit.

Explaining the Exhibits

While the exhibits should be so simple and well arranged as to be easily understood, any exhibit of objects, pictures, and printed words is more enjoyed and appreciated if it is brought to life by a personal interpretation given with enthusiasm. The explainer calls attention to what is displayed much as a chairman introduces a speaker. A good introduction makes the audience more friendly and responsive to either a speaker or an exhibit. The explainer who travels the length of the car with one group can take care of only a few people at a time, and if there is a continuous movement of people through the car only about one-third of them have the advantage of the explanation. If, on the outside or in another car, a lecture or demonstration precedes the reviewing of exhibits, the speaker may close the talk with an explanation of the purpose and character of the exhibits and some suggestions as to what to look for.. With this preparation people may pass through the car unattended and perhaps meet an explainer at the far end who will answer questions and give out literature together with an invitation to take part in the follow-up program. Or the explainer may meet people as they enter the car and give a brief introduction to the exhibits.

Local people, with general information on the subject, can give valuable help in explaining points about particular exhibits which have to be repeated many times. These helpers should receive advance material and in addition should come to the train for coaching before it opens and be stationed at assigned positions.

Staff members who are continually meeting people, work under considerable strain and may easily become tired or indifferent through over-work. So much depends on their enthusiasm and their readiness to offer help that this factor should be carefully checked up, and if any member of the staff shows signs of losing interest or failing to get a response he should be replaced or at least given a period of rest. By relieving staff members of irksome details and by providing in other ways for their comfort, as well as by arranging the schedule of hours so that they do not work beyond their strength in any one period, much can be done to avoid this loss of freshness and enthusiasm.

It was pointed out that the purpose of a tour may be to give information, to create interest in a new movement that is being launched, to revive interest that has become dull, or to serve as an attention-arresting feature of an intensive campaign that aims to produce some immediate results. All of these aims point to the need of planning definite follow-up work. It will not do to let people forget what they have learned or lose interest in it through neglect. If the tour means simply that ideas or facts are dropped down into each community, like seeds scattered by the winds without provision for later cultivating, they have a smaller chance to take root and grow. Psychology has demonstrated that there is a "curve of forgetting." Hollingworth described it as follows:

> When a given appeal is addressed to me, I straightway proceed to forget it. But I do not forget it at a uniform rate, so much being for gotten on each succeeding day until all is for gotten. Instead, I forget the material that has been seen or learned, according to a definite "curve of forgetting," a curve which descends rapidly at first and then more slowly. The larger proportion of material is forgotten in the first day or so. After that a constant decreasing amount is for gotten on each succeeding day.

How may the impression made by the program and exhibits of the train be fixed in the minds of its visitors promptly, so that forgetting may be delayed until results are obtained? Several simple methods suggest themselves. We will take up here mainly those things that can be done while the train is in town or soon after its departure, as we are concerned only with the part that the train tour plays in the whole program of the organization that sends it out.

Getting the Subject Talked About

If the visitors talk about what they saw and heard they are likely to remember it much longer and more accurately than if they do not. The principles discussed elsewhere, of simplicity of form, concentration on one main topic, orderly arrangement, and lack of crowding in both exhibits and programs, have a definite application to getting the subject talked about. People speak vaguely and in general terms about what they have not clearly understood. We may imagine that A, who saw the train, meets B, who did not, and the following conversation takes place:

Hollingworth, H. L.: Advertising and Selling, New York, D. Appleton & Co.

A: Did you see the health train yesterday?

B: No, how was it?

A: Oh, fine! great! You certainly missed it. There was a good crowd out, too.

B: What was it all about?

A: Oh, fresh air and not letting the babies die.

You'd be surprised how many people die that could be prevented. And they say the town ought to have a nurse to look after the school children, and a hospital for see, I've forgotten now about the hospital.

B: I see. Just a scheme of the politicians to make jobs for a lot of people. 1 always thought this was a pretty healthy town and 1 do yet.

A: No, you've got it wrong, B, but 1 can't make it clear to you. 1 can't talk like the fellow at the train. You ought to have heard him. He made a great speech.

If A has no clearer idea than this to pass on to B the next day, he himself is not likely to stay interested and, much less, convinced for very long. One of the best tests of the argument presented at the train is whether the talk about it afterward is general or particular, confused or clear and accurate in repeating facts and reasons. It is worth while to arrange with local cooperators as a part of the follow-up work to sound people as to what interested them and what they think of the suggestions that were made. Many changes, sometimes small ones, but important, nevertheless, can be made on the basis of criticisms brought out in these interviews.

Publicity Following the Train's Stop

There should be a readable account of the train in the first issue of the local paper following its visit. Those who visited it will like to read the account of what they saw and in doing so will be reminded of a number of features of the exhibits and talks that were rapidly slipping from their memories. The train director would do well to see that the local paper receives as good copy for this follow-up story as for advance publicity. The people who came and what they said about it adds to the news value of the story.

Other forms of publicity may be used to advantage immediately following the visit of the train, such as a series of special articles appearing weekly in the local paper, printed matter mailed to a list of people obtained at the train, or a motion picture shown in the local picture theatre, at a meeting or a contest that may reach its climax at some later event, such as the county or state fair.

Organization of Local Forces

Leading men and women to take some action as the result of interest aroused at the train is the surest way to get the message remembered and is the aim of most educational campaigns. This action may be something very simple and concrete, or it may be the entering wedge of some continuous activity. One of the simplest steps, which has already been referred to, is the writing of local people to headquarters for information or for literature. This serves the purpose also of renewing interest when the material sent for arrives and it helps the central organization to make up mailing lists. Local organizations should be encouraged to send for reference material to use in talks and discussions.

Launching or boosting a permanent movement at a meeting held during the train visit is one good way of starting follow-up work. Many an effort that promised much because of local enthusiasm at the start has died a natural death, because after the specialists from the state or national headquarters have departed, local leaders find themselves without any clear-cut program to begin work on or any recognized leadership. An informal meeting of the train staff and local leaders at which temporary committees are formed and definite plans discussed may be one of the most useful features of the train program. It has been suggested elsewhere that the hour of the day least popular with visitors may be a good time for such a meeting. A still better method is an early visit after the departure of the train, of an organizer or consultant who will advise about plans. An interesting report of the follow-up organization work carried on in connection with its health car, comes from the West Virginia Public Health Council:

Wherever possible a temporary committee was formed before leaving the community, this committee being chosen by a group of representative people in a community meeting in the interests of health education at which time child welfare work was emphasized. At this meeting we made an effort to secure the attendance of medical, dental, and nursing professions, of the mayor and town council, school board, and school superintendent and teachers, ministers and Sunday school super-intendents, fraternal organizations, women's clubs, Red Cross, and any other organizations directly or indirectly interested in community welfare work. The temporary committee was appointed to secure a permanent organization based upon the interest and enthusiasm already created, this permanent committee to undertake a definite health program for the community. In addition to this we are keeping in touch with the various communities visited, by frequent correspondence, and the director of the Division of Child Hygiene has already returned to a number of the communities to help in the making of plans, to stimulate interest and enthusiasm, and in every way possible to promote health education and public health nursing. We are now formulating county-wide and state-wide plans for the furtherance of this work through cooperation with the Extension Division of the Agricultural Department of the State University and American Red Cross.

An incidental but important factor in promoting continuous follow-up work is that local representatives of the movement, especially the salaried worker, if there is one, should take an active part in the program of the train, so as to become identified with the impressions and ideas gained here in the minds of the people who visited the train.

Checking up Results

As bearing upon the question of any future use of a similar method of campaigning, "checking up" results is good, although it may not always be easy or bring entirely conclusive evidence. The method described in the account of the Cleveland Children's Year Special, which is a dispensary truck, is suggestive. Cards of invitation to visit the local dispensary were given out at the truck and the number that were turned into the dispensary was noted by the nurses. Nurses also asked new visitors during the following month where they had learned of the dispensary, and recorded it when the visit was directly or indirectly a result of the Special. Reports may be requested from local editors, school superintendents, and others who meet many people, regarding the responsiveness of the people to ideas promulgated at the train. The number and the nature of inquiries received at headquarters from places that have been visited may also serve as an indication of the effectiveness with which the message has been presented.

Finally on the matter of follow-up work, one of the chief criticisms that may be made of much educational publicity is that it is spasmodic and unrelated. This is often due to the fact that the planning of follow-up work is left until the campaign is at its height or until it is over. By that time the workers at headquarters and in the field are too absorbed in the detail of running the affair, or a new project is under way. All the resources and energy have gone into running the campaign and none is left for securing results. In the advance planning of the whole campaign, allowance should be made in the budget for a definite program of follow-up work as well as in the time of staff members needed to carry it out.

Trolley, and Other Travelling Campaigns

The lists below include travelling educational campaigns about which we have obtained reasonably accurate information. The two chief sources of further information about these projects are the state colleges of agriculture and state boards of health. Very little information about tours is available in published form. Articles in class publications giving brief accounts of a few of the tours and a few special reports about tours are listed in Appendix B.

In practically all the train tours, one or more rail-roads have cooperated at least to the extent of supplying cars and free transportation, and sometimes bearing a considerable share of the work and expenses of the tour. Our lists, we realize, do not always give the full credit to cooperating railroads and other participants, but as much is given as it was possible to ascertain and to indicate within the space limits.

We are aware, also, that the list is by no means a complete record of educational tours. Information is coming in continually about tours that we had not known of before. The main purpose, however, is to give a general idea of the purposes, forms, and extent of travelling campaigns in recent years, together with only a few of such details as may help the inquirer decide where to look further for suggestions that may be of assistance in his particular case.

The list does not include tours of trucks or trains for service only, as, for example, library trucks or laboratory trains. Neither does it include "chapel cars," that is, railroad cars, motor vehicles, and boats, for religious services or instruction, such as have been sent out by various religious bodies for many years.

Agricultural and Food Conservation Trains Canada. Better Farming Train. Subject: assistance in every phase of farm life. Saskatchewan Department of Agriculture and the College of Agriculture of the Provincial University cooperated with Canadian Pacific Railway. 1918 and 1919.

Thirteen cars with exhibits or equipment for demonstrations and lectures. Prominent professors and agricultural officials served as demonstrators and lecturers. Sheep Car. Subject: breeding and shearing of sheep. Live Stock Branch, Department of Agriculture at Ottawa. 1919. One car of exhibits. Demonstrations of shearing machine given on farms.

Special Dairy Car. Subject: dairying. Saskatchewan Department of Agriculture, College of Agriculture, and Canadian Northern Railway. 1916. Lecture coach and tourist sleeper for speakers. Exhibits with stereopticon and lectures.

United States. Potiltry and Egg Demonstration Car. Subject: demonstrations of proper methods of handling and keeping poultry and eggs. Bureau of Chemistry, United States Department of Agriculture. 1913 to 1918. Arkansas. Peach Ctilture Demonstration Train. Subject: proper methods of peach tree pruning and spraying. Cooperatively run by Agricultural Departments of Missouri Pacific and Cotton Belt Railroads, American Refrigerator Transit Company, and State College of Agriculture. 1918. Two baggage cars for exhibits; large automobile freight car carried orchard machinery. Exhibits explained by horticulturists, on the cars; lectures and demonstrations given in nearby orchard.

California. Dairy Special. Subject: dairying and hog raising. State

College of Agriculture. 1913 and 1914. Lectures, conferences, and exhibits relative to the industry. Agricultural and Food Production Train. Subjects: methods of stimulating growth of certain crops, interest in increasing food production, and particularly bean culture. State Colleges of Agriculture of Nevada and Utah and Salt Lake Rail-road cooperated with California's State College of Agriculture. 1917. Demonstrations and lectures.

Agricultural and Home Economics Train. State College of Agriculture, cooperated with Southern Pacific Railroad. 1908 and 1909. Ten coaches for exhibits and lectures, a dining car, and sleeper to accommodate demonstrators and lecturers. Demonstrations and lectures. Agricultural and Horticultural Train. Subject: methods of restoring fertility and depleted soils, plant culture, pest and disease extermination, viti-culture, dairying, animal industry, seeding and soil treatment. State College of Agriculture, Southern Pacific and Santa F6 Railroads. Annually, 1908 to 1913. Several exhibit cars, lecture cars, sleeping car, and diner. Good Roads Special. Subject: improvement of roads, Frisco Railway System. 1912. Four coaches and locomotive. Exhibits, lectures and demonstrations.

Georgia. Land Clearing Special. Subject: stump pulling and uses of tractors and other farm machinery. Date College of Agriculture, stump puller companies and tractor manufacturers, Geor Landowners' Association, and the Railroad Administration cooperated. 1919. Passenger coach and four flat cars for lectures and demonstrations, caboose and sleeper for travelling campaigners, and two box cars for equipment and machinery transportation. Motion picture shows, demonstrations, and lectures. Illinois. Home Economics Car. Subject: household science. State College of Agriculture. 1916-1918. Demonstrations and exhibits. Dairy Trains. State College of Agriculture and the Chicago and Eastern Illinois Railroad. 1917, 1919. Three coaches for lectures, automobile car and flat car for demonstrations and exhibits, and a locomotive. Demonstrations of milking machine, lectures and exhibits. Dairy Train. Subject: uses of separators, sterilizers, and other dairy machines. State College of Agriculture and C. C. C. & St. L. Railroad. 1916 and 1917. Lecture coach for motion pictures, baggage car for exhibits, and Arms Palace horse car for cattle.

Dairy Train. Subject: proper use of dairy machinery. State College of Agriculture and Baltimore and Ohio Railroad. 19 16 and 191 7.

Pullman car for attendants; stock car carried cattle, which were taken for demonstrations to some prominent place in towns visited. Lectures in court houses and town halls.

Dixie Jersey Special. Subject: more and better dairy cattle. American Jersey Cattle Club, agents of Department of Agriculture and railroad trade promotion bureaus. In Illinois/Louisiana, Mississippi, and Tennessee. 1920. Arms Palace horse cars for cattle and Pullmans for personnel. Indiana. Seed Com Special. Subject: com culture. Erie Railroad and Purdue University A cultural Experiment Station. 1909. Lecture tram. Alfalfa Lecture Train. Subject: better alfalfa production. Purdue University Agricultural Experiment Station. 1912. Com Improvement Lecture Train. Subject: better corn. Lake Erie and Western Railroad and Purdue University Agricultural Experiment Station. 1911. Dairy Feeding Lecture Train. Subject: better cattle feeding and care. Purdue University Agricultural Experiment Station and several railroads. 1915. Dairy Special Production Train. Subject: increase of dairy production. Southern Railroad and Purdue University Agricultural Experiment Station. April i toy, 1913 Dairy Special Train. Subject: dairying. Monon Railway Company, Purdue University Agricultural Experiment Station, and State Dairy Association. 1907. Baggage car, two lecture coaches, and private dining and sleeping car. Lectures, exhibits, and demonstrations.

Milk Production Special Train. Subject: care and production of milk. Purdue University Agricultural Experiment Station and Erie Railroad. 1909. Seven car train. Lectures and demonstrations. Onion Improvement Lecture Train. Subject: increase of onion crops. Chicago, Indiana and Southern Railroad. 1911.

Seed Com Special. Subject: corn culture. Monon Railway Company, Purdue University Agricultural Experiment Station, Indiana Corn Growers' Association, Indiana Grain Dealers' Association. 1906. Engine, baggage car, coach for lectures, and a coach for the attendants. Lectures, exhibits, and demonstrations.

Wheat Improvement Train. Subject: wheat culture. Southern Railroad and Purdue University Agricultural Experiment Station. 1912. Lectures and demonstrations of culture and fertilization; control of insects and diseases. Iowa. Daily Special. Subject: better dairy products. Illinois Central Railroad. 1916. Three cars for exhibits, demonstrations, and living quarters for speakers. Seed Com Special. Iowa Grain Dealers' Association. 1910.

Sansas. Hessian Fly Special. Subject: control of Hessian fly. State College of Agriculture and Santa Railroad. 1915. Baggage car for equipment, two steel coaches for lectures and demonstrations, and private car for attendants.

Kentucky. Agricultural Exhibit Train. Subject: general education in matters pertaining to agriculture and dairy improvements. State Department of Agriculture. 1912. Four lecture cars, stock car, sleeper, and diner. Lectures, exhibits, and demonstrations.

Louisiana. Dixie Jersey Special

Maryland. Farmers' Institute Train. Subject: dairying. State College of Agriculture. 1913. Lecture car and stock car. Demonstrations and lectures. Michigan. Food Demonstration Train. Michigan Agricultural College. 1917. Minnesota. Advertising Car. Subject: farm and factory products. State Board of Immigration. 1913. One exhibit car. Mississippi. Boll Weevil Special. Subject: extermination of the pests. Illinois Central Kailroadi 1908.

Dixie Jersey Special

Missouri. Patriotic Special. Subject: food conservation and work of Women's Committee. Women's Committee on Food Conservation, Council of National Defence. August, 1917. Lecture and demonstration car. Stereopticon lectures and demonstrations. Nebraska. Agricultural Train. Subject: dairying and seed corn. State College of Agriculture. 1918. Two cars for exhibits and demonstrations.

Conservation Special. Subject: food conservation and preservation. Union Pacific Railroad Company co-cooperated with Nebraska College of Agriculture and others. 1917. Train included business car and living quarters for staff. Illustrated lectures were given in public halls.

Agricultural and Food Production Train

Cooperatively run with State Colleges of California, Nevada, and Utah, and Salt Lake Railroad. 19 16 and 1917.. New Jersey. Save the Surplus Special. Subject: food conservation and other war measures. State College of Agriculture and Lehigh Valley Railroad. 1917. Two coaches, one for exhibits and the other for lectures. Toured New Jersey and Pennsylvania. Demonstrations, lectures, and exhibits.

New York. Victory Special. Subject: introduction of wheat, meat, and sugar substitutes and other food conservation methods. State

College of Agriculture, Food Administration and New York Central, Lehigh Valley, D. & H.7 D., L. & W., and Long Island Railroads. 1917, 1918, 1919. Demonstrations and exhibits on train of two coaches. Apple Packing Train. Subject: instruction in requirements of law relating to apple grading. State Department of Agriculture and New York 'Central Railroad. 1915. Baggage car with equipment, lecture car with capacity of too persons, and car for living quarters.

Better Seed Special. Subject: standard types of seeds; reliable sources; proper methods of controlling common diseases. State College of Agriculture, New York Central, Lehigh Valley, Ontario and Western, Erie, and Delaware and Hudson Railroads. 1919. Exhibits and demonstrations in two coaches. Potato Demonstration Car. State College of Agriculture, County Farm Bureaus, and Lehigh Valley Railroad. 1917. Exhibits and demonstrations.

Sheep Demonstration Train. Subject: breeding, feeling, and care of sheep. State College of Agriculture, New York Central and New York, Ontario and Western Railroads. 1917. Exhibits and demonstrations.

North Carolina. North Carolina Car. Subject: farm machinery and dairying. State Department of Agriculture cooperating with several railroads. Lectures and exhibits with stereopticon slides and moving pictures in baggage cars; demonstrations given out of doors.

Better Fanning Special. Subjects: better dairying, domestic science, food conservation, and sanitary methods. Agricultural and Industrial 'Department of Norfolk and Western Railway, State College of Agriculture of North Carolina, and Virginia Agricultural and Mechanical College. 1915-1916. Nine cars for exhibits, demonstrations, lectures, and living quarters for attendants. Com Growers' Special. Norfolk and Southern Railway and Experiment Station of the Agricultural and Mechanical College. 1908. Farmers' Institutes. Subject: agriculture and domestic science. North Carolina Department of Agriculture, Seaboard Air Line, and Southern Railway. Two railroad cars, one a coach with two of the seats removed and a model kitchen substituted, and a baggage car equipped with farm and dairy machinery. 1908-1910. Lectures and demonstrations on the train and outdoors.

Pennsylvania. Food Conservation Train. Pennsylvania Food Administration, State College of Agriculture, and Pennsylvania Railroad. 1917 and 1918. Two demonstration cars and one exhibit car.

Save the Surplus Special. Toured this state and New Jersey. 1916 and 1917. Agricultural Train. Subject: better farming and foal production. Agricultural Department of Nashville, Chattanooga and St. Louis Railroad. One private car and one lecture car. Exhibits and demonstrations.

Dixie Jersey Special

Texas: Agrictilttiral Train. Subject: dairying. Agricultural and Mechanical College of Texas. Three coaches for lectures, two exhibit cars, automobile car for cattle, flat car with wire fence and canvas top for lecture and demonstration platform, a diner and a Pullman for compaigners. Lectures, exhibits, and demonstrations. Stereopticon slides shown at night in combination with lectures in motion picture theatre or town hall.

Peach: Culture Train. Subject: proper methods of pruning and spraying trees, and extermination of insect pests in orchards. Agricultural Department of St. Louis Southwestern Railroad of Texas, assisted by Agricultural and Mechanical College of Texas and State Department of Agriculture. 1919 and 1920. Two cars for exhibits and one for orchard machinery. Exhibits, demonstrations, and lectures. Similar to train run in Arkansas in 1918.

Utah: Agricultural and Food Production Train. Cooperatively run with State Colleges of California, Utah, and Nevada, and the Salt Lake Railroad. 1916 and 1917. Agricultural Train. Agricultural and Mechanical College of Virginia, and Norfolk and Western Railroad. 1915. Demonstration train.

Better Farming Special

Washington: Agricultural Train. State College of Agriculture. Lectures with stereopticon slides, sometimes in nearby school or hall; exhibits and demonstrations on train.

Good Roads Special: Subject: road and culvert construction and maintenance and general highway improvements. Office of Public Roads of Washington and several railroad companies cooperated. 1912. Two coaches of exhibits and models. Lectures, demonstrations, and exhibits.

West Virginia: Agricultural Train. Subject: better farming. Kanawha and Michigan, Baltimore and Ohio Railroads, and State College of Agriculture. 1912 and 1913. Baggage cars for cattle and coaches for lectures. Lectures, demonstrations, and exhibits.

Wisconsin: Pure Seed and Home Power Special. "Soo" Line, Chicago, Milwaukee and St. Paul Railroad, Wisconsin Bankers Association, and State College of Agriculture. 1917. Two cars for demonstrations and exhibits.

Land Clearing Demonstration Train: Subject: better farming. State College of Agriculture, several land clearing machinery and explosive manufacturers, and several railroads cooperated. 1916-1919. Six cars consisting of a flat car, two box cars for equipment, two bunk cars, and a boarding car for the attendants. Demonstrations and instruction.

Stump Pulling Special: Subject: clearing cutover lands. State College of Agriculture, several land clearing machinery and explosive manufacturers, Chicago and Northwestern, and Chicago, Minneapolis and St. Paul Railroads. 1916. Flat car, two box cars for equipment, two bunk cars, and a boarding car for the attendants. Demonstrations and instruction. Similar trains, with some changes in cars used and in cooperating agencies, were run in 1917 and 1919.

Health Trains

United States: First Aid Train. American Red Cross. 1920. Fully equipped railroad coach to render and teach first aid to the injured. Treatment and instruction.

California. Sanitation Car: Subject: protection of water supply, disposal of sewage, and instruction in disease prevention. State Board of Health. 1909. Continued annually. Exhibits and demonstrations.

Florida. Sanitation and Health Train: State Board of Health. 1916 and 1917. Two exhibit cars. Lectures with motion pictures and slides.

Kansas: Health Car 'barren." Subject: health and child welfare. State Board of Health. 1916. Exhibit car.

Kentucky: Health Exhibit Car. Subject: tuberculosis prevention and cure. 1912. Kentucky Tuberculosis Association and several railroads cooperated.

Louisiana: Health Train. Subjects: child welfare, food, and disease prevention. State Board of Health. 1910. Continuously since then. Four cars including an exhibit car, a laboratory car with garage compartment carrying Ford car for country trips and quick collection of water samples, and two cars for administrative and living quarters.

Missouri: Travelling Car Exhibit. Subject: instruction in anti-tuberculosis measures. Missouri Association for the Relief and Control of Tuberculosis. 1908. One exhibit coach.

West Virginia: Health Car. State Department of Health. 1919. Vestibuled coach, equipped with electrically driven models, posters, exhibits of living bacteria, sanitation exhibits, a moving picture machine, and a small chemical and bacteriological laboratory in one end of the car.

Tuberculosis Exhibit Car. Subject: prevention and cure of tuberculosis. West Virginia Tuberculosis League and several railroads. 1913 and 1914. Car for exhibits and lectures.

Miscellaneous Topics—Trains

Canada: Made-in-Canada Train. Subject: trade extension. Canadian Manufacturers Association. Ten cars for exhibits, demonstrations, and moving picture lectures.

Exhibition Car. Subject: conservation of the forests. Canadiani Forestry Association. 1918 and 1919. Train toured parts of Quebec and New Brunswick. Exhibits of products made from wood.

Southern States: School on Wheels. Southern Pacific Railway. 1919. Baggage car fitted up as modem school room; accommodates teacher and 25 pupils.

United States: Safety First Train. Subject: to show what is being done to promote safety and health. Department of the Interior cooperating with other governmental departments. 1916. Locomotive and twelve exhibit and lecture cars.

Mine Rescue Car. Subject: instruction to miners in first aid and use of oxygen breathing apparatus. Assistance of car apparatus and crew given in case of mine disasters. Bureau of Mines, Department of the Interior, 1910; continuous service since then. Present equipment: eleven specially constructed coaches with exhibits and emergency equipment.

Recruiting Cars. Bureau of Navigation, Navy Department. 1917 and 1919. Three flat cars fitted up respectively with a model of a battleship, destroyer, and torpedo boat. Exhibits and lectures to assist in recruiting and also used for promoting Liberty Loan drives.

War Relic Trains. Subject: promotion of Liberty Loan drives, etc. Federal Reserve Districts of Treasury Department. 1918 and 1919. Flat cars for exhibition of trophies captured from the enemy; baggage car, sleeping car, and a locomotive. Toured the United Mates.

New York. Safety First Car: Subject: instruction in safety measures. New York Central lines. 1919. Two duplicate cars for motion pictures and lectures.

Virginia: Safety First Car. Subject: instruction in safety measures. Norfolk and Western Railroad. 1920. Motion picture and lecture car.

Agricultural and Food Conservation Trucks Canada: Sheep Demonstration Automobile. Sheep and Goat Division, Live Stock Branch, Department of Agriculture, Ottawa. 1919. Demonstrations of shearing by hand and power machines, rolling and preparing of wool for market, dipping of sheep for vermin, and docking and castrating of lambs.

Alabama. Movable School: Subject: agriculture and home economics. Tuskegee Normal and Industrial Institute. 1919. Instruction and demonstrations.

Louisiana. Agricultural Extension Truck Subject: education and agriculture: Louisiana State Agricultural and Mechanical College. 1919. Motion picture and stereopticon lectures.

Massachusetts: Food Conservation and Model then Truck. Subject: canning, food conservation, and substitutes; care and feeding of children in wartime. Woman's Committee, Massachusetts Council of Defence. 1918. Demonstrations and instruction.

Agricultural Truck: Massachusetts Agricultural College. Demonstrations, exhibits, and stereopticon slide lectures.

Food Conservation and Preservation Truck: Bristol County Farm Bureau. In charge of county demonstration agent at Segreganset. Exhibits.

Ohio: Poultry Demonstration Truck. Subject: instruction in proper methods of handling eggs, care of fowl, and better uses of poultry equipment. Ohio State University. 1917. Lectures and demonstrations. Evening lectures with stereopticon slides.

Pennsylvania: Canning Truck. Allegheny County Council of Defence. 1918. Itinerant service to farmers' wives at their homes. Demonstrations, instruction; canning and drying of home products.

Rhode Island: Food Conservation Truck. State Food Administration. 1918. Demonstrations and instruction.

Virginia: Fruit Growers' Automobile Tour. Subject: best methods of orchard culture. Extension Division, Virginia Polytechnic Institute and Virginia State Horticultural Society. 191 8. Automobile tour through Virginia and West Virginia by fruit growers.

Wisconsin: Agricultural Truck. Subject: treatment of grain for smut and a, fanning mill. County agents of the state. 1918. Demonstrations, assistance, and instruction.

Health Trucks

Canada: Travelling Baby Clinic. University Settlement of Montreal. 1919. Weighing, measuring, and advisory service. France. Travelling Exposition. Subject: child welfare and tuberculosis. American Commission for the Prevention of Tuberculosis in France, Children's Bureau of the American Red Cross and, later, the Tuberculosis Bureau, American Red Cross. 1917 and 1918. Trucks carried equipment for lectures, motion pictures, and exhibits.

Italy: Tuberculosis Clinics. American Red Cross Tuberculosis Commission. Seven trucks equipped as clinics. Treatment and instruction.

Dental Trucks: American Red Cross. Three trucks fitted up as dental clinics. Treatment and instruction.

United States: Child Welfare Special. Children's Bureau, Department of Labour. 1919. Lectures, examinations, and well baby clinic.

Connecticut: Baby Special. Subject: infant and child welfare, including care, feeding, measuring, and weighing. Child Welfare Department, State Council of Defence. 1918. Lectures and advisory service. Illinois. Travelling Health Clinic. Subject: tuberculosis. Chicago Tuberculosis Institute. 1919.

Indiana: Travelling Auto Exhibit. Subject: prevention of tuberculosis. Indiana Society for the Prevention of Tuberculosis. 1917. Truck fitted with screen and machine for moving picture shows; also lectures with stereopticon and exhibits. Louisiana. Sanitary Truck. Subject: personal hygiene and disease prevention among Negroes. Louisiana State Board of Health. 1919. Lectures, exhibits, and motion pictures.

Maryland: Public Health Car. Subject: educational and organization work. Maryland Tuberculosis Association. 1916. Motion pictures, lectures, and distribution of literature.

Massachusetts: Child Welfare Track. Division of Hygiene, State Department of Public Health. Lectures, demonstrations, exhibits on all phases of child welfare.

Mississippi: Rural Dispensary Track. Subject: education in general health and tuberculosis. Bureau of Tuberculosis, State Sanatorium of the Board of Health of Mississippi. 1919 — continuous. Motion picture and stereopticon shows, lectures, exhibits, examinations, and distribution of literature.

New York: Health mobile. Subject: general health propaganda. State Department of Health. 1919. Lectures and motion pictures.

Dental Education Car. Subject: dental instruction and dispensary service. Nassau County school authorities and Junior Red Cross. 1920. Ford truck equipped with necessary dental supplies and equipment.

North Carolina: Moving Picture Health Car. State Board of Health. 1916. Lectures and motion pictures.

Health Education Car. Subject: tuberculosis and mouth hygiene. State Board of Health and State Tuberculosis Association, 1920. Truck equipped with lighting system and motion picture machine. Lectures and moving picture shows in the forty-five counties of the state.

Ohio: Cleveland Children's Year Special. Subject: dispensary for child hygiene and welfare work. Children's Year Committee of Council of Defence. 1918. Exhibits, examinations of children, motion picture shows, and distribution of literature.

Washington: Clinic and Exhibit Truck. Subject: tuberculosis diagnosis and education. Truck for transportation of clinic staff and exhibit; clinic held in public halls. Washington Tuberculosis Association. 1919. Lectures, exhibits, and clinic.

West Virginia: Rural Tuberculosis Campaign. Subject: prevention and cure of tuberculosis, and extermination of flies. West Virginia Tuberculosis League. 1917. Automobile tour in charge of a woman physician and her assistant. Stereopticon show and lectures; also first aid demonstration.

Wisconsin: Health Wagon. Subject: health preservation and disease prevention. Wisconsin Anti-Tuberculosis Association. 1916. Motion pictures and lectures.

Motor Transportation Development Tours United States: Transcontinental Tour. Subject: recruiting for Motor Transport Corps, and education regarding good roads. Motor Transport Corps, War Department. 1919. Fleet of motor trucks and passenger vehicles from the Capitol to San Francisco over the Lincoln Highway. Exhibits, demonstrations, and lectures, with moving picture shows.

Georgia. Motor Truck Trains: Subject: Quicker transportation facilities between farms ana markets. Macon Chamber of Commerce. 1919. One hundred and four trucks were divided into four trains; each toured the country routes for a radius of 100 miles. Merchandise carried on outgoing trips and farm produce on return trips. Illinois. Motor Trucks. Subject: uses of motor vehicles on farms. National Association of Motor Truck Sales Managers. 1919. These trucks toured six states and covered over 3,000 miles.

Missouri. St. Louis Motor Truck Expedition: Subject: farm uses of motor-driven vehicles. 1919. Sixteen motor companies cooperated, and the tour covered sections of the north central states.

New York. Rural Motor Truck Express: Subject: uses of motor-driven vehicles on farms and for express delivery. National Automobile Chamber of Commerce cooperated with New York State Department of Farms and Markets. 1919. Demonstration given at State Fair, Syracuse, September, 1919.

Miscellaneous Topics — Trucks England: Cine-Motor Touring Movies. Subject: information relating to war activities shown in rural districts. British Ministry of Information. 1918.

United States: Mine Rescue Auto Trucks. Subject: instruction of miners in first aid and use of oxygen breathing apparatus, and to render assistance in case of mine disaster. Bureau of Mines, Department of the Interior. 1913; continuous service since then. Six such trucks used by Bureau in mining districts.

Connecticut. Victory Conference: Subject: women's war work. Woman's Committee, State Council of Defence. 1918. Exhibits, demonstrations, and lectures.

Georgia. Motion Picture Trucks. Subject: Red Cross activities. Southern Division, American Red Cross. Georgia and Tennes

Maryland: Motion Picture Truck. Subject: Red Cross activities overseas and in America. Potomac Division, American Red Cross, Maryland, Virginia, West Virginia. 191 9. Two lecture and exhibit trucks.

New York: Victory Trucks. Subject: reconstruction and postwar service. Reconstruction Commission of the State of New York, cooperating with the Bureau of Commercial Economics. 1919. One motion picture truck.

Motor Trucks: Subject: go-to-church propaganda. Erie Annual Conference of Methodist Episcopal Church. Two hundred and twenty automobiles toured the state and Pennsylvania in an effort to get people to attend church more often.

North Carolina: Motion Picture Truck. Subject: community welfare. 1919; continuous. State Bureau of Community Service. Semimonthly tour of truck to rural districts for motion pictures and lecture programs and community organization.

Pennsylvania: Motor Trucks. See New York. Tennessee. Motion Picture Trucks. See Georgia Virginia. Motion Picture Truck. See Maryland.

West Virginia: Motion Picture Truck. See Maryland. Miscellaneous Vehicles Used for Tours Canada — ^Motorcycle. Animal Treatment Cars. Subject: encouragement of humane treatment of dumb animals. Toronto Humane Society. 1914. Continuous service since then.

California — House-boat: "The Josephine." Subject: exhibits of animal parasites and working field laboratory. State Board of Health. 1919.

Massachusetts — Trolley Car: Child Welfare and Food Conservation Car. Women's Committee, Council of National Defence. 1918. Exhibits, lectures, and demonstrations.

Michigan — Trolley Car: Children's Year Special. Woman's Committee, Michigan Division of the Council of National Defence. 1918. Car divided into three sections for exhibits, examinations, lectures, and demonstrations.

Vennont— Wagon: Health Exhibit Wagon. State Board of Health. 1913. Horsedrawn vehicle used for moving pictures and health exhibits.

Wisconstn— Motorcycle: 'Tlying Squadron of Health." Subject: propaganda for tuberculosis prevention and cure. Wisconsin Anti-Tuberculosis Association. 1911-1915. Exhibits, stereopticon slides, and lectures.

Survey and Exhibit Series

It is recognized in both surveys and exhibits that a standardized technique has not been fully worked put. Still a beginning has been made. Enough experience has been accumulated to justify recording it and putting it at the disposal of those interested. With a view therefore to increasing the use of investigation in dealing with current community problems and to making such investigations more effective, and with a view also to the widespread employment of better methods of disseminating helpful information, the Survey and Exhibit Series has been planned. The A B G of Exhibit; Planning. By Evart G. and Mary Swain Routzahn. Price, Cloth, $2.00 net. Travelling Publicity Campaigns. By Mary Swain Routzalin. Price, Cloth, $1.50 net.

Other volumes in Preparation

Subscriptions may be entered for the series, new volumes to be sent when issued. Or upon request announcements of new books in the series will be sent as books are issued.

DMP: Background

Domestic tourism accounts for around 70% of total tourism expenditure in Australia. However, recent research has shown that the domestic tourism industry is facing a number of challenges. Australians are not travelling domestically as they once did, due to strong competition for the consumer dollar and for leisure time. Furthermore, the gap between outbound and domestic travel is widening as international destinations become more competitive and low cost carriers make them more accessible.

In August 2007, Tourism Ministers endorsed an Action Plan setting out practical actions to address issues confronting Australia's domestic tourism industry.

The research and consultations that underpin the Action Plan indicate that there is a widening gap between what consumers expect from domestic tourism and what is being offered. The most effective way to address these challenges is coordinated effort from all stakeholders: all levels of government; and industry.

In this context, Destination Management Planning (DMP) emerged as an effective mechanism for improved cooperation and collaboration with local industry and strengthening partnerships with regional economic development agencies/boards and education and training providers.

This document provides a contemporary best practice *Destination Management Planning Framework* to assist all tourism agencies and destinations in ensuring the sustainability and competitiveness of tourist destinations for communities, business operators, industry stakeholders, and consumers. It is based on the large body of work being done on various aspects of DMP both around Australia and internationally.

DMP: International Context

The development of locally and regionally relevant Destination Management Plans (DMPL) is supported by the United Nations World Tourism Organisation (UNTWO), with DMPLs being implemented in many tourist destinations around the world. The UNWTO hosted a Destination Management Conference "Creating Competitive Advantage for your Destination" in Hungary in February 2007.

With the support of the UNWTO, the European Commission has developed an "Action Plan for more Sustainable European Tourism". On the subject of Destination Management Planning, that Action Plan comments:

> *"Many of the challenges set by sustainability, and the actions required, can best be addressed by the different stakeholders working together at a destination level. It is here that the needs of the environment, the local community and businesses come most closely together. It is much easier to take an integrated and holistic approach when working at this level. Furthermore, it is increasingly recognised that the concept of a 'destination', within which a wide range of facilities and activities together make up the complete experience, is critical in influencing consumer choice."*

DMP: Australian Context

The concept of DMP has been strongly supported by the Australian and State/Territory Governments. Through their collective involvement in the development of the above mentioned Action Plan, these agencies have developed this strategic and integrated approach to tourism planning, and encourage tourism organisations at all levels of destination management to integrate the concepts and processes suggested.

The Department of Industry, Tourism and Resources also supports destination development in regional Australia through its Australian Tourism Development Program (ATDP). More than $31 million in ATDP funding has been allocated to 191 projects across Australia, many of which have elements of DMP in their project plans.

DMP: A nationally Consistent Framework

The National Tourism Investment Strategy Consultative Group, in its report to the Minister for Small Business and Tourism in March 2006, encouraged the *"consistent development of destination management plans...that could be assessed collectively to identify economies of scale for private sector investors"*. Additionally, sound DMP provides developers, investors, businesses, and communities with a degree of certainty and predictability about future development in an area.

The Consultative Group also found that *"given the diversity of activities within the entire supply chain of the tourism industry it has often been difficult for Australian and State Governments to adopt a whole of government approach to tourism, tourism marketing and destination planning, particularly in regional areas."*

Development of a nationally consistent DMP framework will facilitate a whole of government approach to tourism, allowing governments to more effectively identify and respond to changing needs for services, infrastructure, education and training throughout regions and facilitate local area and industry engagement with government programs and initiatives.

DMP: Concepts

DMP is a management system that provides a tourism organisation with the tools to produce sustainable and competitive tourism in a destination. DMP is organised around defined visitor destinations, each with its own natural and unique tourism assets, and unique development, marketing, and management needs.

DMP is a step forward from traditional destination marketing roles and provides a more holistic and integrated approach to understanding the tourism potential of each destination, and the best methods of maximising that potential. DMPLs are developed after a comprehensive process of research within the destination, consultation, feedback, planning, and review. Grass roots level participation from local tourism organisations, tourism boards, local government, and operators is essential in the preparation of DMPLs. DMPLs should be linked upward to State/Territory level strategic tourism plans.

Destination Management Planning is defined here as being inclusive of all of the practices and principles known as:

— Destination *development planning:*

- Critical assessment of the destination's tourism potential and monitoring of progress;
- Effective consultation and collaboration with all stakeholders;

- Focus on attracting investment and infrastructure projects;
- Workforce planning to generate local employment and to ensure that there are adequate workers to service demand; and
- Long term tourism strategies to grow the industry.

— Destination *marketing:*

- Ongoing research;
- Identifying and targeting the correct markets, including new and emerging markets;
- A raised awareness in the target market(s) of the qualities of the tourism destination; and
- Increased visitation and yield.

— Destination *management:*

- Protection of the natural and unique tourism assets of the destination;
- Ensuring quality visitor experiences;
- Industry leadership; and
- Growing a unique and sustainable tourism industry within the destination.

Management Planning Framework (DMP Framework) encompasses the economic, environmental and community practices and principals called on in the above three disciplines and is considered to be 'Best Practice' in DMP.

DMP: Benefits

The potential benefits for destinations, communities, business operators and tourism agencies that can be achieved through an effective and nationally consistent approach to DMP include:

- *Improved destination competitiveness;*
- Increased destination appeal resulting in increased visitation and yield;
- Advantage over other destinations; and
- Ongoing investment in tourism;
- *Increased visitor satisfaction;*
- Delivering on the brand promise;

- Increased repeat visitation; and
- Enhanced destination reputation.

Economic, social and environmental sustainability

- Increase in tourism's contribution to destination's economy;
- Community support for tourism development;
- Controlling tourism's environmental impacts; and
- Long term industry viability;
- Destination Development Planning;
- Critical assessment of tourism potential;
- Consultation and collaboration;
- Investment and infrastructure.

Destination Management

- Protection of assets,
- Quality experiences,
- Sustainable growth.

Destination Marketing

- Research,
- Target markets,
- Awareness,
- Visitation and yield,

Effective partnerships

Strong partnerships (community, industry, government, development agencies etc) are an important factor in many better performing tourism regions. The benefits include:

- Avoiding duplication of resources;
- Bringing a focus to developing the full visitor experience from arrival through to departure;
- Increasing the profile of tourism in regional destinations; and
- Minimising conflicts between tourism and other sectors.

Continuous Improvement

This Framework encourages the implementation of DMP as a process of continuous improvement rather than a once off "set-and-forget" activity. The benefits include:

- Early awareness of emerging trends;
- Development of innovation and new technology; and
- Constant refreshing of destination brand.

DMP: Key Characteristics

Although it is recognises that no two destinations are the same, and that each destination or region will require those aspects of DMP that best suit its unique tourism assets and circumstances, the following points are provided to assist destinations in tailoring a DMPL that will ensure their sustainability and competitiveness.

The core of effective DMP is the commitment of all those that will be implicated in the outcomes of the DMPL, and involves them in the decision-making and implementation of the DMPL, including establishing a strategic vision and setting objectives that:

- Clearly contribute to achieving the vision;
- Are realistic, achievable and measurable, and are based on the best available information;
- Take a holistic and integrated approach to the broader social, environmental and economic development goals for the destination;
- Identify global forces that may have an impact on the destination;
- Include both short and medium-term activities, as well as long term planning;
- Deliver economic benefits:
- tourism potential: identifies the destination's key success factors, strengths of current tourism supply/demand, external factors and constraints, and opportunities for growth;
- business operations: improves potential for business operators (tourism and non-tourism) to improve profitability and operational efficiency;
- local supply chains: maximises the proportion of tourism income that is retained locally;
- employment: improves the quality of jobs in tourism and how the sector is perceived as a career choice;
- enables economic growth in an area and, where relevant, assists in the restructuring and/or diversification of local economies; and

- identifies and facilitates private-sector tourism investment opportunities within the destination.
- Align with community aspirations: manages the pressure of change in the interest of the overall well-being of the community. This may include managing:
- challenges to the quality of life for local residents;
- provision of infrastructure and public amenities;
- local residents' willingness to welcome visitors; and
- responsible behaviour by tourists towards local communities.
- Strengthen environmental management:
- contributes to the conservation and enhancement of natural and cultural heritage assets;
- identifies appropriate carrying capacities and visitor management plans;
- encourages energy and water-use efficiency;
- promotes and facilitates reduction, reuse and recycling of waste materials;
- seeks to minimise pollution, traffic congestion and litter; and
- encourages responsible behaviour by tourists towards the environment.
- Encourage innovation:
- Increases business productivity and efficiency; and
- Drives economic growth.
- Facilitate collaboration:
- Enabling effective leadership and partnerships within which the different stakeholders can communicate and work together.
- Encourage and facilitate continual improvement (capacity building in the destination) This may include:
  - For individual businesses: improved business practices;
  - For the destination: improved management skills for destination managers; collection of data to facilitate performance benchmarking; and
  - For the labour force: enhanced opportunities for skill development, employment and career options; future planning for a sufficient available workforce.

- Develop business operators' and destination managers' ability to anticipate and respond to risk and crisis; and
- Encourage political will for an ongoing, progressive and innovative approach to tourism DMP.

DMP: Overview of a Typical Process

Although the processes and outcomes of Destination Management Planning (DMP) will vary between regions and destinations, a 'typical' process would take the following steps:

Current Situation-Research and Assessment

- Demand-side research: identification and profiling of target tourism markets (existing and emerging); visitor expectations and satisfaction; consumer perceptions; effectiveness of current marketing communications; assessment of external factors affecting the markets.
- Supply-side research: assess the full range of tourism activities (products, services, experiences, partnerships) already undertaken in the destination.
- Gap analysis: between supply and demand.
- *Identify Stakeholders*: Those with an interest in and/or ability to influence the outcomes of a DMP process for the destination. This list would broadly include:
- private sector – tourism and non-tourism businesses;
- local community interests;
- tourism organisations – local, regional, state/territory and national;
- local and regional economic development agencies and Area Consultative Committees;
- industry and consumer associations and peak bodies;
- environmental and cultural heritage bodies;
- local education and training bodies; and
- whole of government: local, state/territory and national.
- *Stakeholder Consultations*: Identify stakeholders' interests and issues, ability and/or constraints to participating in a DMP process, and preferred outcomes. The facilitation of this stage of DMP can benefit greatly from the involvement of experts in the field.

Stakeholder consultations should consider all of the design and development elements of DMP as described above, that are relevant to the destination.

- *Strategic Choices*: based on outcomes from research and consultation.
- Stakeholder consensus on the tourism potential for the destination, and whether DMP will benefit the destination. Note that in some cases where an assessment is made that there is insufficient tourism potential for DMP to be useful, it could also be argued that a DMP process could assist in fostering a fledgling tourism industry in a destination; and
- Determine the key strategic objectives for the DMPL.
- *The DMPL:* Capture these outcomes in a Destination Management Plan, taking account of consistency with (and adding value to) existing non-tourism development and management strategies and plans operating at the state, regional and local levels.
- *Leadership:* Establish all necessary leadership roles, ongoing relationships, management systems, research and reporting processes necessary to implement the development, management, and marketing activities identified.
- *Resources:* Where the process highlights additional resources are required to implement DMP activities, the means of providing or attaining those resources must be identified.
- *Review:* DMP should include a continuous process of monitoring against the agreed objectives and regular review in the light of results achieved and changing circumstances, both externally and within the destination.

Implementation

A key element of the Action Plan endorsed by Federal, State and Territory tourism ministers in August 2007 calls for:

The research and consultation undertaken in the development of the Action Plan identified that many destinations would benefit from the implementation of a comprehensive DMPL, and access to appropriate expertise and advice to assist with that process.

The specialist experience and advice that can assist tourism agencies in the implementation of DMP already exists in the market place. It resides with practitioners in the private and public sectors that have worked for a number of years and have valuable experience in developing and implementing contemporary DMP in many destinations around Australia.

That experience and expertise can be accessed by sharing experience and existing best practice processes between State, Territory and Regional Tourism Organisations, some examples of which are outlined below. A number of useful links have also been provided for further information and assistance in developing DMPL for your destination.

Conclusion and Reflections: The Future of Educational Tourism

Tourism is a hallmark activity of the postmodern world. As such, it is a significant factor in world-making and people-making. The same can be said for universities – they are major enterprises and can be sources for innovative thinking and change. The intersection of tourism and universities is, therefore, a powerful nexus of potential influence. However, tourism educational systems are in need of radical change in order to meet the challenges of the next few decades. The Tourism Education Futures Initiative (TEFI) was born in 2007 to meet this challenge.A number of innovators concerned about the future of tourism education first met in Vienna, Austria to discuss the status of tourism education. During this meeting, a process emerged that provides a framework for the growth and development of TEFI. Subsequent meetings in Hawaii, USA and in Lugano, Switzerland built on the work in Vienna. TEFI is organized around a process which is both proactive and action oriented, focusing on translating the core values articulated by the participants into implementation to bring about fundamental change in tourism education.

Leisure, Sport and Tourism

There can be little doubt that, for the UK, the government White Paper *The Future of Higher Education* will have a significant impact on the development of higher education in general. But there are also some special issues that may affect Hospitality, Leisure, Sport and Tourism (HLST) subjects. With this in mind this editorial will focus on three key areas where there are particular issues for the HLST subjects:

- the opportunities, threats and issues emerging from the White Paper;

- areas overlooked by the White Paper; and
- implications of the White Paper for pedagogical research and related activities.

Opportunities, threats and issues emerging from the White Paper

Perhaps the first point of celebration should be that, in a White Paper dominated by science and technology paradigms, one of the HLST subjects-tourism-gets a specific mention on page 23. There are several other specific opportunities that merit discussion. Many of these require HLST lecturers to engage with specific agencies and to anticipate and plan for new initiatives. In the former category Regional Development Agencies (RDAs) and Sector Skills Councils (SSCs) assume increasing significance. The government states in the White Paper that it wishes to 'build stronger partnerships between Higher Education Institutions and RDAs' and 'help Sector Skills Councils forge stronger alliances between business and relevant departments in universities and colleges'. In terms of initiatives, the Higher Education Innovation Fund (HEIF) is to have an expanded role and play a key part in developing a new proposal. Here the government intends to '[strengthen] the HEIF ... to encourage especially the non research intensive universities to work with employers locally, regionally and nationally' and specifically to '[fund], through HEIF, 20 knowledge exchange centres'. Another initiative that our subject areas may wish to participate in is the 'Aim Higher programme to build better links between schools, colleges and universities'.

There are also a range of initiatives involving teaching, students and quality that can evoke a positive response from the HLST sector. Institutions will be expected to have human resource strategies 'that explicitly value teaching and reward and promote good teachers'. Whilst many of the characteristics of good teachers are generic there are clearly subject-specific aspects where HLST pedagogic research and reflection can offer guidance. HLST lecturers should be encouraged to apply for the National Teaching Fellowship Scheme which is to be expanded. The White Paper has also announced that 'Centres of Excellence in Teaching will be established'. However, currently, the Learning and Teaching Support Network (LTSN) for Hospitality, Leisure, Sport and Tourism works well in promoting good practice across its subjects and there is therefore scope for confusion, conflict and competition over funding with Centres of Excellence. It is hoped that successful LTSNs will be given a clear role in working with Centres of Excellence. A more comprehensive sampling of student feedback and a strengthening of the external examiner system are also areas where HLST specialists can provide valuable input.

Perhaps the biggest threat to the HLST subjects comes from the new policy directions on research evident in the White Paper. There is a cluster of related issues here. First, the government intends to concentrate research funding in departments which are excellent and large. For example, the White Paper notes that there are 'benefits ... from concentrating the best research in larger units' and that 'the government intends to improve the position of research by focusing resources more effectively on the best research performers'.

The creation of the 6* category to reward submissions which scored 5* in each of the last two research assessment exercises (RAE) represents the first step along the road to greater research funding selectivity. Second, the government is proposing a break from the tradition that research is a central and defining feature of a university and intends to '[steer] non-research active institutions towards other parts of their mission'. Third, the government is sceptical about the relationship between teaching and research and states that 'the connection between an institution's research activities and its teaching is indirect'. Fourth, the training of PhD students is being rethought. Ideas in the White Paper include 'larger graduate schools in fewer HEIs' and 'a model where postgraduate degree awarding powers are restricted to successful research consortia'. This should be read in conjunction with recent Higher Education Funding Council for England (HEFCE) proposals to restrict PhD teaching to departments scoring an RAE rating of 3a or above. All this has particular relevance for HLST subjects because of their paucity of 5/5*/6* ratings in the RAE and its aftermath.

However there is much research in HLST subjects that was rated 3b to 4 in the RAE. It should be remembered that a 3b rating demonstrates national excellence in more than half of all the research activity submitted whilst a 4 rating demonstrates national excellence in virtually all research activity submitted. Hence much HLST research of national significance would be lost under the increased research selectivity envisaged by the White Paper. Increased research selectivity would cause negative effects beyond the loss of the research itself. These include loss of motivation and incentive; loss of role models to students and staff; loss of research culture; loss of dynamism; ossification of knowledge; the collapse of important academic networks and subject infrastructure and expertise; and loss of many features associated with a university experience. The HLST subject area also supports a small but growing number of PhD students. This programme would be threatened by proposals to restrict supervision of PhD students.

Crucially, the White Paper also holds out a lifeline for research in HLST subjects. It states that 'the government will develop new incentives to support emerging and improving research' and that 'we must make sure that the allocation of funding overall encourages and rewards promising departments with comparatively low research ratings, particularly for work in new research areas, so that they have the resources to develop and improve'. This has been translated into action in the 2003-2004 research grant awards from HEFCE who designated Unit of Assessment (UoA) 69 (Sports-related subjects) an area of emerging and improving research (one of seven such designations) and offered exceptional funding arrangements to fund research rated 3b and 3a (ratings that elsewhere attract no funding). This was good news for Sports subjects. Whether it was good news for Hospitality, Leisure or Tourism subjects depended on which UoA they had submitted under. Many tourism and hospitality submissions were included in Business and Management (UoA 43) where 3a and 3b ratings are not funded.

As well as a move towards greater research selectivity, in various parts of the White Paper the following are suggested. First, the government proposes to 'allow universities to set their own rates for graduate contributions, between £0 and £3,000 a year.'. Second, the White Paper underlines the government commitment to 'continue to increase participation towards 50 per cent of those aged 18-30, mainly through two-year work-focused foundation degrees'. Third, the White Paper signals the need to reward talented researchers and teachers. Bringing these things together creates a powerful cocktail where the potential for serious and divisive fault lines within higher education emerge as the following plausible scenario illustrates. At one end 6* research ratings create excess student demand enabling top end £3,000 fees to be charged. These institutions become resource rich from both teaching and research incomes and are able to offer pay incentives to recruit the best staff.

A virtuous circle is created. Of course the complete opposite set of circumstances will create a vicious circle of resource poverty and decline. Because of their relative immaturity, HLST subjects tend to be taught in new universities and attract lower research ratings. There is therefore a strong possibility that much HLST provision will end up at the Cinderella end of higher education. A key issue for HLST subjects is that of widening access. The government has underlined its intention to increase participation rates in HE to 50 per cent. It is planning to ensure that there are resources available to support this 'so that universities and colleges will be properly funded for the extra costs of attracting and retaining students from non-traditional backgrounds'. The clear challenge to those interested in HLST pedagogy is to determine what are the appropriate interventions (particularly those which are subject-specific) for this group of students.

Areas Overlooked by the White Paper

There can be few involved in higher education that have not had their minds concentrated on aims, particularly through course validations and Quality Assurance Agency (QAA) visits. Aims come before, and guide objectives. Yet readers of the White Paper, despite its sweeping title *The Future of Higher Education,* will search in vain for a coherent exposition of what the government sees as HE's aims or purposes. There are many objectives but no clear aims. This poses a fundamental problem. For if we are not clear what universities are for, we can tinker with them and even radically change them with impunity. Only a clear idea and statement of the purposes of higher education will offer us an evaluative framework to test the validity and consequences of proposed changes.

It is because the White Paper offers no clear or convincing insight into the aims of higher education that it is able to suggest two radical reforms which will by themselves redefine the purpose of higher education. These reforms are first the notion that many universities become research-free zones with the de-coupling of knowledge creation from knowledge transmission, and second, the rapid expansion of Foundation Degrees. Both of these imply a narrow vocationalist view of higher education. Institutions where research withers away and Foundation Degrees flourish effectively revert to technical college status whilst retaining the title 'university': it is tempting to redefine them as 'post-universities'. Their business will be that of training, and HLST subjects are likely to become heavily implicated in this movement if they are unable to retain a credible research profile. A final irony may be discerned in terms of access. Whilst access may be raised to 50 per cent the scenarios described above may see perhaps 8 per cent of students educated in elite universities whilst the other 42 per cent gain places at 'post-universities'. A neat example of back to the future which would take us roughly back to the situation of the 1960s.

Ron Barnett's seminal work *The Idea of Higher Education* should be required reading for policymakers in this sector. In the introduction Barnett states: 'The aim of this book is quite simple. Its focus is higher education, and its purpose is to ask: What is it all about?'. In his conclusion Barnett outlines six minimal educational conditions for an educational process to justify the title 'higher education'. These are:

1. "A deep understanding, by the student, of some knowledge claims,
2. A radical critique, by the same student, of those knowledge claims,
3. A developing competence to conduct that critique in the company of others,
4. … some form of independent inquiry,
5. The student's self-reflection, with the student developing the capacity critically to evaluate his or her own achievements, knowledge claims and performance,
6. The opportunity for the student to engage in that enquiry in a process of open dialogue and cooperation.

It is not suggested that these criteria are adopted wholesale by the government-but rather that it gives some serious thought to the purposes of higher education. The default position implicit in the White Paper is that higher education is for the economy, industry and employment-a narrow conception indeed.

Implications of the White Paper for pedagogical research and other activities The proposals in the White Paper are wide ranging and will cause considerable change in HLST higher education. From the above discussion there are a number of implications for the HLST community. First, the need for the HLST community to understand the implications of the White Paper and to make a reasoned response underlines the importance of pedagogical research and reflection. For without this we are less able to make a convincing case and contribute to the beneficial development of the subject areas. A clear example of this is the White Paper's assertion about the lack of relationship between research and good teaching. There does not yet appear to be research in HLST subjects to evaluate this assertion. However there is published research on aspects of HLST provision such as aims, RAE results and e-learning that enable us to offer evidence-based evaluations of other White Paper proposals. Indeed this edition of the journal offers insights into teaching methods (Armstrong), evaluating the student experience, the purposes of education, gender and education, virtual learning and quality.

Second, if the HLST community is to have an impact and input into national policy-making commensurate with the size of educational provision and importance of the subjects to the economy it must organise itself and educate itself and others. Here the activities of information gathering, dissemination, lobbying and networking come into play. In Australia, tourism research has never been stronger thanks to the creation of the Centre for Sustainable Research in Tourism at a national level.

In the UK, tourism research looks vulnerable post RAE and White Paper. There is a clear role for subject associations-ATHE (Association for Tourism in Higher Education), BASES, CHME, and LSA in conjunction with the LTSN for Hospitality, Leisure, Sport and Tourism to drive up the importance of HLST subjects at the national level.

The designation of all HLST subjects as areas of emerging and improving research is perhaps the most urgent item of a joint-lobbying agenda. This would offer HLST subjects a more dynamic future in the heart of higher education rather than ossification at its fringes.

5

Exploring the Future of Australian Educational Tourism

Introduction

Improving communication between scholars and the tourism sector requires us to explore the emerging possibilities of scholarly interaction with Australian educational tourism companies, as well as to understand the challenges for academics to engage with teaching and learning in this domain.

Challenges

136 of the academics surveyed expressed an interest in participating in educational tourism in the future. This included 79 who had previously participated, indicating that the experience was positive for most that had done so in the past. As with prior experiences, being a guest lecturer on a tour was the preferred experience. Significantly, being a tour leader was the least preferred experience for the future, despite being the second most common experience previously experienced.

Just as significantly, 47 academics indicated they would not be interested in participating in educational tourism; including 13 who had previous experience. Broadly speaking, the reasons concerned a series of perceptions about educational tourism that fell into the following categories.

Description

As tourism matures as an academic subject and the number of tourism higher education providers continues to expand worldwide, there is an increasing interest in its educational aspects. At the same time the development of research into education issues related to tourism means that there is now a developing literature on the subject. This international handbook offers a timely evaluation of the sate of the art of tourism higher education.

Its global survey of tourism education offers a comprehensive basis for comparative review. In addition to setting out the development and current provision of tourism education it also addresses cutting edge issues such PhD education, non-formal education, cultural issues in learning, research and teaching, e-learning and e-assessment. It offers practical advice for the design, delivery, evaluation and resourcing of courses and concludes with a reflective agenda of issues for the future.

Education Tourism: A Strategy to Sustainable Tourism Development in Sub-Saharan Africa

Countries in sub-Saharan Africa are faced with bleak economic and grave human conditions. Protracted civil wars, political instability, and falling prices for agricultural and mineral exports have combined to wreak havoc on the economies in the sub-region.

These countries are saddled with huge debt burdens resulting from foreign loans. Consequently, scarce resources needed for economic development are diverted to service these loans. According to Vice-president George Saitoti of Kenya, sub-Saharan Africa's debt in 1999 exceeded 250% of its export earnings, a figure that is over the 200% that the World Bank and other multi-lateral financial institutions consider sustainable for economic development.

The combination of a crippling debt burden, political instability, civil wars and falling export prices is that living standards are lower today in sub-Saharan Africa than they were at the time of independence in most countries.

Attempts are being and continued to be made by leaders in the sub-region to alleviate these conditions. Promotion of mass tourism is one of several strategies that has been tried. However, sub-Saharan Africa is still not a significant player in the world tourism industry. The sub-region accounted for less than one percent of the world's total tourism receipts in 1997.

This paper suggests education tourism as an alternative strategy to the mass tourism development efforts. It calls for a coordinated, sustained and organised approach to education tourism to realise its social and economic potential.

What is Education Tourism? The term education tourism or edu-tourism refers to any "program in which participants travel to a location as a group with the primary purpose of engaging in a learning experience directly related to the location". It is comprised of several sub-types including ecotourism, heritage tourism, rural/farm tourism, and student exchanges between educational institutions. The notion of travelling for educational purposes is not new and its popularity in the tourism market is only expected to increase. Sub-Saharan African countries can increase their tourism earnings by tapping into this growing market phenomenon. The sub-region is endowed with abundant tourism resources that could serve as the basis for education tourism. These resources may be categorised into the following dimensions: cultural/historical, ecotourism/nature based tourism/rural tourism, and study abroad programs. Examples of themes that may be used for education tourism include: studying dolphins in South Africa to discover their ecological limits; monitoring bird migration to restore declining populations and manage habitat change; tracking the habitats of rare endemic carnivores; measuring the impact of public health education and clinical testing of intestinal parasites of remote villages; surveying traditional herbalists to preserve indigenous knowledge; finding the connection between global warming and termites by investigating South Africa's insect engineers. Cultural and historical themes include: arts and crafts, architecture, language, archaeological sites, music, dance, slave trade, etc.

Markets for Education Tourism in Sub-Sahara Africa The size of the word market for international education travel is estimated to have increased from 4.8 million trips in 1985 to almost 8 million trips in 1996. This figure represents more than a 66% increase. Over the same period, spending travel increased by 73%.

The Sub-region is currently not a major education tourism destination. The significant global edu-tourism destinations. However, trends from the U.S. market indicate the sub-region is increasingly becoming at destination of choice of many American students. The Open Doors Report 1998/1999 published by the Institute of International Education (IIE) indicated that the number of American students travelling to Africa increased by 20% between 1997 and 1998.

Markets for education tourism in sub-Saharan Africa may be grouped into four categories:

(a) intercountry (domestic),
(b) intra-regional,
(c) European, and
(d) North American.

Countries in the sub-region cannot expect to develop a sustainable edu-tourism based solely on foreign tourists. These countries need to build and nurture the domestic capacity critical for the long-term success of edu-tourism. Education policies should be revamped to incorporate edu-tourism programs in school curricula from primary to tertiary levels. Students in these institutions should not only learn about these attractions/resources in their courses, but they also should be actively encouraged and required to make field trips to these sites. This is particularly important because research suggests that interest in the activities that most people engage in as adults were first developed during childhood and adolescence Consequently, by encouraging the involvement of school children in their formative and impressionable years, sub-Saharan African countries will be creating a cadre of future clients to sustain edu-tourism.

The second edu-tourism market results from intra-regional travels. According to the WTO, intra-regional travel, which is travel by Africans to other African countries, constitutes the most common form of tourism in the region. In 1998, almost 40% of tourist arrivals in Africa came from the continent. This figure represents a staggering increase of almost 118% compared with 1989 (WTO). Countries within the sub-region can tap into this vast potential market via education tourism.

To stimulate intra-regional edu-tourism travel, member countries can overhaul and strengthen existing travel and immigration protocols of their respective regional blocs to facilitate easy movement among nationals within the sub-region. Furthermore, conscious promotional efforts will have to be undertaken within the sub-region to heighten public awareness of available edu-tourism opportunities and their accessibility. In addition, national tourism organisations and universities will need to work in a coordinated manner to design and create edu-tourism programs that engender interests of nationals of the sub-region. For instance, in the area of foreign languages, universities in the sub-region rather than sending their students to metropolitan European capitals for practical experiences, may elect to send them to universities within the sub-region. Students from English-speaking African countries rather than travelling to Paris for their French language experience may travel to the Ivory Coast, Togo, Senegal, etc. Conversely, those from the French speaking African countries may travel to Ghana, Nigeria, Sierra Leone, Liberia, etc. for their English language requirements instead of to London. In addition. Countries with similar colonial experiences may encourage intra-regional travels by their nationals to learn more about their common colonial experiences and heritage.

The third edu-tourism market is represented by the European Union (EU). This region is a large tourist-generating market for Sub-Saharan Africa. Most of the countries in the sub-region still have strong ties to these former colonial powers. Education tourism could benefit from this market through several bilateral and technical agreements. Sub-Saharan African countries can negotiate with European institutions of higher learning to encourage European students to travel to the sub-region.

The fourth market is the North American market. It comprises of universities and institutions offering area studies relating to sub-Saharan Africa, Historically Black Colleges and Universities (HBCUs), and the largely untapped African-American market. Promotional efforts and direct contacts will have to be made with these entities to stimulate and tap into these latent markets currently under exploited by sub-Saharan African countries.

Organisational Framework for Implementing Education Tourism at the Country
Unit

Countries in sub-Saharan Africa have to pursue the goal of education tourism separately as well as in a coordinated and structured way through regionalism. At the country level, each country through their National Tourism Organisations (NTOS), universities/colleges and tourism stakeholders will be responsible for identifying appropriate themes to form the framework for the education tourism strategy. In addition, inputs may be solicited abroad from universities/colleges travel agents/tour operators to shape the themes and course content.

Conceptual Framework for Implementing Education Tourism

Strategy at the Country Unit. The NTOs will set the tourism development policies with advice from the universities and tourism stakeholders. The universities will have the responsibility of providing facilities and equipment, expertise and the necessary academic environment to facilitate learning. The stakeholders will make available the tourism attractions, lodging and transportation. Governments of these countries will provide the infrastructure and super-structure needed to facilitate the smooth operation of the strategy.

The universities collaborating with tourism stakeholders, will produce a workable education program. This program will be divided into two sections: a) classroom experience and b) on-site experience. The program schedule should specify the length of the classroom segment and the on-site practical experience. The governments, through their NTOs, will provide resources to set up Community Communication Centres (CCC) in the various attraction sites.

These centres will have a resident expert on tourism attractions and subject matter in the curriculum to assist with the dissemination of on-site instruction. In addition, these centres will have up-to-date technological links to the universities. Lessons in education tourism could be delivered through distance learning, the Internet and email. Learning can take place in two phases. In the first phase, participants will spend some time in the university classrooms that are linked to the community centres. This arrangement makes it possible to provide participants the knowledge-base and the perceptual view of what is involved in the next phase. The second phase is the on-site experience where participants travel to the attraction location to actively participate and acquire skills that will reinforce the knowledge acquired in the classroom.

Organisational Framework Needed to Implement Regional Education Tourism

Strategy

The implementation of the education, tourism at the regional level will be based on the existing frameworks of regional blocs or institutions in the sub-region. Regionalism seeks to combine and coordinate efforts and functions of different sub-Saharan countries. The regional blocs include: (ECOW S (Economic Community of West African States), EAC (East African Cooperation) and SADC (Southern African

Development Community). According to Dieke (1998), the benefits of regional strategies are as follows:

(a) they provide countries a more co-ordinated approach to negotiations and strengthens their bargaining position with multinational corporations;

(b) create a sizeable regional market-this is particularly important because over 40% of tourist flows in the sub-region resulted from intra-regional travel by residents to other sub-Saharan African countries); and

(c) an increasing number of foreign tourists visiting sub-Saharan Africa are opting for tour circuits rather than resort holidays (the regional approach will prepare countries in the sub-region for this new demand).

The secretariats of the regional blocs, working with member countries, will create a composite education tourism product which is reflective of the region's diversity. The theme, curriculum, course content and schedule will be the outcome of joint efforts by both the regional secretariat and the individual countries. In addition, input may be solicited abroad from universities/colleges, travel agents/tour operators etc.

To facilitate the delivery of the tourism education program, the regional blocs can take advantage of the new African Virtual University (AVU) established by the World Bank to serve countries in the sub-region. It is an interactive-instructional telecommunications network set up to build capacity and support economic development. AVU is currently in the pilot phase and is being implemented and tested in 14 English-speaking and 8 French-speaking universities across sub-Saharan Africa. The regional blocs may request AVU to include education tourism in their course offerings.

Description of the Process for Regional Tourism Education

The courses in education tourism from member countries will be transmitted at the regional level through the AVU. The regional blocs will serve as the link between A VU and: the sub-Saharan countries to facilitate this process. Each country will be responsible for providing the facilities, communication centres, local experts and other critical resources essential for linking that country with the AVU. Potential tourists may experience education tourism through Interactive Video Network

Systems operated by the A VU and actual on-site visitations to the respective countries.

Interactive Video Networks allow for two-way voice activated video systems to transmit live, high-quality audio and colour video between several sites. An instructor or trainer at the home site is able to see and hear the students in a remote site. Conversely, students in remote sites are able to see and hear the instructor and other participants.

Pricing of Education Tourism Package

The tuition for the education tourism program at both the country and regional level may be calculated by, factoring in the cost incurred providing the education infrastructure and personnel. It should also be guided by competitive prices for similar attractions elsewhere in the world. At the country level, profit-sharing between entities involved will be determined by the size of each entity's investment and also by negotiations. A written contract should be signed by all parties before inception of the program.

Potential Problems and Possible Solutions

Potential problems associated with the education tourism strategy include:

1. limited financial resources to procure equipment, parts and other technology hardware;
2. lack of skilled personnel to facilitate the tourism instruction delivery via the Information Super highway; and
3. the sub-region's negative image in the tourist generating markets.

Countries and regional blocs can address the problem of limited financial resource by taking advantage of the World Bank's proposed loan and grants for Internet projects.

In addition, governments will have to liberalise their over-regulated markets to foster competition and attract potential external Internet providers. Skilled personnel may be trained through technical aid from the World Bank and other international agencies. In addition, countries could recruit qualified nationals residing abroad through the Reintegration of Qualified Nationals (ROQAN Program) based in Geneva. It was established to assist African countries to recruit their nationals who have acquired skills abroad through studies and work experience. ROQAN provides airfares, family support and luggage allowances to the individuals to help with their transition in their home countries. The negative image problem can only be effectively addressed through cooperative efforts of all the countries in the sub-region.

These efforts may be supplemented by the activities of the African Centre International (ACI) recently launched to give African business people an opportunity to trade in the U.S. According to its chairman, Emmanuel Chileshe, the centre would operate as a trade and tourism promotion initiative.

Set the rules of behaviour for the visit. Emphasize the importance of the school or organization's reputation, local pride and the repercussions of the actions of any one person.

Prepare lists of DO's and DONTs covering such areas as good manners, their role as ambassadors, curfews, and use of drugs, cigarettes and alcohol. You might also want to elaborate on the following topics:

- Hotel behaviour: curfews, keys, phoning other rooms, running from room to room, etc.
- Restaurant behaviour: noise level, staying seated at the table, manners, etc.
- Amount of luggage, essential items to pack, amount of spending money, shopping time, etc.
- Always listening to the directions and other information given by the group organizers, chaperones, SEVEC-RVC guides or any other guide,
- Respecting meeting times set by group organizers, chaperones and guides,
- Wearing a watch and keeping track of time, and if some do not have one make sure they are with a friend who does,
- Never going anywhere alone! Never leaving their buddy! Waiting for each other when going to the washroom or stopping to buy anything ,
- Being responsible for their own personal belongings and being careful with their back packs, cameras and jackets,
- Not using an IPod, cell phone or other personal electronic device during scheduled activities,
- Knowing the procedures to follow if lost. For example, participants should always have the emergency telephone

numbers and a few quarters in their wallet in case they have to make an emergency phone call,

- Sticking to the schedule and remaining with the group. Participants understandably look forward to opportunities for souvenir shopping, but shops at museums and attractions are often busy and there may not always be time to visit the gift shop.

Code of Conduct

Make sure all group members understand the consequences of bad behaviour In extreme circumstances, they can even be sent home at their parent's expense.

Itinerary and City Map

All participants should have a copy of the itinerary in their handbook, plus any background information they have collected about any of the sites and attractions to be visited. A city map is also very useful.

What to Bring

The best kind of luggage is the lightest. Participants should not bring luggage or accessories that they cannot carry themselves. We suggest one piece of luggage so that participants are able to carry their own bag. It is recommended that you consult the airline you are travelling with to confirm their luggage policy. Here is a useful checklist of personal items that you will want to customize for your trip:

For all Seasons

- toiletries,
- camera/film/batteries,
- light backpack,
- bathing suit/towel,
- money belt/fanny pack,
- lock,
- watch,
- spending money.

Winter

- warm sweaters,
- hat,

- mittens/gloves,
- scarves,
- winter coat/hooded parka,
- winter boots,
- wool socks,
- long underwear.

Fall/Spring

- warm sweater,
- wool socks,
- walking shoes,
- rubber boots,
- waterproof rain jacket.

Summer

- light clothing,
- shorts and tee-shirts,
- walking shoes,
- wind breaker/waterproof rain jacket,
- sunhat,
- sunglasses,
- sunscreen.

Useful Vocabulary

It may be useful to have participants make a list of vocabulary and sentences that they may want to refer to during the trip.

Word Games, Puzzles, etc.

Word puzzles, crosswords and other games are great to occupy participants on the bus, train or plane.

Souvenir Page

Participants may want to have a few pages in their handbook to keep special souvenirs from their visit.

Autograph Page

Having an autograph page always seems to be very popular.

Participant Journal

Having participants write about their daily activities helps them remember what they have learned and makes for interesting reading in later years.

Emergency Procedures and Phone Numbers

Even with constant supervision, participants can occasionally get lost. It is a good idea to discuss this possibility with them beforehand, and to have them take note of the proper steps to follow if it happens.

Tourism

Tourism is travel for recreational, leisure or business purposes. The World Tourism Organization defines tourists as people who "travel to and stay in places outside their usual environment for more than twenty-four hours and not more than one consecutive year for leisure, business and other purposes not related to the exercise of an activity remunerated from within the place visited".

Tourism has become a popular global leisure activity. In 2008, there were over 922 million international tourist arrivals, with a growth of 1.9% as compared to 2007. International tourism receipts grew to US$944 billion in 2008, corresponding to an increase in real terms of 1.8%. As a result of the Late-2000s recession, international travel demand suffered a strong slowdown beginning in June 2008, with growth in international tourism arrivals worldwide falling to 2% during the boreal summer months, and this negative trend intensified as international tourist arrivals fell by 8% during the first four months of 2009. Thereafter this declining trend was exacerbated in some regions due to the outbreak of the influenza AH1N1 virus.

Tourism is vital for many countries, such as the U.A.E, Egypt, Greece and Thailand, and many island nations, such as The Bahamas, Fiji, Maldives and the Seychelles, due to the large intake of money for businesses with their goods and services and the opportunity for employment in the service industries associated with tourism.

These service industries include transportation services, such as airlines, cruise ships and taxis, hospitality services, such as accommodations, including hotels and resorts, and entertainment venues, such as amusement parks, casinos, shopping malls, various music venues and the theatre.

Definition

Hunziker and Krapf, in 1941, defined tourism as people who travel "the sum of the phenomena and relationships arising from the travel and stay of non-residents, insofar as they do not lead to permanent residence and are not connected with any earning activity." In 1976, the Tourism Society of England's definition was: "Tourism is the temporary, short-term movement of people to destination outside the places where they normally live and work and their activities during the stay at each destination. It includes movements for all purposes." In 1981, the International Association of Scientific Experts in Tourism defined tourism in terms of particular activities selected by choice and undertaken outside the home.

The United Nations classified three forms of tourism in 1994, in its "Recommendations on Tourism Statistics: Domestic tourism", which involves residents of the given country travelling only within this country; In bound tourism, involving non-residents travelling in the given country; and Outbound tourism, involving residents travelling in another country. The UN also derived different categories of tourism by combining the three basic forms of tourism: Internal tourism, which comprises domestic tourism and in bound tourism; National tourism, which comprises domestic tourism and outbound tourism; and International tourism, which consists of in bound tourism and outbound tourism. *Intrabound tourism* is a term coined by the Korea Tourism Organization and widely accepted in Korea. Intrabound tourism differs from domestic tourism in that the former encompasses policy making and implementation of national tourism policies.

Recently, the tourism industry has shifted from the promotion of in bound tourism to the promotion of intrabound tourism, because many countries are experiencing tough competition for in bound tourists.

World Tourism Statistics and Rankings

Most Visited Countries by International Tourist Arrivals

The World Tourism Organization reports the following ten countries as the most visited in between 2006 and 2008 by number of international travellers. When compared to 2006, Ukraine entered the top ten list, surpassing Russia, Austria and Mexico, and in 2008 surpassed Germany. In 2008 the U.S. displaced Spain from the second place. Most of the top visited countries continue to be on the European continent.

International Tourism Receipts

In 2008, there were over 922 million international tourist arrivals, with a growth of 1.9% as compared to 2007. International tourism receipts grew to US$944 billion in 2008, corresponding to an increase in real terms of 1.8% on 2007. When the export value of international passenger transport receipts is accounted for, total receipts in 2008 reached a record of US$1.1 trillion, or over US$3 billion a day.

The World Tourism Organization reports the following countries as the top ten tourism earners for the year 2008. It is noticeable that most of them are on the European continent, but the United States continues to be the top earner.

International Tourism Expenditures

The World Tourism Organization reports the following countries as the top ten biggest spenders on international tourism for the year 2008. For the fifth year in a row, German tourists continue as the top spenders.

Most Visited Cities

History

Wealthy people have always travelled to distant parts of the world, to see great buildings, works of art, learn new languages, experience new cultures and to taste different cuisines. Long ago, at the time of the Roman Republic, places such as Baiae were popular coastal resorts for the rich. The word *tourism* was used by 1811 and *tourist* by 1840. In 1936, the League of Nations defined *foreign tourist* as "someone travelling abroad for at least twenty-four hours". Its successor, the United Nations, amended this definition in 1945, by including a maximum stay of six months.

Leisure Travel

Leisure travel was associated with the Industrial Revolution in the United Kingdom – the first European country to promote leisure time to the increasing industrial population. Initially, this applied to the owners of the machinery of production, the economic oligarchy, the factory owners and the traders. These comprised the new middle class. Cox & Kings was the first official travel company to be formed in 1758.

The British origin of this new industry is reflected in many place names. In Nice, France, one of the first and best-established holiday resorts on the French Riviera, the long esplanade along the seafront is known to this day as the *Promenade des Anglais*; in many other historic resorts in continental Europe, old, well-established palace hotels have names like the *Hotel Bristol*, the *Hotel Carlton* or the *Hotel Majestic* – reflecting the dominance of English customers.

Many leisure-oriented tourists travel to the tropics, both in the summer and winter. Places often visited are: Cuba, the Dominican Republic, Thailand, North Queensland in Australia and Florida in the United States.

Winter Tourism

Major ski resorts are located in the various European countries, Canada, the United States, Australia, New Zealand, Japan, Korea, Chile and Argentina.

Mass Tourism

Mass tourism could only have developed with the improvements in technology, allowing the transport of large numbers of people in a short space of time to places of leisure interest, so that greater numbers of people could begin to enjoy the benefits of leisure time.

In the United States, the first seaside resorts in the European style were at Atlantic City, New Jersey and Long Island, New York.

In Continental Europe, early resorts included: Ostend, popularized by the people of Brussels; Boulogne-sur-Mer (Pas-de-Calais) and Deauville (Calvados) for the Parisians; and Heiligendamm, founded in 1797, as the first seaside resort on the Baltic Sea.

Adjectival Tourism

Adjectival tourism refers to the numerous niche or speciality travel forms of tourism that have emerged over the years, each with its own adjective. Many of these have come into common use by the tourism industry and academics. Others are emerging concepts that may or may not gain popular usage. Examples of the more common niche tourism markets include:

1. Agritourism,
2. Culinary tourism,
3. Cultural tourism,

4. Ecotourism,
5. Heritage tourism,
6. LGBT tourism,
7. Medical tourism,
8. Nautical tourism,
9. Religious tourism,
10. Space tourism,
11. War tourism,
12. Wildlife tourism.

Recent Developments

There has been an upmarket trend in the tourism over the last few decades, especially in Europe, where international travel for short breaks is common. Tourists have higher levels of disposable income and greater leisure time and they are also better-educated and have more sophisticated tastes. There is now a demand for a better quality products, which has resulted in a fragmenting of the mass market for beach vacations; people want more specialised versions, such as Club 18-30, quieter resorts, family-oriented holidays or niche market-targeted destination hotels.

The developments in technology and transport infrastructure, such as jumbo jets, low-cost airlines and more accessible airports have made many types of tourism more affordable. WHO estimates that up to 500,000 people are on planes at any time. There have also been changes in lifestyle, such as retiree-age people who sustain year round tourism. This is facilitated by internet sales of tourism products. Some sites have now started to offer dynamic packaging, in which an inclusive price is quoted for a tailor-made package requested by the customer upon impulse.

There have been a few setbacks in tourism, such as the September 11 attacks and terrorist threats to tourist destinations, such as in Bali and several European cities. Also, on December 26, 2004, a tsunami, caused by the 2004 Indian Ocean earthquake, hit the Asian countries on the Indian Ocean, including the Maldives. Thousands of lives were lost and many tourists died. This, together with the vast clean-up operation in place, has stopped or severely hampered tourism to the area.

The terms *tourism* and *travel* are sometimes used interchangeably. In this context, travel has a similar definition to tourism, but implies a more purposeful journey. The terms *tourism* and *tourist* are sometimes used pejoratively, to imply a shallow interest in the cultures or locations visited by tourists.

Sustainable Tourism

"Sustainable tourism is envisaged as leading to management of all resources in such a way that economic, social and aesthetic needs can be fulfilled while maintaining cultural integrity, essential ecological processes, biological diversity and life support systems."

Sustainable development implies "meeting the needs of the present without compromising the ability of future generations to meet their own needs".

Medical Tourism

When there is a significant price difference between countries for a given medical procedure, particularly in Southeast Asia, India, Eastern Europe and where there are different regulatory regimes, in relation to particular medical procedures, travelling to take advantage of the price or regulatory differences is often referred to as "medical tourism".

Educational Tourism

Educational tourism developed, because of the growing popularity of teaching and learning of knowledge and the enhancing of technical competency outside of the classroom environment. In educational tourism, the main focus of the tour or leisure activity includes visiting another country to learn about the culture, such as in Student Exchange Programs and Study Tours, or to work and apply skills learned inside the classroom in a different environment, such as in the International Practicum Training Program.

Creative Tourism

Creative tourism has existed as a form of cultural tourism, since the early beginnings of tourism itself. Its European roots date back to the time of the Grand Tour, which saw the sons of aristocratic families travelling for the purpose of mostly interactive, educational experiences. More recently, creative tourism has been given its own name by Crispin Raymond and Greg Richards, who as members of the Association for Tourism and Leisure Education (ATLAS), have directed a number of projects for the European Commission, including cultural and crafts tourism, known as sustainable tourism. They have defined "creative tourism" as tourism related to the active participation of travellers in the culture of the host community, through interactive workshops and informal learning experiences.

Meanwhile, the concept of creative tourism has been picked up by high-profile organizations such as UNESCO, who through the Creative Cities Network, have endorsed creative tourism as an engaged, authentic experience that promotes an active understanding of the specific cultural features of a place.

More recently, creative tourism has gained popularity as a form of cultural tourism, drawing on active participation by travellers in the culture of the host communities they visit. Several countries offer examples of this type of tourism development, including the United Kingdom, the Bahamas, Jamaica, Spain, Italy and New Zealand.

Dark Tourism

One emerging area of special interest tourism has been identified by Lennon and Foley (2000) as "dark" tourism. This type of tourism involves visits to "dark" sites, such as battlegrounds, scenes of horrific crimes or acts of genocide, for example: concentration camps. Dark tourism poses severe ethical and moral dilemmas: should these sites be available for visitation and, if so, what should the nature of the publicity involved be. Dark tourism remains a small niche market, driven by varied motivations, such as mourning, remembrance, macabre curiosity or even entertainment. Its early origins are rooted in fairgrounds and medieval fairs.

Growth

The World Tourism Organization (UNWTO) forecasts that international tourism will continue growing at the average annual rate of 4 %.With the advent of e-commerce, tourism products have become one of the most traded items on the internet. Tourism products and services have been made available through intermediaries, although tourism providers can sell their services directly. This has put pressure on intermediaries from both on-line and traditional shops.

It has been suggested there is a strong correlation between tourism expenditure per capita and the degree to which countries play in the global context. Not only as a result of the important economic contribution of the tourism industry, but also as an indicator of the degree of confidence with which global citizens leverage the resources of the globe for the benefit of their local economies. This is why any projections of growth in tourism may serve as an indication of the relative influence that each country will exercise in the future. Space tourism is expected to "take off" in the first quarter of the 21st century, although compared with traditional destinations the number of tourists in orbit will remain low until technologies such as a space elevator make space travel cheap.

Technological improvement is likely to make possible air-ship hotels, based either on solar-powered airplanes or large dirigibles. Underwater hotels, such as Hydropolis, expected to open in Dubai in 2009, will be built. On the ocean, tourists will be welcomed by ever larger cruise ships and perhaps floating cities.

Latest Trends

As a result of the Late-2000s recession, international arrivals suffered a strong slowdown beginning in June 2008. Growth from 2007 to 2008 was only 3.7% during the first eight months of 2008. The Asian and Pacific markets were affected and Europe stagnated during the boreal summer months, while the Americas performed better, reducing their expansion rate but keeping a 6% growth from January to August 2008. Only the Middle East continued its rapid growth during the same period, reaching a 17% growth as compared to the same period in 2007. This slowdown on international tourism demand was also reflected in the air transport industry, with a negative growth in September 2008 and a 3.3% growth in passenger traffic through September. The hotel industry also reports a slowdown, as room occupancy continues to decline. As the global economic situation deteriorated dramatically during September and October as a result of the global financial crisis, growth of international tourism is expected to slow even further for the remaining of 2008, and this slowdown in demand growth is forecasted to continue into 2009 as recession has already hit most of the top spender countries, with long-haul travel expected to be the most affected by the economic crisis. This negative trend intensified as international tourist arrivals fell by 8% during the first four months of 2009, and the decline was exacerbated in some regions due to the outbreak of the influenza AH1N1 virus.

6

The Educational Origins of Tourism

Tourism was used at key points in British history to educate people. It is possible to argue that it was filling an educational role most of the time, at least in its early stages. Virtually all forms of tourism began for educational reasons. Most currently available work under plays this fact, with the possible exception of discussions on the Grand Tour. Holloway makes a statement about "tourists and locals alike widening their horizons" almost as an afterthought to a short discussion of sociocultural problems. Cooper et. al. refer to myths surrounding tourism which "should be broken", pointing out "Tourism is not purely for the purposes of leisure. It also includes business tourism, pilgrimages and tourism for health purposes". A later chapter on "The Future of Tourism" makes only passing mention to 'new' tourists looking for "rewarding activities to fill their leisure time and to satisfy their cultural, intellectual and sporting interests", but it is only in the context of the needs of certain market segments in "multi-interest travel". Voase (1995) in an interesting and useful book touches on many aspects of tourism which relate to education, without dealing with it as a perspective. A chapter about the future discusses economics, global warming, people in tourism, sustainability, transport and fashions, but not tourism as an educative activity.

Ryan's "The Chase of a Dream, the End of a Play" refers to tourism as an educative process within the context of sociological discussion. The historical references consider tourism largely as leisure and escapism. Hollinshead's "Heritage Tourism Under Post-modernity: Truth and the Past" in the same collection as Ryan (1997), shows how great a gap there is between the sociological critic on the one hand and the teacher of history on the other, as the scholarship of Samuel's

"Theatres of Memory" (1994) illustrates. Hollinshead paints a pessimistic picture of a world in which all history teaching outside the classroom or library appears impossible since it long ago succumbed to a conspiracy by various forces of darkness. There is little illumination in this kind of writing for the history teacher working out of the classroom. History teachers know well that all interpretations-including books and academic papers-of the world take particular viewpoints, selecting, interpreting and presenting reality as they see it. Even so, a re-assessment of tourism which hopes to be accepted at a higher academic level will have to establish a credible, theoretical and practical counter-argument to the Hollinshead kind of view.

Weiler and Hall edited a collection of papers in "Special Interest Tourism" (1992) which look at a number of case studies and review some sectors. They point to the "diversity of market segments and products... encompassed within the rubric of `special interest tourism'" and "the limited amount of research that has been done". The book unfortunately suffers from being more a collection of snapshots of relevant areas, but the opening chapter does attempt an overview. Sadly, it remains only a collection of separate perspectives such as marketing, ethics and green tourism, rather than shining a well-focused new light on the whole issue.

Within the book, the paper on "Educational Travel" is particularly disappointing in its attempt to take a historical perspective. It makes only two references, the first to the Grand Tour as the originator of educational travel and second to 'Chautauqua'. "The modem-day learning vacation concept seems to have originated at Chautauqua, a residential institution in New York. Initiated in 1874 by a Methodist minister and an Ohio businessman, Chautauqua blends the concept of an outdoor recreation setting with social activities and learning opportunities". This American example is interesting and important as it led to some 12,000 similar centres within the United States, but they were largely centres where general educational activities took place, rather than centres where people discovered their (temporary) new environments through first-hand contact. As a perspective on educational tourism it is disappointing. Another look must be taken at the history of tourism forms.

The pilgrimage was an early form of informal education as it brought devotees closer to knowledge of sacred sites and introduced them to new experiences and knowledge, but not in any didactic way. Prehistoric pilgrimages took place to centres associated with magical properties and religious beliefs, and specifically Christian pilgrimages were undertaken at least from the late fourth century AD. Around 610 AD pilgrims could buy a guide to the churches of Rome-an early aid to visitor interpretation. The Canterbury Pilgrims, following a well-used route from Winchester or London to Canterbury Cathedral relied on a growing infrastructure of tracks, inns and stables in order to make their journey. In Poland, the monastery of Jasna Gora in Czestochowa, founded in 1382, received thousands of pilgrims each year to see an image of the Blessed Virgin Mary housed there: by 1682 it was around 140,000, and by the present day it sometimes welcomes a million in a single year. Historically, each visit was part of a process of communication and teaching in which what the pilgrims had seen and experienced was fed back to others in their own villages and towns.

The nature of the Grand Tour as an education for the sons of the English gentry has been well covered. Rooted in the explorations of Queen Elizabeth I's age, the Grand Tour was encouraged by her as a means of training men for government. Feifer quotes James Howell's "Instructions for Forraine Travel" (1642) comparing the stay-at-home with the traveller. "To run over and traverse the world by hearsay... other men's eyes... is but a confused and imperfect kind of speculation, which leaveth but weak and distrustful notions" said Howell of the former, and praised the first-hand view of the latter: "the eye... as through a clear and crystal casement we... in one instant comprehend half the whole universe".

Though the later Grand Tourists were more interested in pleasure than in being educated, the whole experience remained educational in the widest of senses. Even time spent in a brothel would teach the young buck about life. The part played by Grand Touring in British culture is well documented, but there was an important influence on industry and technology, too.

Thomas Cook's entry into the history of travelling was made by a desire to educate. The 1841 railway excursion from Leicester to Loughborough took five hundred people to an open space where Cook, a Baptist preacher, could educate them about the evils that he saw in alcohol. However successful he might have been in his chosen aim, he was certainly successful in his method. With a combination of the excitement of open-wagon rail travel, the leisurely nature of the day, and the ambience of a different environment, the Leicester folk must have been in a receptive and tolerant mood. No consumer motivator could ask for more. Thomas Cook's contributions were all about packaging travel, an attention to detail, and the providing of quality experiences, but above all the enjoyment by his customers of discovering new places.

The growth of seaside holidays is also well documented. From them it can be seen that even the hedonism of the seaside existed alongside the wonders of discovery. In 1788 Catherine Hutton from Birmingham wrote home about the people she encountered in Blackpool: "The Boltoners are sincere, good humoured and noisy. The Manchestrians reserved and purse-proud, the Liverpoolians free and open as the ocean upon which they get their riches". And while Blackpool was a place of social encounter, it was also one with an Opera House, an Aquarium, a Menagerie, a Winter Gardens with "high class concerts", and its famous Circus. From 1910 even the Pleasure Beach had its "edutainment" in devices like the Naval Spectatorium which used 360-degree film projection and mechanical devices to present representations of the American Civil War, and later, World War I naval battles. Such devices were the norm for resorts which wanted to entertain their visitors, and indeed, Scarborough retains its "Naval Warfare" event to this day.

Presenting the wonders of the world has been a foundation for entertainment ever since the earliest bards told their stories. In due course the resorts of the industrialised world built fair grounds, theatres, museums, galleries, menageries and gardens drawing upon the culture, artefacts, flora and fauna of the world around them. Fairs like the Kursaal at Southend-on-Sea, Dreamland at Margate, and the Paradium at Great Yarmouth derived excitement from representations, however distorted, of reality. The huge Coney Island parks in New York almost became international expositions in their own right by building theatres, cinemas and other shows. They were in direct line of descent from the London, Paris, Vienna and Chicago Exhibitions long before Disney.

Visiting great houses and museums, and the educational value that related to such excursions, has been a recent subject of analysis. Ousby says that "Travel was a leading instrument of that post-Reformation spirit of enquiry which valued empirical knowledge over abstract speculation or book-learning derived merely from tradition".

It was during the middle years of the nineteenth century, and in parallel with the beginnings of formalised education for various age groups from young to old, that the practice was established of townspeople and city dwellers making day visits to the country. These were not only for what we might term 'escapist' entertainment, but for 'self-improvement'.

Local newspapers of the time are full of the accounts of annual outings by social groups from chapels or work-places. There are detailed accounts preserved of the organisation required for the bigger trips, such as the well-known railway excursions from the Bass Breweries. These show how guide books and visits of an 'improving nature' were made integral to the excursions by those who organised them. One quotation from the 40-page booklet distributed to 8,000 participants in the 1914 visit to Scarborough will give a flavour:

"The improvements made since our last visit in 1910 consist of deepening the old or West Harbour by about three to four feet, so as to accommodate and give more room for fishing craft of a larger size and to the increasing number of Steam Drifters now engaged in the Herring Fishery, in addition to the Sailing Herring Fishers. The West Pier, where the fish is landed, sold and packed, has been widened-70 feet being added-and now provides excellent curing and packing spaces for the herring curers and exporters".

A videotaped account given by a retired worker from John Crossley and Sons' carpet mills in Halifax shows in anecdote some of the cultural effects. Mrs Florence Waite took part in a long railway excursion over 30 hours to Edinburgh, Glasgow and the Isle of Bute in 1934 with Crossley's Social Club. The impact made by Edinburgh's particular historic character, and the Clyde's glorious scenery, are clear even after sixty years.

Delgado has shown how important the annual excursion was as an escape from the industrial city. In 1912 the Duchess of Sunderland foresaw "A day that is a glimpse of Paradise to the poor little mites who live in the darkness of squalid back courts and the mean streets of our cities", when raising money for a charity sending children on a countryside excursion.

Thomas Cook had religious motives (it was his son John Mason Cook who went fully commercial in tourism), believing that through his tours "man has been brought nearer to man and nearer to his Creator". It must be stressed that Cook began as an evangelist, a communicator, and not a tour operator. However unconsciously, he succeeded because he removed his audience from the stress of everyday life, induced within them a receptive and relaxed frame of mind, and then tried to persuade them to adopt a new lifestyle based on Christianity and, in particular, teetotalism. This aligns with Turner's analysis of the pilgrimage with its ideas of separation, liminality and communitas. But it also aligns with the principles of propaganda and persuasion of the use of group psychology, removing his audience to a different setting, creating a receptive mood and using crowd psychology to persuade individuals to adopt new attitudes. Cook's Loughborough excursion operated in terms of communication between people, and between people and environments, depending on the contrasts between Leicester (a city full of the stresses of everyday life), the thrills of the railway journey (excitement, empowerment, and innovation) and the Loughborough destination (comparative arcadia, relaxation, and enjoyment). Cook's aim was to educate, and educate effectively.

A similar set of motives inspired the Reverend T A Leonard. The Congregational minister preached a sermon at Dockray Street Church in Colne in August 1891 in which he criticised the habit some people had of 'laking' about-playing-saying that "the devil wields no small influence over holiday times". Holidays should be taken sensibly, sacredly indeed. Leonard's view was "Speak to the earth and it will teach thee". The idea of education within holidays was present when Leonard went on to encourage a group of thirty men to organise a holiday in Ambleside in 1891, and Caernarfon the next. By 1893 he was Secretary "of a scheme which embodies a new idea of summer holidays", inviting adult education classes and Pleasant Sunday Associations to join in visits to Ambleside and Keswick, walking by day and enjoying music and `lecturettes' in the evenings. The rambles were conducted by a University companion guide appointed by the National Home Reading Union. This was the beginning of the Co-operative Holidays Association, now the Countrywide Holidays Association and operating many holiday homes for its members.

Formal education out of doors is little covered in tourism books, yet it is one which by its variety and early encounter by students must underlie so much of their subsequent interest in travel. A very early example of this activity is that of the herbarizing organised by the Society of Apothecaries of London. This was the practical means by which apprentice apothecaries could be taught to recognise plants which would have medicinal values. The first one known took place in May of 1620, beginning at 5.00 am with a rendezvous at St Paul's in the City. The day was spent out in the country, then relatively close by. Within a short while six excursions a year were being held. After a while a paid official known as the Demonstrator of Plants was employed to lead the excursions, and in 1673 the Chelsea Physic Garden was established as a permanent demonstration area. It has since become an important tourist attraction in its own right. Herbarizings continued up to 1824 when it was decided London was too big to allow for day excursions to open countryside, and the educational practice was abandoned. By then, many botanists had received their introduction to the subject through these events.

In 1732 The Society of Dilettante was formed from a group of men who had been on the Grand Tour. The Society helped to pioneer archaeological field study. Geology field teaching was in turn developed from 1804 by Robert Jameson of Edinburgh who took formal field classes as far away as the Western Isles. Geography field teaching in the UK got off to a relatively late start and in 1938 a survey of London schools showed that "hardly a half are able to conduct outdoor field work". This was despite John Ruskin having said that "the country will become an outer and uncovered classroom, a Divine museum utilised by our teachers". Excursions were the exception, rather than the rule. One did occur in 1886, when Scott Keltie reported to the Royal Geographical society that the children of Gordon's Hospital School, Aberdeen, were "taken out into the country and in a simple, rough but effective, and to them, interesting and instructive way, are taught to draw maps of a small area for themselves". On the other hand, adult geographers made group excursions quite early. The Manchester Geographical Society went to inspect the new docks in Preston in the autumn of 1887 for example. It should be remembered that individual adult travellers were being drawn towards industrial locations to see the changed landscapes presented from at least the 1780s onwards, as has been seen above. Field Societies, Scientific and Literary Societies and Geographical Societies continued through the nineteenth and twentieth centuries to make such excursions.

The practice widened out in the twentieth as manufacturers like Cadburys and Wedgwoods, anxious to promote their methods and products, opened their doors to all kinds of groups. Lever Brothers joined with the LMS railway company to promote tourism to their factory in Port Sunlight in 1926. In the 1950s and 1960s both companies handled thousands of adult and school visitors. The present author recalls making visits to factories such as Lotus Shoes in Stone, British Rail Engineering in Crewe, a Co-op Dairy in Llangadog, the Velindre Tinplate Works and the Steel Company of Wales, Port Talbot. The steel and engineering companies used visits for general public relations purposes, the consumer goods makers used them to sell their wares. Even tiny manufacturers got involved, for example Joseph Dobson and Sons of Elland who from 1980 welcomed visitors in order to raise their profiles against their big competitors.

Indeed, Marling has recently shown how even that great icon of theme park tourism, Walt Disney, began with ideas for a "kiddies park". Disney's new Burbank studio of 1939 was laid out on production-line principles. Having seen Snow White, people were asking to see how the animation was done. Disney thought that those who did visit found the whole process boring, and in any case there was none of the fairy tale magic on the production floor. So he began to plan a special area which would show both magic and motion picture production.

Early in the twentieth century it took people like James Fairgrieve, training geography teachers in the 1920s, to foster an interest in school excursions and holidays. He suggested children in east London could begin by finding out "information about the commodities that their fathers are handling". They could look at the doors of Fleet Street to see listed the newspapers of the British Empire as a starting point for discussing its geography. They would continue by making excursions to other places. "This is a benefit not only to the understanding of other lands but to the understanding of the homeland also. In a very real sense the homeland is measured by other lands: also, unless it is seen in its world setting, it is not really understood". Factory visits were being added by progressive teachers at least from the late 1940s.

The nineteenth century was the great age of self-improving societies, often growing out of church or chapel groups who began to investigate interesting subjects. Others were specifically for self-help. The earliest, and still thriving with its private museum and lecture programme and visits-was the Spalding Gentlemen's' Society, founded in 1710. There were Mechanic's Institutes and worker's educational groups, and the subject societies for literary and scientific pursuits, from botany to geology and geography, many of which organised and ran their own excursions. In the United States similar self-help groups emerged in the diverse and often isolated settlements further west, while in the east urban groups sprang up, and the Chautauqua, already mentioned, had an important effect.

The original Chautauqua started as a summer vacation and training centre for Sunday School teachers at Chautauqua Lake, near to Lake Erie, in New York State. It developed as a place for discussion and debate on classical and current topics. Scholars, actors, speakers and exhibits were arranged, plays put on, great speeches re-made and debates staged. Home-reading circles became part of the system, and for a time participants could study for a degree at a Chautauqua University.

The idea was imported to Britain largely through the work of J B Paton, who had been involved in setting up a University Extension in Nottingham. In 1887 Paton formed a small committee with John Percival, Headmaster of Rugby School, and from 1888 they organised Summer Meetings at Oxford with educational courses. This line continued as the growth in the UK of adult education.

By the late nineteenth century the ideas of Frederic Le Play and then Patrick Geddes had formed the basis for sociological field work with a strong geographical basis. Geddes' ideas has particularly interesting features in the context of the present paper. In Paris in 1878 he visited the International Exhibition and was enthusiastically inspired by the display of the reconstruction of Paris after the Franco-Prussian war of 1870. Returning to Edinburgh he became immersed in ideas of planning and improvement, one step in which was the purchase by him of the old Observatory at the lower end of the Castle Esplanade. It housed (and still does) a camera obscura which was used to project views of the city onto a white 'projection table' for visitors to study.

Renamed the Outlook Tower and using whatever small funds and voluntary help that he could muster, Geddes began to create a kind of regional museum. He was also involved in teaching at the Edinburgh Summer Meetings or schools, linking the educational work with the displays in his Outlook Tower and excursions into Edinburgh to encourage city renewal.

Helen Meller, in Patrick Geddes: "Social Evolutionist and City Planner", shows how he absorbed ideas from the efforts of museums to collect and classify social knowledge. The Musee Sociale in Paris built on ideas which had been shown at the Paris Exhibitions of 1867, 1878 and 1889 about the study of people and their environs. The International Bibliographical Institute in Brussels was systematically collecting and classifying human knowledge in order to act as a centre of study. Geddes devised an idea for an `Index Museum' in his Outlook Tower with a kind of three-dimensional encyclopaedia of the world installed in it.

Geddes again went to an Exhibition in Paris, this time in 1900, organising a huge programme of lectures and tours in a Summer School there. "Eight hundred classes were held in just 120 days, and the average attendance at these was between 40 and 502". And there at the Exhibition were pavilions and buildings from around the world. Geddes wanted to save them as a permanent `Index Museum', a centre of study of the world's cultures and societies. It failed to happen for reasons of cost and ownership.

Within the Paris Exhibition of 1900 the strands of education, tourist attraction (the displays) and inspiration for progress (the ideas communicated by the displays and the School) came together. It did not become permanent: that would happen in museums and inter-activity centres in another age, perhaps more related to heritage than to visions of the future as Geddes wanted, but the principles, firmly based in educative forms of tourism, were all there.

A different-though related-reason was behind the origins of the Scout and Guide movement, which turned mere country visiting into an organised, structured, educationally-motivated activity. "Our business is not merely to keep up smart `show' troops, but to pass as many boys through our character factory as we possibly can: at the same time, the longer the grind that we can give them the better men they will be in the end". Scouting was one of the occupations which, along with inspirational books like "Bevis: The Story of A Boy" and "Swallows and Amazons" created the idea of adventure holidays which is at the heart of modem children's activity tourism. Jefferies educated his readers about the countryside: Baden-Powell trained his, through "Scouting For Boys" into adventurers who grew inwardly through their interaction with the rural environment.

As Michael Rosenthal shows, much of scout culture drew upon the works of the Anglo-American author, Ernest Thompson Seaton. Between the 1880s and the 1900s Seton spread ideas of what he called Woodcraft' as a way for young American males to learn from, and be entertained by, life in the great outdoors. He based his philosophy on the native North American culture and outlined a national movement based on features from his reading of native life, with a liberal dash of European chivalric ideas thrown in. Baden-Powell's movement adopted some of the ideas, but Seton's Woodcraft Indians continue still as a separate organisation. There was also an influence on the European Woodcraft Folk movement which grew amongst people who wanted a youth organisation which avoided what they saw as Baden-Powell's establishmentism and military leanings. Within one sector of tourism therefore it is possible to follow the development of a clear political/ philosophical strand. During the nineteenth century the growth and diversity of schooling allowed experimentation in terms of organisation and curriculum. Influenced by Rousseau's ideas about the importance of an individual's development some innovations were made which tried to relate teaching environments to the pupil's needs. In England, Cecil Reddie founded Abbotsholme School in 1889 as somewhere which could take a boy "to train him how to live". This meant daily, outdoor activities such as drill, sports, river bathing, running, carpentry and gardening.

Just after World War I Kurt Hahn co-founded Salem School in Germany with Prince Max von Baden, in which the development of character and selfdiscipline were foremost. Abbotsholme had an influence. With the arrival of Nazism Kurt Hahn was forced to leave, and he moved to Britain_ In late 1933 he opened Gordonstoun School in Scotland, with a disciplinarian programme which included ideas of service to the nearby community. From 1935 onwards boys were enrolled as HM Coastguards, and they later operated a small fire brigade. The 'Moray Badge' scheme was devised with tests in athletics, expeditions, and life-saving, partly in response to a national debate about the poor quality of fitness in young people. It is interesting to note the similarities to matching fears expressed at the turn of the century about the health and character of boys which helped lead to the Boy Scouts.

Out of the Badge scheme came three experimental; residential summer schools in Invemess-shire and Morayshire. Their success led in turn to the formation of the Outward Bound schools, this time in Wales, at Aberdovey, to which Gordonstoun had been evacuated on the outbreak of war. From 1941 an Outward Bound Sea School commenced operation, offering courses to young men from industry, not only in maritime activities, but also 30-mile mountain country expeditions. The Outward Bound movement has also grown and expanded its activities to a number of British and European centres.

In Germany the idea of the school excursion had gained ground rapidly from 1907 and the formation of the 'wandervogel' at Jena in January that year. Its aims were "to promote rambles and excursions of German boys in their own and other neighbourhoods, and thus to awaken in them a taste for the beauties of nature, and to give them opportunities of learning to know their German homeland and its people at first hand". Local associations were set up and older children encouraged to qualify as guides. Books and maps were bought and could be hired out to non-members. Travel and overnight accommodation were to be simple-fourth-class rail and country barns.

Earlier still, the Eberfeld 'Realgymnasium' was one of several schools which held indoor lessons until noon and then gymnastics or excursions. On six afternoons in the summer term the whole four hundred children at Eberfeld would march out of town behind a band, the older children going the furthest, and teachers instructing the pupils along the way. Games would round off the excursion, for which six hours was allowed. The government extended the Whit holiday to allow higher classes make longer journeys to places like the Westerwald, Taunus and Eiffel districts. Up to twenty boys and their masters might make a fortnight's visit to somewhere like Italy. The days started early and consisted of long walks followed by evening recreation ("beer and songs") and summaries by the boys of what they had done-often given in foreign languages. The pupils paid themselves in advance, with poorer boys charged less, but "for poor masters no funds were provided". It is noteworthy that German interest in exploring environments seems to have underpinned the country's ideas in gestalt psychology, to which reference will be made later.

Another organisation began in Germany in the same year, 1907, that Baden-Powell was holding his first scout camp on Brownsea Island in Poole Harbour. A teacher, Richard Schirmann, opened his school to a group of children from slum areas, so that they could enjoy a countryside holiday. Two years later Altena Town Council and a local businessman gave money to turn Burg Altena into a hostel. It was the start of the 'wandervogel' movement, anti-militarist, anti-machinery, pro-country life. Britain set up its first hostel in 1930 though a water-supply problem forced it to close soon afterwards. The YHA dates from that year, and the next year saw no fewer than twenty hostels open. Country life, exploration and adventure were the aims of all their visitors.

In Britain all of these strands became woven together after 1945 and new ones were added. The Field Studies Council in Britain opened its first centre in Suffolk in 1946, and the first local authority centre, White Hall near Buxton, opened in 1950. National Parks, open air museums, commercially-run adventure centres, stately homes and historic houses, castles and wartime defences, zoos and sea-life centres, gardens and country parks, heritage centres and inter-active science centres, factory tours and craft demonstration units made their appearances on ever larger scales. Were these just part of a heritage industry making new money, or an extension of the very long growth of educational tourism? School visits, especially when linked to the National Curriculum, can provide the bread-and-butter visitor income that they need to survive.

This account of some of the educational aspects of tourism is not complete, nor could it be within the confines of a discussion paper. Nor does it attempt to discuss in detail who benefited from each, nor just how much benefit there was, nor how prejudiced or enlightened any of it might have been. What is important here is the acknowledgement of the frequent close liaison that there has always been in tourism with education. It is fair, and appropriate, to say that all forms of information and opinion, whether expressed between individuals, through the mass media, or in education, are subject to limitations on access, quality and objectivity. The point is that tourism is just as good, or just as bad, as they are. But it has, like them, a potential for being beneficial.

Educational Tourism in Thailand

Imagine studying in a country like Thailand... Imagine rewarding yourself with a weekend on the beach after a hard week's study, or trekking through the jungle as soon as your exams are over! Whether for full blown degree programs or short vocational courses, more and more people are making Thailand part of their educational objectives and becoming 'Educational Tourists'.

With fewer Thai students studying abroad over the last decade, foreign universities opened campuses in Thailand or made agreements with Thai universities to run 'Dual' (or 'Twinning') degree programs-foreign degrees run at Thai universities. As a result, Thailand has a huge choice of international-level education options and is a major draw for students all over the world looking for world-class education.

Of course, to benefit from higher education at an 'English-medium' university, students must understand English well. For many years there has been a booming domestic market for English language courses in Thailand; a market driven by Thai students who appreciate the benefits of studying with a native English speaking teacher. As a result, there are countless teaching jobs available to foreign teachers in Thailand, both at commercial language centres and within the state system. Such is the demand for teachers that visitors often include teaching English as part of their itinerary for a trip to Thailand. Would-be-teachers do though need training and as a result of there has been a dramatic rise in the number of English teacher training courses available in the Kingdom. Whether it's short courses that give you the basics, or detailed internationally recognized courses that offer a stepping stone into the English teaching profession, there is certainly a course in Thailand to meet your needs.

English though is not the only language you can study in Thailand. As the country takes its place on the international stage, its influence grows around the world. Increasingly, people take Thai language lessons for business and educational purposes, or simply build a short language course into their stay in the country for fun. As a result, a number of commercial Thai language centres catering for expatriates and visitors have emerged to give people an insight into the language.

Of course, with the rise of tourism to Thailand the world is now interested in all things Thai – particularly Thai food. There is an abundance of centres in Thailand teaching foreigners the intricacies of preparing Thai cuisine… and very popular they are, too! With the worldwide boom in Spas and 'Wellness', the demand for masseurs able to offer Thai massage is increasing and the number of visitors studying massage in Thailand growing. Likewise, more and more visitors take courses in traditional Thai medicine to become practitioners in their own countries. What follows is a sample of courses for 'Educational Tourists':

University Courses in Thailand

Although traditionally every young Thai person's dream has been to study abroad in a country like the USA, Britain or Australia, the realities of issues like the financial downturn of the late 1990s, '9-11' and war in Iraq forced many to reconsider their educational goals. As a result, numbers of Thai students studying abroad plummeted as many chose to stay at home. Losing valuable revenue streams, foreign universities got creative. Rather than fighting over fewer Thai foreign students, they changed tactics and began to look at opportunities actually here in Thailand. As a result, some of the world's leading universities now either have a campus in Thailand or are attached to a Thai university where they offer 'International' degree programs. The benefits to Thai students of having world-class higher education on their doorstep are obvious, but there have been substantial benefits for Thailand as a whole – the Kingdom has become a hub for foreign students who want to receive an international-standard higher education. Students from places like China, Taiwan, former Eastern bloc countries, Scandinavia, and increasingly, Europe, the United States and Great Britain, take university courses in Thailand to enjoy the benefits of standard, lower cost (particularly in terms of cost of living and educational fees) and the ability to simply be able to enjoy Thailand while they study. Most universities require some formal indication of English language capability and increasingly this means students taking an IELTS test. Click here to learn more about the IELTS listening, reading, writing and speaking test. What follows are details of some of Thailand's leading universities offering 'International' programs:

7

Famous Educational Tourists

Talking To Visitors: Whitby Abbey

Whitby Abbey is associated not only with the history of Christianity but also the origins of the story of Dracula, the life of fishermen over the centuries and the early life of Captain James Cook, the explorer. It stands high above the east cliffs at the top of a long, flight of steps climbed by thousands of tourists and people From the nearby community. So it has many stories to tell.

English Heritage Care for the site and organise the interpretation of these stories through a visitor centre and guide books, and also an up-to-the-minute personal digital player. Carried by the visitor who holds an earpiece close to his or her head, the unit replays recorded words and sound effects chosen by the user according to at which point they are standing. Rechargeable batteries and no moving parts mean much more reliable units than the simple cassette players available in the late 1970s. The capital cost might be high, but it's relatively easy to revise messages. The human voice has e strong resonance for the listener. In addition, different languages and messages suitable for different ages can be added quite easily.

Travel to Understand-Cities

It's noticeable that the pioneers of outdoor education discussed below turned to the countryside and the wilderness as the places of educational value. The explorers recorded by Richard Hakluyt would have had few cities to discover in their sailing the world's oceans. Cities were not what they were looking for, anyway-they wanted to find tracts of country that could be easily commandeered and colonised. The later pioneers were usually advocating escaping from the city, all too often seen as cess pits of social problems and ill health.

Tourism at first targeted the cities for its destinations, as Grand Tourists went to Paris and Rome. Many rich city dwellers would head for smaller urban areas, the spas like Bath, Bad Harzburg or Karlovy Vary. Coastal resorts-Trouville, Brighton, Monaco for example-grew with the railways. These were the destinations for several days or, with railway access, long single days. Yet for many people an excursion out of the town and city into quite close-by countryside was all that they had available in the nineteenth century, making the trip by horse-drawn wagonette or local timetabled train. Under the influence of religious leaders, who saw in the countryside something of the clean paradise of the Garden of Eden, whole congregations and Sunday Schools would troop out into open fields and hills. The 'leaders into the field' described on these pages were either part of this culture or connected with it.

Metropolitan areas always attracted travellers and tourists, Grand or not so Grand. There was business to be done as well as leisure to be enjoyed. So, too, did the old cathedral and abbey towns and the university centres such as York, Oxford, Heidelburg and Uppsala. Thomas Cook organised hundreds of trips to cities, and not only London but more unusual ones-Liverpool has been mentioned in the posting below, for instance.

There is an interesting mix of attraction and promotion in cities today. Prestige must be maintained. Trade must be promoted. New sources of income must be found to replace that of declining industries. Alongside the older museums and art galleries, sports and arts venues and shopping streets there has been a strong growth in educational and cultural attractions. Urban renewal schemes have often been given some kind of prestigious flagship to give them a boost: the Cite des Science in Paris as part of the redevelopment of the Parc de la Villette complex is a good example. Or in Barcelona the redeveloped docks area with a large sealife aquarium.

Boston is a good illustration of the kind of range of interest which draws the modern urban explorer. It has the older Art Museum and it has the newer Science Museum. Faneuil Hall is an important historic landmark-with shops-as part of the Quincey Market regeneration project. Within that development are many shops, restaurants and bars which reflect Amercian, and especially Bostonian, cultural norms-the 'Cheers' bar is a representation of the popular TV series setting (and a distance away from the famous exterior which was shown in the series). Around Boston are other places for the explorer of cities and their urban margins-Saugus Ironworks noth of the city and-further out to the south-places like Plymouth Harbour with its replica of the Mayflower ship of 1620. Urban regions have never been as popular and rewarding as they are now. I wonder what Rousseau and Ernest Thompson Seton would have made of them?

The Coming of the Guide Book

Early travellers who were not 'on business'-government, military or trading-were mainly pilgrims. Within the Christian world there are records of pilgrims going to Jerusalem late in the fourth century AD at least. They were shown places with biblical associations and some returned with souvenirs such as stones from the hill at Calvary.

Early in the seventh century pilgrims going to Rome were able to buy basic guides-simple block prints showing the route around the main churches. Not until printing with movable type was established in Europe in the late fifteenth century-Gutenberg began commercial work around 1450 in Mainz; Caxton set up in Westminster, London in 1476-was guide book production feasible, but the market was small, especially as there was only a poor distribution infrastructure. Travellers' guides would only appear much later. In addition, maps and pictures would be very crude compared with what a traveller needed to be useful. It is noteworthy that it was only in 1570, during Europe's great effort to discover other continents, that the first Atlas appeared. Published by Abraham Ortelius and printed by

Christopher Plantin, it contained 53 copperplate maps. Atlases in the early days were productions for wealthy people to have on show in their private libraries, large works of art rather than something to slip into the pocket or even cabin trunk.

In 1699 Joseph Addison set out from England to tour Europe and gather material for a guidebook on its various countries based on the writings of Horace and Virgil. He must have been one of the very first travel writers.

The first English guide book aimed at describing routes to take and what there was to be seen came in 1817-18. It consisted of a two-volume "Tour of Picturesque Rides and Walks with Excursions by Water Thirty Miles Around the Metropolis" and was written and published by John Hassall.

A number of factors came together to create a rapid growth of guide book publishing in the early nineteenth century, which also established some of the key firms in the trade. It was becoming easier to travel-more could afford to do so, the roads were being improved and railways spread after about 1830. The relatively rich had time to travel for leisure and exploring places became a fashion in the wake of the Grand Tour. Steam power, cylinder-printing and typesetting machines were equipping the printing trade far better than before so that large runs of book production were possible, potentially reducing unit costs. Finally, the new railways provided a fast distribution system, not only to bookshops around the country but direct to the rail traveller through station bookshops such as those of W H Smith, whose pioneering news stand was opened on Euston Station in 1848. Passengers wanted something to read, and some wanted books that satisfied their curiosity about the places they saw out of the carriage window.

The great pioneer in guide book publishing was Karl Baedeker, whose books were highly researched and packed with detail, including fine maps on thin, fold-out sheets of paper. In 1829 his first such book was a guide to the town where his press was situated: Koblenz. Britain's main published was John Murray. He produced his first Handbook for Travellers on the Continent in 1836. Murray joined with Karl Baedeker to publish the first Baedeker guide in English, in 1861. It was a book about travelling along the Rhine. France had its great published of detailed guides, too. In the early 1850s Louis Hachette added travel books to his wide range of general publishing. Detail and accuracy were again their hallmark, and later the Hachette company would also enter into joint production with British publishers, this time Muirheads, in 1918-Muirheads had bought the John Murray imprint earlier.

One other important date: in 1857 the first English book illustratated with photolithographs from nature was published. It was John Pouncey's 'Dorsetshire'.

Leaders into the Field: Ernest Thompson Seton

Ernest Thompson Seton (1860-1946) was a highly influential figure in the growth of what we now know as Scouting. Although there is some controversy over the matter, it is clear that Seton's ideas helped to shape those of Lord Robert Baden-Powell about how to deal with the wild areas of the world and the animals, plants and trees within it.

Seton was born in South Shields, England, but emigrated with his family at the age of 6 to Canada. It is said that he spent time in the woods near his home playing and sketching in order to avoid his abusive father. His knowledge of animals and their habitats grew and Seton became a skilled naturalist, a writer and artist. He moved to New York City and then Greenwich, Connecticut, where over one weekend he dealt with some local vandals by inviting them to the land he owned and telling them stories about North American native peoples. In 1902 he formed a youth group, 'Woodcraft Indians' for local boys. The stories he told became articles in a magazine, the Ladies' Home Journal, and later they were assembled in his book 'The Birch Bark Roll of the Woodcraft Indians'. This appeared in 1906, coincidentally the year before Baden-Powell's famous camp held on Brownsea Island in Dorset, which was followed by his book 'Scouting for Boys' the next year. Daniel Beard, the subject of the previous posting on this page, had already published several books developing the theme of self-reliance and adventure in the outdoors of America-two of these came out in the same year, 1906, one of them being the 'Field and Forest Handy Book'.

Baden-Powell read a copy of 'The Birch Bark Roll' in the year of its publication, was taken by the ideas and met Ernest Thompson Seton to discuss them. When Scouting became established over the next few years in Britain, Seton and Beard joined in by merging their organisations with it. Seton became the first Chief Scout of the Boy Scouts of America, and Beard one of the first commissioners.

In the foreword to one of his books published in 1921 Seton wrote the following about the idea of Woodcraft that he had been advocating for some twenty years:

"By Woodcraft I mean outdoor life in its broadest sense and the plan has ever been with me since boyhood. Woodcraft is the first of all the sciences. It was Woodcraft that made man out of brutish material, and Woodcraft in its highest form may save him from decay".

Leaders into the Field: Daniel Carter Beard

Daniel Carter Beard (1850-1941) was one of three men in the USA and the UK, who shared very similar decades and who created organisations for boys aimed at getting them out into the countryside in order to learn about life and to develop their characters. Ultimately two of them, Beard and Ernest Thompson Seton, would channel their own organisations into merging with those of the third man, Robert Baden-Powell, the founder of the Scouting movement.

Beard was also known as 'Uncle Dan', a reference to his skill at storytelling and inspiring boys to take up life in the open air. He was born in Cincinnati, Ohio, living in Covington, Kentucky, across the river from his birthplace during his childhood. There he could explore the valley of the Licking River as it flowed into the Ohio, and he learned stories of the pioneers who settled the area. Beard became an engineer and learnt to survey, then he attended art school in New York City. Soon he was to take up writing as well, producing articles for popular family magazines. As a competent illustrator he drew for books written by Mark Twain. Then he became an editor, of 'Recreation' magazine for which he penned a monthly article aimed at youth.

His interest in, and enthusiasm for, frontier traditions led to his founding the Sons of Daniel Boone in 1905. By this time he had met Ernest Thompson Seton who was working along similar lines, as the next posting will show. Beard's column moved twice to different magazines, and because an arrangement with one of them had meant he did not have the rights to the name 'Sons of Daniel Boone' Beard renamed his organisation the Boy Pioneers of America.

Daniel Carter Beard me Lord Robert Baden-Powellsoon after the latter founded his Boy Scouts movement, and in 1910 Beard merged his group into a new Boy Scouts of America which was formed. He became one of the first National Scout Commissioners and served the Boy Scouts for thirty years.

Beard wrote and illustrated many books, among which were The American Boy's Book of Camp-Lore and Woodcraft (1920) which is still in print, and Wisdom of the Woods (1926) and Buckskin Book for Men and Boys (1929). The titles give a taste of the particular American frontier idiom of pioneering self-reliance. While they were in keeping with the style of the times and aimed at the males in the population, Beard was also supportive of moves (by his sister, for example) to open up some part of this culture to girls. He died in 1941, as did Baden-Powell, and only five years before Ernest Thompson Seton.

Leaders into the Field: Pioneers of Outdoor Education

Under the inspiration of many writers and innovators, the later nineteenth and early twentieth centuries saw ideas develop to take teaching and learning into the world outside the school and home. Some, like the Boy Scouts movement, were aimed at building the individual psychologically and socially. Others were related to academic subjects or a mix of the two ideas. Some important examples are shown here.

Dr. Cecil Reddie founded Abbotsholme School in Staffordshire as a place to develop both the minds and bodies of its pupils in pleasant surroundings. Working within a community was important. Reddie had been influenced by Rousseau and John Ruskin and he admired the German secondary schools which emphasised involvement in the outside world. Even so, in an example of a long period of idea-swapping between the United Kingdom and Germany, he in turn inspired one of his teachers, Hermann Leitz, to return home to set up a similar school at Ilsenberg in 1899. Others followed in Germany as Leitz built up his activities.

Robert Baden-Powell counted British and American influences amongst his antecedents when he ran his famous camp for boys from contrasting communities in 1907. Out of that event on Brownsea Island in Poole Harbour, Dorset, came the Boy Scout and Guide Guides, Cubs and Brownies movements which were not outdoor classroom activities but educationally-aimed nonetheless.

Just after the First World War a German educator, Kurt Hahn, was employed as Secretary to the last Chancellor of Imperial Germany, Prince Max von Baden. In 1920 Hahn set up Salem School which also had aims of developing character and self-discipline. Hahn stood against the rise of Nazi control during the early 1930s and in 1932 was forced out, having written to his pupils to say they had to choose between the school's principles and those of the Nazi party. Kurt Hahn fled to England. Two years after leaving Salem he founded Gordonstoun in Scotland. The new school had its own strong blend of personal and social development set in the Highlands communities close to Inverness. The present Prince of Wales would become its most famous (though apparently reluctant) alumnus. Hahn was to have another achievement in Britain. As the Second world War broke out, Gordonstoun moved to Plas Dinan in North Wales. Sharing a similar concern that had motivated Baden-Powell much earlier, Hahn and Lawrence Holt of the Blue Funnel shipping line began another school, at Aberdovey. This would attempt to improve the mental and physical qualities of boys entering the merchant navy. It was the first centre of the Outward Bound movement. As such it would expand into a series of centres and be used by many organisations anxious to train employees to be self-reliant and successful by using demanding physical and team-building techniques. There is a strong element here that also led towards much more informal adventure holidays, notably through companies like PGL after the war.

The last example of outdoor education shown above is the Field Studies Council which began life in 1947. It has already been the subject of a separate posting. The Council grew out of the observation of the difference between London children and their new neighbours when they were evacuated early in the war to Cambridgeshire. However, its work was not primarily aimed at individuals and human communities but at knowledge about the natural environment. Many field centres were opened and helped in the academic education of thousands of pupils and students.

Leaders into the Field: Frederick Gunn

In nineteenth century Britain there was nowhere really that was unknown to people. The exploration mode was already moving towards that of ordinary individuals setting out for themselves to see what others had already discovered. Thomas de Quincey camped for nine nights in a tent he had made himself in order to walk from Manchester to North Wales in 1802. John Wilson used a tent on a walking tour in 1815. In North America, on the other hand, in the great plains and northern wastes of Canada and the western USA there was much still be seen, at least by settlers of European origin if not for native Americans. They knew their country and they lived with it intimately in a relationship that would not be known or understood by the white man for many decades to come.

The European settlers were moving north towards the Arctic Circle and west towards the Pacific, besides progressing further up the Pacific coast from Mexico and along the sea routes. Driven by reports of adventure and wonders to be seen, even the longer-established communities of the Atlantic coast harboured aspirations of exploration and desires to meet the challenges of the open spaces. When the United States Civil War broke out in 1861 the news was greeted with an upswelling of patriotic feeling on both sides. As the years went by and the dreadfulness of the war machine ground onwards these feelings became less intense. At the start, however, the boys of a school in Connecticut were keen to march and camp just like the soldiers. Frederick William Gunn and his wife ran what they called the Gunnery School in Washington in that state. They seized the chance to introduce activities that would develop the boys physically and morally. In August of 1861 they took the whole school on a two-day, 40-mile trip to Welch's Point on Long Island Sound. A horse-drawn wagon carried tents and two donkeys were on hand for younger children less able to walk the whole way. On arrival they swam and fished and at night stories were told and songs enjoyed by the light of camp fires. Accounts of the expedition suggest that the Gunns probably held discussions about the causes of the war and the likely outcomes for the country. Similar events were held in 1863 and 1865 and then camps were switched to a site on Lake Waramaug seven miles from the school. Academic subjects were introduced at Lake Waramaug. The camps were finally discontinued in the 1870s, but for some years afterwards, alumni from the school held reunion holidays at the spot. The Gunnery School still thrives, and each year a commemorative hike is made to the Steep Rock Reservation near to Washington, Connecticut.

Frederick Gunn is considered to be the originator of leisure camping in America. Other people developed their own camps of different kinds during the century. One of these was founded by Ernest Balch and some friends on Burnt Island, Squam Lake in New Hampshire. Called Camp Chocorua, it did not have a ready-assembled group of users of the sort the Gunnery School had, but it attracted boys whose parents spent their own holidays in resorts which Balch considered socially less desirable for children. Again, the aim was to develop healthy activities in a well-ordered community. Camp Chocorua lasted only eight years but had a long-lasting influence on many other pioneers of education in the open air, and it and the Gunnery camps sparked off what would become a very active part of the American tourist industry.

Eells, E (1986) Eleanor Eell's History of Organised Camping: The First Hundred Years, Martinsville, Indiana

Leaders into the Field: William Gordon Stables

Dr. William Gordon Stables (1840-1910) has been described as "having invented pleasure-time caravanning". This is owed to two accomplishments by Dr. Stables in the 1880s. First, he had built for himself a wooden caravan called 'The Wanderer' which was styled after traditional roma ('gypsy') caravans. He then toured England in the caravan, which was pulled by two horses and staffed – yes, staffed – by a coachman, John, and a valet, Alfred. There was also a parrot and a dog. Oh, and a bicycle. Dr. Stables supervised the activities, wrote up a log of his journeys and generally enjoyed leisurely life. The coachman looked after the horses, sleeping at inns where he could keep an eye on the horses. Alfred erected a washroom tent, cooked the meals and cleaned the caravan. Dr. Stables, ate, rode his bike and wrote his account of the trip.

The second accomplishment of the doctor was to write books about travelling. The main one described "The Cruise of the Land Yacht Wanderer: or 1,300 Miles in My Caravan" and was published in 1886. Dr. Gordon Stables was a qualified doctor and had been a Royal Navy surgeon between 1863 and 1871. Even more than that, for thirty years up to his death he wrote adventure books for boys at the rate of about one every three months. These were imperial-era tales of derring-do and by including caravan journeys as 'land-cruise' adventures Stables was raising the slow progress of horse-drawn vehicles into a realm of excitement which must have drawn many youngsters to commercially-produced caravans as soon as they appeared. In later postings we will see how later writers in Britain and the United States did the same for other forms of transport – motor cars, bicycles, canal boats and sailing boats, for example.

Geographical Societies

John Bartholomew's role in the Royal Scottish Geographical Society points to the growth of these public bodies in the mid-nineteenth century. The first of these was the society formed in Paris in 1821 after which others followed in several continents. The Royal Geographical Society in London was formed in 1830. By 1885 it has been estimated that almost a hundred existed round the globe with over 50,000 members.

Geographical societies at the time were interested in exploration of places unknown to the people in the societies. The great age of exploration of the 1900s was in full swing. These organisations must also have been nationalistic-as most of groupings at the time-and that turned their attention to imperial power and economic gain, rather than any questions of theories and local studies. Later, the idea of such societies spread to schools so that a continuous strand of world exploration through talks and, in due course, travel films, was fostered with a powerful influence on public knowledge. School holidays and expeditions abroad reinforced the interest; package holidays for the family added to it post-world war II. Schools' use of outdoor adventure training from the 1950s onwards (in Britain) continued in the same strand-though that was also encouraged by activities like scouts and guiding and Outward Bound.

Leaders into the Field: John George Bartholomew

John Bartholomew (1860-1920) was the third of four men of that name, his grandfather, father and son all being known that way. His grandfather founded a map-making business in Edinburgh that would become famous and still exists. His father continued the work, he did himself – with even greater success – and his son did, too.

This John Bartholomew introduced street maps of large cities, maps for the railway timetables and maps for car owners. He introduced special ways of helping users to see the shape of hills and mountains by adding coloured contour-layers to the map. There were specialist atlases, too – for meteorology and zoogeography. The first Times Atlas of the World was his work, though first published posthumously, in conjunction with the newspaper. It still continues.

His importance lies not only in this work, however, but also in his related interests and activities. He began to work for his father's business in 1880 and four years later was the co-founder of the Scottish Geographical Society, becoming its secretary, a post he held until his death. 1888 saw him elected to the Royal Geographical Society in London; four years after that he became secretary of one of the sections of the British Association for the Advancement of Science. King George V appointed him Cartographer Royal in 1910.

While the Ordnance Survey remained the national surveyor during his lifetime, it was Bartholomew who used the marketing of maps in such a way as to popularise their use and encourage travelling, before the OS itself put effort into making its own maps more readily available by selling them through bookshops in attractive covers that appealed to the walker, cyclist and car owner.

Leaders into the Field: John Muir

John Muir (1838-1914) was one of the most important naturalists in the USA during the nineteenth century. His influence is still great through the Sierra Club which he founded and the books that he wrote. His love of the natural world and his efforts at arousing knowledge and concern for it have made him a key figure in education as well as travel. The modern environmental movement, which is usually seen as a product of the 1960s, has to acknowledge him as one of its forerunners.

Muir was Scottish by birth and from a large family which moved to Wisconsin in 1849. Inspired by a fellow student at the University of Wisconsin-Madison who talked about the relationship of wild flowers to garden vegetables, John Muir became a self-confessed enthusiast for the natural world. He withdrew from his course after several years of part-time study and walked from Indiana to Florida. His plan had been to go on to South America but illness forced him to abandon the idea and he turned to California instead. Once there Muir took himself to the Yosemite Valley, a place which overawed him. "No temple made with hands can compare with Yosemite, the grandest of all special temples of nature", he later wrote.

After a number of jobs John Muir became a shepherd in the Yosemite area, taking up climbing and hiking to explore the wilderness. He moved to become the manager of a sawmill, building a cabin on Yosemite Creek. It was during these early days that he began to develop ideas of how this landscape had been formed – in his view, glaciers has sculpted many of the features. It was an opinion which clashed with that of Josiah Whitney, head of the California Geological Survey, who, like many geologists of his day thought that a catastrophic earthquake had formed the Yosemite scenery as it now appeared. Over time it was Muir's interpretation that gained acceptance and his ideas were published in the first of many writings in papers and books.

Having married into a family owning a large ranch in Martinez, the shepherd turned mill manager now became the manager of orchards and vineyards on the ranch. His travels, explorations and writing increased with several books to his credit which have since been read by millions of people. Prominent Americans like Ralph Waldo Emerson, railroad president E H Harriman and President Theodore Roosevelt travelled to meet him and spending time walking in the mountains or travelling by ship along the north-west coast. Through such meetings he was able to convince national figures of the need for federal control of the Yosemite wilderness areas through the system of national parks. The Sierra Club, which now has millions of members, was founded by John Muir to campaign for conservation and education in matters to do with the environment. His books, like 'The Mountains Of California' and 'My First Summer In The Sierra' stand alongside the Sierra Club and the creation of Yosemite as a national park as memorials to a remarkable pioneer.

Leaders into the Field: Thomas Cook

Thomas Cook (1808-92) is today considered to be the founder of one of the world's most successful travel agencies. And so he was. But that was not what he set out to do, and it in a way places him in too modern a context when he was a really part of the religious fervour of the early nineteenth century. Britain was fast becoming industrialised; factories, railways and cities were changing the landscape. Damaging social conditions had been created through overcrowded housing, pollution and harsh industrial conditions. Poverty, crime and drunkeness were often the result. Cook was a cabinet maker. He published Baptist leaflets and in 1828 became a Baptist minister in Melbourne, Derbyshire. As one of a movement who campaigned for temperence in drinking habits-usually by giving up alcohol entirely-he preached against the evils that resulted and published leaflets to support the efforts of his fellow campaigners.

The flash of inspiration which was to change his life came while travelling by road in Leicestershire, but thinking about the railways which were being built around the country. Cook was a preacher, a publisher and a propagandist. His aim is life was evangelical-to unite man with man, and man with God. He and others believed the way to God lay along a path of good human behaviour, and that meant among other things giving up the alcohol, the cause of drunkeness, violence and other antisocial problems. Cook knew that communicating these ideas would be easier and more effective on a large scale if those he wished to have in his audience when preaching were feeling at their most receptive and positive. It would be good to take the people away from their normal surroundings full of industry and toil and put them somewhere more pleasant, let them relax and enjoy good fellowship, perhaps play some healthy games-even to have a decent picnic provided. There could be music provded by a brass band, some hymn-singing of the sort they enjoyed in church and chapel. What a marvellous thing it would be if they were not only entertained by food and play but perhaps excited by something new, something exciting, spectacular even.....

The railway could supply some of the answers to the main needs that he was seeing. On 5 July 1841 the event he had begun to shape that day out in the countryside took place. It was also the event that would launch a whole new set of activities and the employment which went with them: mass travel, tour operations and-the heart of what Thomas Cook was seeking-travel as education.

On that day he had hired a train from the Midland Counties Railway to take 570 passengers from Leicester to Loughborough at a cost of one shilling (5p) per person. In a field in the town the crowd had food, non-alcoholic drink, music and games-and speeches on the joys of temperance. The excitement of having made an eleven-mile journey in the open wagons of a train must have been immense. The day was judged a success all round, so much so that Cook made further excursions over the next few summers for temperance groups and Sunday-school pupils. In 1845 he took a party to Liverpool, booking evrything needed at an all-in price and offering trips by sea along the north Wales coast. Information booklets about the journey and the destination were circulated to evryone. In 1846 he escorted 350 people from Leicester to Scotland. In 1851 he ran a number of trains carrying 165,000 visitors to the Great Exhibition in London. There were failures-a bankruptcy which had to be overcome-but persistence established Thomas Cook as the pioneer that we know of today-a pioneer of tourism as education whose business would take people across continents and exploring around the world.

Ggantija Temples

Here are pictures of the oldest free-standing structures in the world-older than Stonehenge, the Pyramids and anything else you care to name. But pretty much unknown.

On the left is a model of the remains of the temples which is part of the small, but excellent National Archaeological Museum in Valletta, Malta's capital. Ggantija is only one of a whole number of ancient temples in the country-Tarxien, Mnajdra, Hagar Qim, Skorba and others-and is itself on the island of Gozo. Next picture: a timeline for the Ggantija temples in the Museum-they're at the top at around 3,400BC. Then: a group of visitors in 2004 listening to a Maltese guide (pointing) at the site. Right-hand: part of the temple walls are propped up with scaffolding as they have been for several years.

The archaeology is little-known world wide and the 'earliest remains' fame hasn't yet arrived. Ggantija is in great need of more suitable conservation and visitor facilities which are limited to someone selling tickets and a few pieces of interpretation-leaflets, postcards and interpretive panels. A small exhibit in the entrance to the National Archaeological Museum says that an internationally-supported plan for improved treatment of all the temple sites is out for public consultation, which "will be complete by 2007"..... no mention of the outcome. Malta is, of course, the EU's smallest country with limited resources. All the more reason for getting cracking, raising the profile and standard and bringing in more tourists who want to understand just how important this tiny republic has been in Mediterranean history.

Exploring the Old and the New: Malta-Mdina

Not on the Grand Tour trail in the eighteenth century but with a longer span of history on show, Malta is a popular Mediterranean resort and of course has featured regularly on this web site, thanks to the residentials that Leeds Met ran for nine years.

In fact Malta has a longer human history to show than virtually anywhere else in the world-at least until archaeologists prove there are earlier human artefacts somewhere else. The Ggantija Temples on Gozo, the second-largest Maltese island, date from earlier than Stonehenge, the Pyramids or any other ancient remains. But they are not well known. The tourist group above was being shown around Malta's early capital city, Mdina, a tiny and very attractive city indeed yet with its fortified entrances through the city walls and the main cathedral-that in the modern capital, Valletta, is described as the Co-Cathedral. On hand inside Mdina's gate is one of the horse-drawn carriages which take visitors around, and one of the colourful buses that ply the roads of Malta. These are popular with visitors but not so popular with image-conscious Maltese people. Outside they're beautiful but inside old fashioned and not always the most comfortable. On the other hand, thay're part of the Maltese story along with much else to tell visitors about from the country's five-thousand-years-plus history.

Leaders into the Field: Adam Sedgwick

Adam Sedgwick (1785-1873) was born in Dent, Yorkshire, and attended the nearby Sedbergh School. After becoming a student at Trinity College, Cambridge he took holy orders, in 1817, but the following year moved on from being a Fellow of Trinity College to becoming the Woodwardian Professor of Geology in the University of Cambridge. "Hitherto I have never turned a stone" he is reputed to have said on his appointment, "henceforth I shall leave no stone unturned".

Sedgwick's importance in the general area of education out of the classroom was in the field excursions he organised for his students and other interested people. In these he inspired many-including women, who he allowed in to his classroom lectures, unusual for the time-to take an interest in exploring the countryside. He wasn't the first to lead geological excursions, William Buckland of Oxford having done so in 1832, Sedgwick following in 1835. The Cambridge professor's trips into the Fens were immensely popular, however, with sometimes up to 70 students following him on horseback in order to hear five lectures in a day.

Adam Sedgwick was also influential in choosing the young Charles Darwin as a field assistant. Darwin studied geology after achieving his first degree. When he made his famous voyage in HMS Beagle he sent rocks and fossils from South America back to Sedgwick and kept up a correspondence with him. They were to disagree on the matter of religion and evolution but the fact remains that Sedgwick had contributed to Darwin's exploration skills and scientific knowledge just as he had with many other people. The study of geology in the field was some way ahead in Britain of that of geography and Sedgwick was one of the reasons why.

Leaders into the Field: Carl Ritter

The importance of German efforts within geography is shown by Carl Ritter (1779-1859) who was a close contemporary of his fellow countryman, Alexander von Humboldt.

Ritter was not an explorer of new lands, however. He was a collector of knowledge through constant with men who did travel. What he did do outside the classroom and lecture hall, however, was to be a propagandist against slavery and racism. He corresponded with the Royal Geographical Society in London, who were mainly interested in exploration to further the economic gains of Britain. He had taught Heinrich Barth who explored northern and western Africa and who worked on behalf of the British government to eradicate slaving.

Carl Ritter began to publish his great series of books called 'The Science of the Earth in Relation to Nature and the History of Mankind' in his earliest days as a teacher. It reached 19 volumes but by the time of his death it had covered only Asia and his particular interest, Africa. It was Ritter who promulgated the view that geography was a kind of comparative anatomy of the world, and that its mountains, deserts, glaciers and river valleys were instrumental in shaping the history of mankind. "The earth is a cosmic individual with a particular organisation, an 'ens sui generis' with a progressive development: the exploration of this individuality of the earth is the task of geogarphy" he wrote. Ritter was casting the shape of geographical thinking for the next several decades.

Leaders into the Field: Alexander von Humboldt

Alexander von Humboldt (1769-1859) was a German naturalist and explorer who was an early pioneer in the growth of interest in travel amongst Germanic peoples. Along with men like Carl Ritter he encouraged through his explorations and writings the German love of discovery. His modern-day countrymen and women are amongst the great travellers of Europe, making expeditions across many continents in order to experience places and peoples and to learn about the world in general. German schools have a long tradition of excursions and holidays with the same aims, well before most other countries including the United Kingdom. This is partly due to Humboldt.

His early travelling included England, Vienna and a tour of Switzerland and Italy studying the botany of those places. Then he spent five years in Latin America between 1799 and 1804, observing and describing the countries he saw in a new, scientific manner. His account of the travels were published over 21 years in a monumental set of books.

It was Humboldt who first suggested that South America and Africa were once joined, long before the Atlantic Ocean was formed. In 1845 towards the end of his life he wrote the five volumes of his work 'Kosmos' which set out to draw together different areas of scientific knowledge. Darwin, Goethe, Jefferson and many others regarded him as one of the most prominent of scientists. Humboldt inspired later generations to travel and explore like he did-even if they were to use more comfortable means of touring to do so.

Leaders into the Field: Johann Heinrich Pestalozzi

Johann Heinrich Pestalozzi was a Swiss teacher and educational reformer. He was born in Zurich in 1746 and died in Brugg, Switzerland in 1827. Like Rousseau he wrote a book on education but unlike Rousseau he was a busy teacher for many years, first in Birr, then Stans, next Burgdorf and finally Yverdon.

Pestalozzi was not so much a teacher advocating outdoor education but rather one remembered as a general educational reformer who placed the pupil at the centre of education. He once said "The role of the teacher is to teach children, not subjects". His most important book was called "How Gertrude Teaches Her Children". Pestalozzi's ideas were based on starting from the simplest steps and progressing to the more difficult. Observation was to be used, followed by conscious thought about what was observed, and finally the use of speech to discuss the results within a general system of knowledge. Measuring drawing, writing, numbering and reckoning would come after that. At the heart of observation was the idea of 'Anschauung' which could be translated as 'sense impression', the 'experience' which resulted from the observation. This concept would be a key element in German, as well as Swiss, ideas about travel. 'Doing' leads to 'knowing' said Pestalozzi, so it can be said that Anschauung contained within it an active process on the part of the observer-it was not a simple, passive procedure. Seeing, hearing, touching etc had to be thoroughly performed, multiple activities, such as looking at a thing from different points of view. The knowledge gained had to be related to other knowledge so that an integrated picture would emerge like (as we might see it) the growing completion of a jig-saw puzzle.

Children helped each other in Pestalozzi's class. He said "I put a capable child between two less capable ones. He embraced them with both arms, he told them what he knew and they learned to repeat after him what they knew not". His experience in the early days at Stans, where he was teaching orphans gathered together after suffering during the French invasion of 1798, was crucial. Of this he said:

> *"I learned, as never before, the relation of the first steps in every kind of knowledge to its complete outline; and I felt, as never before, the immeasurable gaps that would bear witness in every succeeding stage of knowledge, to confusion and want of perfection on these points. The result of attending to this prefecting of the early stages far outran my expectations. It quickly developed in the children a consciousness of hitherto unknown power, and particularly a general sense of beauty and order. They felt their own power, and the tediousness of the ordinary school-tone vanished like a ghost from my rooms. They wishes, tried and persevered, succeeded, and they laughed. Their tone was not that of learners, it was the tone of unknown powers awakened from sleep; of a heart and mind exalted with the feeling of what these powers could and would lead them to do".*

So Pestalozzi was describing classroom teaching, but those principles that he was identifying would become the basis of out-of-the-classroom education as well. A later posting in this series will describe the writings of Freeman Tilden in 1957 about heritage interpretation in American National Parks. Tilden's principles of interpretation owed much to the ideas formulated by Pestalozzi, as did many of the ideas of educationalists in the years between.

Leaders into the Field: Jean-Jacques Rousseau

Jean-Jacques Rousseau was born in Geneva in 1712 and died in France in 1778. He was an important philosopher, writer and composer who has exerted a great influence on world life and culture. His writings certainly contributed to the development of political ideologies of all shades of opinion. His ideas on education have had a profound effect on both theory and practice at all levels, even though some aspects of them were quickly rejected as being impractical. Some years after his death he was reburied in the French Pantheon in Paris as a national hero.

For someone considered to have added much to the ideas about educating children it is ironic that Rousseau had five and sent them to an orphanage where they might not have survived to adulthood. His defence was apparantly that they would have done better there as he would have been a poor father. Since orphanages had high mortality rates that view must have been questionable at the very least.

Rousseau's thoughts about education were set out in his book 'Emile', a semi-fictitious account in which the author brings up a young boy in the countryside. To Rousseau the city is a place where children would learn bad habits, mental as well as physical. Emile has a tutor who teaches him on a one-to-one basis reminiscent of those tutors who accompanied young men of wealth on the Grand Tour. The boy is educated through three stages of life. The first is up to the age of twelve when complex thinking was thought to be impossible and the child behaved according to animal instincts. From 12 to 16 reasoning begins to develop. From 16 upwards adulthood is achieved and useful skills like carpentry are acquired. Working with wood demanded skill and creativity but would not compromise the child's morals. Rousseau thought that Nature was a good and effective teacher. He wrote "Nature exercises children continually, it hardens their temperament by all kinds of difficulties, it teaches them early the meaning of pain and sorrow".

In another section he wrote: "Men are devoured by our towns. In a few generations the race dies out or becomes degenerate; it needs renewal, and it is always renewed from the country. Send your children to renew themselves, so to speak, send them to regain in the open fields the strength lost in the foul air of our crowded cities. Women hurry home that their children may be born in the town; they ought to do just the opposite, especially those who mean to nurse their own children. They would lose less than they think, and in more natural surroundings the pleasures associated by nature with maternal duties would soon destroy the taste for other delights".

It was through this kind of idea that Rousseau became an inspiration for education outside the town or city, or if the child were country-born it was about learning about himself or herself and their relationship to society.

Leaders into the field: John Locke

John Locke was an English philosopher who influenced many thinkers and writers in the seventeenth century when he lived (1632-1704), and subsequently many others such as Rousseau, Voltaire and David Hume. For these postings on education out of the classroom and, informally, through travel and tourism, his importance lies in his essays "An Essay On Human Understanding" and "Some Thoughts Concerning Education". Unlike his contemporaries in the church he believed human beings started life without inborn knowledge-like a 'tabula rasa' or blank page-on which knowledge gained in life would be inscribed. In "An Essay Concerning Human Understanding" he wrote that knowledge came from external sources, which to us would mean our general environment with its stores of information and the wider world to be explored. His style is that of a man writing about philosophy in 1690. Here is an example:

> *"The notice we have by our senses of the existing of things without us, though it be not altogether so certain as our intuitive knowledge, or the deductions of our reason employed about the clear abstract ideas of our own minds; yet it is an assurance that deserves the name of knowledge. If we persuade ourselves that our faculties act and inform us right concerning the existence of those objects that affect them, it cannot pass for an ill-grounded confidence: for I think nobody can, in earnest, be so sceptical as to be uncertain of the existence of those things which he sees and feels".*

In "Some Thoughts Conerning Education" Locke develops the idea that learning must not be a matter of absorbing facts by rote, but one of aquiring skills which can be used to learn, and that the whole process must be enjoyable in order to succeed. He writes of many things including the curriculum for learning by skills acquisition. As just one example he describes the usefulness of drawing :

> *"When he can write well and quick, I think it may be convenient not only to continue the exercise of his hand in writing, but also to improve the use of it farther in drawing; a thing very useful to a gentleman in several occasions; but especially if he travel, as that which helps a man often to express, in a few lines well put together, what a whole sheet of paper in writing would not be able to represent and make intelligible. How many buildings may a man see, how many machines and habits meet with, the ideas whereof would be easily retain'd and communicated by a little skill in drawing; which being committed to words, are in danger to be lost, or at best but ill retained in the most exact descriptions?"*

The connection with being educated away from home and possibly out of doors is made. People were already making the Grand Tour of Europe from Britain and Locke's comments helped to encourage sketching and painting as a way of recording what the traveller encountered.

Leaders into the Field: Richard Lassels

The term "Grand Tour" was first used by the French-'le grand tour'-and then introduced into English usage by Richard Lassels. He wrote a book called "The Voyage of Italy" (sometimes refered to as "An Italian Voyage") in 1670. The word 'tourist' stemmed from it but was not used until the early nineteenth century.

Lassels was only one of a number of writers about the Grand Tour but it seems to have been his book which stimulated much of the early travellers in the seventeenth century-when the practice was already a century or so old but with much smaller numbers of travellers.

Richard Lassels listed four benefits that English partakers would gain: those of the intellectual, the social, the ethical or moral, and the political. He was actually writing about two established, but more localised, tours-the French grand tour and the Italian Giro. What emerged was a tour with a fairly common set of destinations even though individuals (accompanied by a tutor) were making their own way where they thought fit. The route would take in Calais, the Loire valley, Paris, Geneva (or, taking a different route, the Rhone valley to Avignon) and across into Italy for Venice, Florence and Rome. A frequent return leg went north into modern Austria and Germany and then west towards Amsterdam and then back to the UK. Some tour-makers went the opposite way round, but whichever way they travelled Rome was the high point of the journey, which could be spread over two, three or more years. Lassels was a writer who really led hundreds, if not thousands, out into the field of European society for the good of their education.

Leaders into the Field: Richard Hakluyt

The next series of postings will be about people in relatively modern history who have helped persuade others to explore the world for themselves. So it will not be about the primary explorers, the original pioneers, but about those who inspired more ordinary folk to explore. It will be an eclectic mix from writers like Rousseau to TV presenters like David Attenborough. It won't be comprehensive-how could it be with such a wide field? It won't attempt to provide more than a glimpse of their lives and work: there are plenty of published, detailed studies of each of them. The purpose of these postings is merely to draw together some of the main figures of importance to the development of tourism as education. Several of them were nothing to do with tourism as it is now known, but all of them had an influence on it. Tourism as education has its theories and its practices, even if these have yet to be codified in any form. These people have shaped some of them.

Richard Hakluyt (1152 or 1553-1616) was an ordained priest holding important positions in Tudor England which allowed him to influence national affairs. He did this through the contacts he held and the books that he wrote. Among his achievements, albeit in collaboration with others, were the founding of English colonies in Virginia and the growing interest in world exploration, largely for political and economic reasons. Hakluyt became chaplain and secretary to Sir Edward Stafford, the English ambassador to the French court, enjoying the patronage of the Stafford family until his death. He also became personal chaplain to Sir Robert Cecil, who opened up important posts for him at Westminster Abbey.

His early education had been at Westminster School. His parents had both died when Richard was young so he was given a guardian, his cousin who was also named Richard Hakluyt. On a visit to his guardian he was shown "certain bookes of cosmographie, an universall mappe and the Bible" which inspired an interest in acquiring knowledge, especially of exploration. At Oxford Hakluyt read voraciously amongst manuscripts and printed works on voyages and discoveries.

His first book was a translation of a French account by Jacques Cartier of that explorer's second visit to Canada, although some confusion as to publication dates might mean that it was a book by Hakluyt himself which appeared first. This was 'Divers Voyages Touching the Discovery of America and the Lands Adjacent to the Same' which appeared in 1582. Several other books would follow. He used his contacts to meet and interview sea captains, merchants and other mariners, 'making diligent inquirie of such things as might yield any light unto our westerne discoverie in America'. Time spent with the english ambassador in Paris was partly used to collect information about the Spanish and French activities in that direction. Further books appeared over the years about voyages and the values of overseas possessions. Exploration and later, empire, would prove to have been stimulated by Richard Hakluyt, and his promotion of the colonisation of Virginia and the trading of the East India Company helped turn that interest in geography into national economic growth.

A tradition of discovery through travelling was, thanks to his books, the lasting legacy of this Tudor churchman and scholar. The Hakluyt Society, which was formed in 1846 for printing accounts of voyages and world travelling still publishes material each year today.

Blackwells, who run university bookshops, produce a set of five pocket-size booklets useful to university students. They are written in conjunction with the University of North London and have been around for nearly thirty years, but are still highly relevant today. Shown are four of them. They cost £1.00 each. The set consists of:

- Taking Notes From Lectures,
- Reading for Study,
- How to Write Essays,
- Citing References,
- Grammar book.

Each book is clear and simple, without demanding the longer reading that a full text book on studying at university would demand. It does mean that they can't be comprehensive, but students have basic needs when studying and these booklets are aimed firmly at addressing those problems.

A lot of problems in undergraduate life revolve around the inescapable fact that higher education is a numbers game. In the UK the aim is for around 50% of the population to have taken a post-secondary university course. The result of this political decision is that course management, and therefore teaching, is becoming unwieldy, even uncontrollable. There is a shift of responsibility being made towards students having to educate themselves in ways that made dubious sense when only the very best went to university. 'Distance learning' is often the claimed panacea: not just of students miles away from their tutors doing everything via a computer terminal, but in the sense of large numbers of students with little individual tutor contact time given slabs of reading, group activities, multiple-choice assessment and mechanised feedback-standardised computer codes for common errors or misapplications. All of these can be helpful and do have a place in university. The danger is that they reduce the goals of higher education to a whole series of mechanical instructions about absorbing and then applying knowledge. That is what schools do in the lower and middle grades. Universities are about the handling of concepts and ideas.

University education is about making sense of knowledge through a process of transactions between teachers, students and a stunning range of information sources. Better education demands more discussions, debates and the testing of ideas, not through bullet-point rehearsals of 'facts' but the challenging development of ideas in well-integrated expressions of thoughts. At the heart of the process are two activities which must be in symbiotic relationship: distilling ideas from sources and expressing those ideas anew in essays and verbal debate.

The Blackwell/University of North London booklets concentrate on those activities and it would be well if schools prepared their pupils for higher education by using them as well.

All Roads Led to Rome-1955

This is not a full guide book as such but a free brochure issued by Thomas Cook's to its customers visiting Rome. It contained basic information in three languages-English, Spanish and French. As a production of the 1950s it was internally in two colours but had a full-colour graphic on the cover. Photographs of some of the main sites were accompanied by brief descriptions.

The main aim seems to have been to promote visits and tours organised by the company. The page spread on the right introduces four pages with four tours "by motor coach with guide-lecturer". Of course anyone visiting Rome for leisure was likely to be sightseeing and in need of historical information, but Thomas Cook's had from the very start in 1841 been aimed at educating in an entertaining, informal style. Another sign of the times was the offer of cars ("Go as you please by private automobile"-aimed at American tourists, perhaps) for hire as well as the use of coaches for group tours. The advert opposite the title page (centre) is a reminder that by now, post war, air transport was becoming dominant rather than railways for European travel. It was three years later that more passengers crossed the Atlantic by air rather than ship.

All Roads Led to Rome-1886

By the later nineteenth century the Grand Tour as such was long gone. The Napoleonic Wars had made foreign travel more difficult-though not impossible. From the 1840s the coming of railways made for a shift in the social structure of travel. It became less expensive. Journeys were becoming much faster with the result that there was a much more clear-cut division between the travelling and the destination. A coach had to stop more frequently to change the horses and to spend nigh time at an inn. The journey was interspersed with lots of little destinations as each stop was encountered. Railway trains could run for several hours and through the night if needs be. Dining cars and sleeping accommodation would be added in due course leaving the need for intermediate stops behind. For the most part of the nineteenth century though the restaurant and the overnight hotel would remain as requirements. As the rail network increased the distances and destinations open to choice multiplied. Countries which figured little on the Grand Tour-Spain and some of the German states for example-were available. Steamers working the Mediterranean and Baltic seas were extending the scope of travel further still. The days of the travel agent had arrived-in Britain Thomas Cook, Henry Frame, Dean and Dawson arranged everything necessary and could supply a tour manager capable of handling a few dozen people. The one-to-one approach of the tutor with his solitary student had gone. As mass education spread at the end of the century so did mass tourism. Both movements increased the mental horizons of whole populations, even if they could only experience elementary education and short excursions with their own regions.

The guide book industry expanded to meet a growing demand. Travel books could deliver some kind of satisfaction even to those unable to do any actual travelling. Armchair tourism has always outpaced actual tourism and the enjoyment of spending time reading about a wide choice of places to visit is a necessary precursor to the buying decision. W H Smith's railway bookstalls sold guide books (and others) to the passengers who needed to while away the hours spent travelling. The level of information packed in to the new books became enormous in both scope and depth. While few travellers ventured abroad following their own itinerary and arrangements, they would at least have been better able to make their travel agency journeys better informed. On their return home they would have been equippped to regale their friends and neighbours with not only the places they saw with their own eyes but a very good number that they had only read about.

Karl Baedeker's publishing business began in Koblenz in 1827 when he reprinted a guidebook to the River Rhine. This was followed by the publishing of one of his own. It was successful, so others followed and the name Baedeker became almost synonymous with that of 'guide book'. "Look it up in your Baedeker" is said to have been a phrase in common use, interesting because it also reflected the fact that his books were little travel encyclopedias.

Shown above are a few pages from the ninth edition of "Italy: Handbook for Travellers-second part-Central Italy and Rome", of 1886. This is the English version available through the agency of Dulau and Company of Soho Square in London. It contained 8 maps, 31 plans, a panorama of Rome and masses of other details of places to see, hotels to use and dozens of shops selling statuary, paintings, engravings, books, artists' materials, artists' models with fashionable costumes, furniture, clothing, prints of photographs (postcards were not in common use then), places to hire carriages, places to obtain the services of porters, post offices, churches, events, museums and so on. Itineraries to suit short or long visits were detailed, as were books about the history, culture and current life of the places to be seen. The book itself has a finely-detailed eight pages of history of Rome alone with a chronology of the emporers and popes and page upon page of descriptions of places. It has fold-out maps and plans, but it is text-heavy and lacks the jundreds of colour drawings, photographs and maps that a modern book would have. Even so, it is much more a work of reference than most modern guide books. Only the French series by Hachette, published in Britain by the AA but not available for many years, have attempted anything like the Baedeker detail.

All Roads Led to Rome-1746

"A man who has not been in Italy" said Dr. Johnson in 1776 "is always conscious of an inferiority from his not having seen what it is expected a man should see". Samuel Johnson was referring to the fashion of taking the Grand Tour, the long journey across Europe to complete a young man's education and to prepare him to take his place in society as a figure of power and influence. Usually accompanied by an older man as his tutor, the grand tourist would probably see Paris and other parts of France before crossing the Alps into Italy and spending time in the great centres of the peninsula such as Venice, Florence, Sienna and, of course, Rome. Here lay, to Dr. Johnson's mind, one of the four great sources of England's laws, politics and culture (the Assyrian, Persian, Greek and Roman empires). A catalogue of cities with their churches, palaces and assorted ruins would have to be seen and admired. Foreign habits, some to be copied, others to be avoided, had to be studied. Cultural norms and customs were to be noted, all the more to turn the young milord into an acceptable leader of society once back in England. There were many guide books and histories to help. Then as now they could be read while abroad or studied at home before being placed prominently on the home library shelves to impress the neighbours. They were books like any others of the time-the same sizes, bindings, text styles and mode of illustration would be found. Today a guide book might be pocket sized with waterproof plastic cover and carefully planned referencing system to make them easier to dip into. The early guide books were largely set out for reading cover to cover though they did have contents pages and perhaps indexes for finding important information. Good ones had line drawings made from copper engravings and plans or maps. They often mixed heavy history in with the descriptions of sites to be seen.

Shown above is a copy of one such-Basil Kennet's 'Guide to the Antiquities of Rome" of 1746. It was actually the eleventh edition of a very popular work still to be found by collectors in the lists of dealers. The left-hand picture is of the spine of one copy: the front cover is opened to the right. The leather is worn but still protects the book. The gold-leaf lettering and lining is almost gone and yet it shows something of its old attractiveness and dignity. Opposite the elaborate title page is an engraving of the Duke of Gloucester to whom the book is dedicated (in flowery prose over four subsequent pages). Inside are illustrations on single pages or else printed on thin, folded paper sheets which open out. The maps and plans are collections of tiny sketches of buildings placed roughly in the correct relationship to each other. Other pictorial work shows classical figures drawn from statues or the images struck on coins. Pages of text have ornate drop-capitals at the start of chapters. There are strange items of typography such as linked letters and the letter 's' in three different forms-the normal version that we use and others looking like long or short 'f's, making it more difficult for us to read. The writing style is, to our eyes, over-elaborated and long winded. Image standing in front of the Colosseum on a windy day trying to distill from this kind of description everything you needed to know about what was in front of you. It was a style more suited to the long hours spent in a library when there were few distractions around.

Glossary

Accommodation capacity: The measure of accommodation stock at a defined destination. May be given by various different measures: e.g. number of establishments; number of main units within an establishment (e.g. rooms, caravan stances); capacity in terms of residents (e.g. bedspaces).

Accounting period: Normally one year, the period for which accounts are drawn up.

Accreditation: A procedure to establish if a tourism business meets certain standards of management and operation.

add-on: any component of a package tour that is not included in the package price.

Advanced ecotourism: A level of accreditation consisting of all core criteria as well as some of the advanced certification criteria.

adventure tour: a tour designed around an adventurous activity such as rafting or hiking.

Adventure tourism: A form of tourism in natural areas that incorporates an element of risk, higher levels of physical exertion, and the need for specialised skills.

affinity group: a group sharing a common interest, usually from an organization. See also preformed group.

after-departure charge: expenses such as telephone charges that do not appear on a guest's account at check out.

agent: one who acts or has the power to act as the representative of another. Most frequently in travel anyone other than a principal, such as a retail travel agent, receiving agent, ticket agent, local operator or wholesaler (usage uncommon in No. America).

air sea: a cruise/travel program which includes both air/sea arrangements. Often combined with local hotel arrangements for pre/post stays

airline classes of service: variety of terms used to express a particular type of aircraft cabin service. Classes vary with types of compartments, seating comfort, and amenities, with variation between domestic and international flights, and denoted by a fare code on the ticket.

airline fare: price charged for an airline ticket. Some of the categories are as follows: advance purchase excursion (APEX): heavily discounted excursion fare available on many international routes. Reservations and payment will be required well in advance of departure, with varying penalizes for cancellation; excursion: individual fares that require a round-trip within time limits, discounted from coach fare, limited availability; group: discounts from regular fares for groups; and regular or normal: any unrestricted fare.

All-inclusive: A form of package holiday where the majority of services offered at the destination are included in the price paid prior to departure (e.g. refreshments, excursions, amenities, gratuities, etc).

Allocentric: Of a minority of tourists: adventurous, outgoing, self-confident, independent, needing little tourist infrastructure. Enjoys high contact with locals.

Alternative tourism: In essence, tourism activities or development that are viewed as non-traditional. It is often defined in opposition to large-scale mass tourism to represent small-scale sustainable tourism developments. AT is also presented as an 'ideal type', that is, an improved model of tourism development that redresses the ills of traditional, mass tourism

American plan: type of rate that includes the price of the hotel room, breakfast, lunch and dinner. AP is the common abbreviation. See also room rates.

Antifoul: applied to ship's hull to prevent encrusting of barnacles, seaweed, and other marine organisms.

Artefact: An object; an item of material culture.

Assets: Something of value that will provide future benefit or utility, can be used to generate revenue. Usually owned, so simply described as 'things we own'.

association executive: A full-time professional administrator who is employed by an association and is responsible for planning and promoting annual conventions and association meetings.

attraction: a place, event, building or area which tourists want to visit.

attraction: a natural or man-made facility, location, or activity which offers items of specific interest to tourists.

Auditing: A process to measure and verify the practices of a business.

average room rate: the total guest room revenue for a given period divided by the number of rooms occupied for the same period. Since it can be related to investment, this statistic is frequently used as a measure of economic feasibility.

back to back: term used to describe tours operating on a consistent, continuing basis, usually without time between.

Backpacker: A visitor, for the purpose of a holiday or special event, who stays in a backpackers lodge/hostel.

bed and breakfast: (B & B) overnight accommodations usually in a private home or boarding house, with a full American-style or continental breakfast included in the rate, often without private bath facilities.

Benchmarking: Measuring performance against that of best in class companies, determining how the best-in-class achieve those performance levels and using this information as a basis for your own company's targets, strategies and implementation (Pryor, 1989).

Benchmarking: Process of comparing performance and activities among similar organizations either against an agreed standard or against those that are recognized as being among the best.

Benchmarks: Points of reference or comparison, which may include standards, critical success factors, indicators, metrics.

Best Practice: Operational standards considered the most effective and efficient means of achieving desired outcomes.

bias: preferential display on a reservations computer of a host carrier flight schedule.

biodiversity: a variety of wildlife in an area.

Biological diversity (biodiversity): The variety of life forms and genes they contain, and the ecosystems they form. Biodiversity is usually considered at four levels; genetic diversity, species diversity, community diversity, and ecosystem diversity.

block: a number of rooms, seats, or space reserved in advance, usually by wholesalers, tour operators, or receptive operators who intend to sell them as components of tour packages.

bonding: the guarantee of protection for a supplier or consumer. In the travel industry, certain bonding programs are mandatory. The ARC insists that travel agents be bonded to protect the airlines against defaults. Professional operators and agents buy bonds voluntarily to protect their clients.

bulk fare: fare available only to tour organizers or operators who purchase a specified block of seats from a carrier at a low, non-commissionable price and then have the responsibility of selling the seats, including a commission in their marked-up price.

Bureaucracy: An organisation typified by formal processes, standardisation, hierarchic procedures, and written communication.

business plan: an action plan that entrepreneurs draw up for the purpose of starting a business; a guide to running one's business.

Business Travel or Business Events: Travel for commercial rather than leisure purposes. Business travel is sometimes used as a cover-all to include what are sometimes referred to as the "MICE" markets – meetings, incentives, conferences and exhibitions.

Business travel: Travel for a purpose and to a destination determined by a business, and where all costs are met by that business.

Business Travel: Travel of 1: 365 days duration for the purpose of attending a convention or training, conducting official/government or private business.

cafeteria: a food-service operation of a limited menu, in which customers carry their own trays to seating.

Capacity management: A process that seeks to ensure that their organisations operate at optimum capacity whilst maintaining customer satisfaction levels.

Capital expenditure: The cost of long-term assets; such as computer equipment, vehicles and premises. Importantly these are bought to use over several years and not to resell.

carrier: transportation company such as an airline, motorcoach, cruise line, or railroad which carries passengers and/or cargo carrying capacity: the amount of tourism a destination can handle.

Carrying capacity: The amount of visitor activity that a site or destination can sustain.

Carrying-capacity analysis: Originally a term applied in ecology referring to the maximum number of animals of a given species that a particular habitat could support. In the context of tourism, it refers to the maximum number of tourists a destination can support.

cash flow: monies available to meet the company's daily operating expenses, as opposed to equity, accounts receivable, or other credits not immediately accessible.

Certified Tour Professional: CTP: a designation conferred upon tour professionals who have completed a prescribed course of academic study, professional service, tour employment and evaluation requirements. It is administered by the National Tour Association.

Chain of distribution: The means by which products (package holidays in this instance) are distributed from producers (principals) to consumers (tourists), often via wholesalers and retailers (tour operators and travel agents).

charter operations: (1) term referring the transportation of preformed groups which have the exclusive use of the vehicle. (2) An operator authorized to arrange transportation, however, is not limited to dealing with preformed groups, but can itself form the tour group.

Charter: A legal contract between an owner and an organisation for the hire of a means of transport for a particular purpose. An individual traveller will use an intermediary to arrange to be carried on the transport. Often applied to a flight which is the result of a charter.

charter: to hire the exclusive use of any aircraft, motorcoach, or other vehicle.

circle trip: a journey with stopovers that returns to the point of departure.

city guide: a person who has a speciality of guiding in the city only.

closeout: finalization of a tour, cruise, or similar group travel project after which time no further clients are accepted. Any unsold air or hotel space is released, and final payments are sent to all suppliers.

Coach Tour: A guided bus tour for a group of holiday makers that follows a scheduled itinerary. Visitors purchase all arrangements from the Inbound Tour Operator prior to arrival in NZ.

Code of conduct: Guidelines advising a tourism stakeholder, including tourists, on how to behave in an environmentally responsible manner.

Code of Ethics/Conduct/Practice: Recommended practices based on a system of self regulation intended to promote environmentally and/or socio-culturally sustainable behaviour.

commercial rate: a special rate agreed upon by a company and a hotel. Usually the hotel agrees to supply rooms of a specified quality or better at a flat rate to corporate clients.

commercial recreation system: recreational products, services, and facilities created and operated by privately owned businesses or corporations as opposed to public facilities.

commission: the percentage of a selling price paid to a retailer by a supplier. In the travel industry, travel agents receive commissions for selling tour packages or other services.

common carrier: a privately owned carrier which offers transportation for a fee.

complimentary room: a guest room for which no charge is made. Complimentary rooms with a tour group are usually occupied by the tour manager or driver.

Computer reservation systems (CRS): Computerised Reservation Systems used for inventory management by airlines, hotels and other facilities. CRSs can allow direct access through terminals for intermediaries to check availability, make reservations and print tickets.

concessionaire : a firm which, under contract rights, operates for another party (in many cases, a government agency) food and beverage services, lodging facilities, and other services on-site at an attraction.

concierge: a hotel employee who handles restaurant and tour reservations, travel arrangements, and other details for hotel guests.

conditions: the section or clause of a transportation/tour contract which specifies what is not included and which may spell out the circumstances under which the contract many be invalidated.

conductor, and (in Europe) courier: Tour manager/guide-both terms have roughly the same meaning and are used interchangeably. A person with this title is usually at a professional, well trained level.

confidential tariff: a schedule of wholesale rates distributed in confidence to travel wholesalers and agents. Better known as a net rate.

configuration: the interior arrangement of a vehicle, particularly an airplane. The same airplane, for example, may be configured for 190 coach-class passengers, or it may hold 12 first-class passengers and 170 coach passengers, Configuration is also used in conjunction with how the plane is arranged such as three seats on each side or in larger planes two seats on each side with four middle seats.

confirmed reservation: an oral or written agreement by a supplier that he has received and will honour a reservation. Oral confirmations have no legal weight. Even written or telegraphed confirmations have specified or implied limitations. e.g.: a hotel not honouring a reservation after 6 pm., unless late arrival has been guaranteed in some manner.

Conservation: Can be broadly interpreted as action taken to protect and preserve the natural world from harmful features of tourism, including pollution and overexploitation of resources.

Conservation: The protection and maintenance of nature while allowing for its ecologically sustainable use.

consolidation: cancellation by a charter tour operator of one or more tours/flights associated with a specific charter departure or departure period, with the transfer of passengers to another charter tour/flight to depart on or near the same day.

consolidator: a person or company which forms groups to travel on air charters or at group rates on scheduled flights to increase sales, earn override commissions or reduce the possibility of tour cancellations.

consortium: a loosely knit group of independently owned and managed companies such as travel agencies, tour operators, hotels, or other suppliers, with a joint marketing distribution process.

continental breakfast: at a minimum, a beverage (coffee, tea or milk) and rolls or toast. Fruit juice is often added.

continental plan: a hotel rate which includes a continental breakfast with the overnight room stay.

contract: a legally enforceable agreement between two or more parties.

contractor: an operator who provides services to wholesalers, tour operators and travel agents.

convention and visitors bureau (CVB): a non-profit local organization supported by transient room taxes, government budget allocations, private memberships, or a combination of any of these funding mechanisms. A CVB typically encourages groups to hold meetings, conventions, and trade shows in its area.

Convention or Conference Bureau: Usually a publicly funded organisation charged with the promotion of a town or region for conferences, meetings and exhibitions.

co-op tour: a tour which is sold through a number of wholesalers, cooperatives, or other outlets in order to increase sales and reduce the possibility of tour cancellations.

Cost-benefit analysis: Full analysis of public and private costs and benefits of project.

costing: the process of itemizing and calculating all costs the tour operator will pay on a given tour. Costing is usually the function of the operations manager.

Cost-plus pricing: A method of pricing where an amount, to cover profit, is added to costs to establish the selling price, this is an internally orientated pricing method.

coupon, tour: a voucher that can be exchanged for a travel product.

courier: a European definition for tour manager/guide.

cover charge: a fee, usually a flat amount per person, charged to patrons to cover the cost of music and entertainment.

Critical incident point (CIP): A critical incident point or 'moment of truth' is any event which occurs when the customer has (or even perceives that he has) contact with a service organisation.

Cultural Authenticity: Ensuring the appropriate dreaming stories, spiritual beliefs, history, ceremony and art is attributed to the relevant area.

Cultural tourism: Travel for the purpose of learning about cultures or aspects of cultures.

culture: people's customs, clothing, food, houses, language, dancing, music, drama, literature and religion.

Culture: A set of shared norms and values which establish a sense of identity for those who share them. Typically applied at the level of nation and/or race.

Culture: The sum total of ways of living by a group of human beings that is transmitted from one generation to another.

Customer: "An organization or a person that receives a product" (ISO, 2000a: 10).

customized tour: a tour designed to fit the specific needs of a particular target market.

customs: the common term for a government agency charged with collecting duty on specified items imported into that country. The agency also restricts the entry of persons and forbidden items without legal travel documents.

cut-off date: designated day when the buyer must release or add commitments to their event or tour.

day rate: a reduced rate granted for the use of a guest room during the daytime, not overnight occupancy. Often used when someone needs a display room, office, or is in-transit due to odd airline schedules.

Day visitors: Visitors who arrive and leave the same day, irrespective of why they are travelling.

Decision-making unit (DMU): The combination of inputs to a purchasing decision.

Degradation: Any decline in the quality of natural or cultural resources, or the viability of ecosystems, that is caused directly or indirectly by humans.

deluxe tour: in travel usage, presumably of the highest standard.

Demographic Profile: Characteristics used in research such as age, gender, occupation, income, marital status, place of residence, etc.

departure tax: fee collected from the traveler by the host country at the time of departure.

Dependency theory: This theory maintains that developing countries are kept in a position of dependency and underdevelopment due to existing economic and institutional power structures sustained by leading Western nations. Dependency theorists argue that the policies and activities of multinational corporations, national bilateral and multinational aid agencies such as the World Bank and the International Monetary Fund (IMF) tend to widen the gap between rich and poor countries and perpetuate the dependency of developing nations.

deposit policy: a specified amount or a percentage of the total bill due on a specified date prior to arrival.

deposit: an advance payment required to obtain confirmed space.

deregulation: the act of removing regulations from the travel industry. The Airline Deregulation Act of 1978, which amended the Federal Aviation Act of 1958, provided for the end of the Civil Aeronautics Boards regulating authority over domestic airlines on January 1, 1985, for removing travel agent exclusivity, thus paving the way for carriers to appoint and pay commissions to non-travel agents, and for the removal of antitrust immunity for travel agents. The motorcoach industry was deregulated in 1982.

Designation: The act of conferring a legal status on a building which requires compliance with specific legislation on conservation and preservation.

destination: the end point of a journey.

Destination Management Company (DMC): A company working in a specific destination to handle all bookings and arrangements for tours or conferences, including hotel accommodation, transfers, sightseeing, meetings and special events. Tour operators or conference planners are likely to use the services of a DMC because of their specialist local knowledge.

destination management company: (DMC) a company that provides on-the-scene meetings assistance for corporations and associations.

destination marketing organization: (DMO) a category of membership of the National Tour Association which includes state or provincial tourism offices, convention and visitors bureaus, and chambers of commerce which promote a city, region, or state as a travel destination.

destination: the place to which a traveller is going. In the travel industry, any city, area, or country which can be marketed as a single entity for tourists.

dine-around plan: a plan that permits tourists to dine at a variety of restaurants using vouchers and coupons on a tour.

direct spending: money that goes directly from a tourist into the economy of the destination.

director, tour: a person, usually employed or subcontracted by the tour operator, who accompanies a tour from departure to return, acting as a guide and troubleshooter and performing all functions to make the tour operate. Also see tour manager or escort.

Discretionary income: Money received from employment or other sources which can be freely spent on leisure pursuits (such as travel and tourism) after general living costs, taxation etc. are taken into consideration.

Discrimination: Unequal treatment of persons on grounds which are not justifiable in law, e.g. in the UK, discrimination on the grounds of sex or race.

Distribution: The process employed to provide customers access to the product. For travel products distribution focuses largely on the ways in which the customer can reserve or purchase the product.

Disturbance: Accelerated change caused by human activity or extreme natural events.

Diversification: The process of developing new products for new markets, in order to achieve business growth.

diversity: variety; multiplicity; range; assortment.

domestic escorted tour: a packaged, pre-planned itinerary, including the services of a tour manager (escort) within a traveller s own country.

domestic independent tour: DIT: a custom-made tour of a part of the USA planned exclusively for a client by a travel agent

Domestic supply of tourism commodities: Domestic supply of tourism commodities is defined as the total production in Canada of the tourism commodities which are mainly produced by tourism industries. Not all of domestic supply is purchased by visitors, so that supply exceeds tourism demand for the national tourism indicators (NTI). For example, visitors purchase only a small proportion of food and beverage services, with most going to local consumption. Also, supply does not include imports. For example the sale of a ticket on a non-Canadian airline is excluded from supply.

Domestic tourism: Travel within the country of residence.

Dominant scenic alteration: An alteration in the scenic landscape that is visually obtrusive.

double-occupancy rate: the price per person for a room to be shared with another person; abbreviated ppdo and most often quoted in the industry.

double-room rate: the full price of a room for two people (twice the double-occupancy rate).

downgrade: to move to a lesser level of accommodations or a lower class of service.

Due diligence: Taking what is considered in law to be reasonable care.

Dwell time: Length of time a visitor spends at an attraction or destination. Dwell time is often taken into consideration when setting admission fees as a way of ensuring perceived value for money.

Earth Check™ indicators: Proprietary system belonging to Green Globe 21, which uses carefully selected indicators to measure and benchmark key environmental and social impacts, as well as operational efficiency.

Ecologically sustainable: Using, conserving and enhancing the community's resources so that ecological development is maintained, and the total quality of life can be sustained now and in the future.

eCommerce: Internet facilitated commerce, using electronic means for promoting, selling, distributing, and servicing products.

economy fares or services: in U.S. domestic airline operations, passenger carriage at a level below coach service; in international operations, carriage at a level below first class.

ecosystem: an area where living and non-living things interact.

Ecosystem: A dynamic system of plant, animal, fungal and micro-organism communities, and the associated non-living physical and chemical factors.

ecotourism: a combination of tourism and the environment (e.g. planning before development; sustainability of resources; economic viability of a tourism product; no negative impact on either the environment or local communities; responsibility for the environment from developers, the tourism industry and tourists; environmentally-friendly practices by all parties concerned and economic benefits flowing to local communities).

Ecotourism: Defined by The International Ecotourism Society as 'responsible travel to natural areas that conserves the environment and sustains the well-being of local people'.

Ecotourism: Ecologically sustainable tourism with a primary focus on experiencing natural areas that foster environmental and cultural understanding, appreciation and conservation.

educational tour: tour designed around an educational activity, such as studying art.

endangered species: in severe danger of becoming extinct in the near future unless immediate steps are taken to protect the species.

Energy conservation: Positive initiatives to reduce the consumption of energy to the minimum level required.

environment: the diverse community activities and cultures of a country's inhabitants, as well as its scarce and sensitive natural resources.

Environmental auditing: Inspection of a tourism organisation to assess the environmental impact of its activities.

Environmental education: Formal and informal learning processes that are designed to raise awareness and teach new values, knowledge and skills, in order to encourage more sustainable behaviour.

Environmental impact assessment: A study undertaken to assess the effect of an action upon a specific environment or the social or cultural integrity of a community.

Environmental impact statement: The report resulting from an environmental impact assessment.

Environmental impact: The effects that a community has on the environment as a consequence of its activities.

Environmental management systems: Systems established by tourism organisations with the aim of mitigating negative environmental impacts.

Environmental scanning: The process of collecting information to carry out a systematic analysis of the forces effecting the organisation and identifying potential threats and opportunities with view to generating future strategies.

errors and omissions insurance: insurance coverage equivalent to malpractice insurance, protecting an agents or operators staff if an act of negligence, an error, or an omission occurs which causes a client great hardship or expense.

escort: (1) a person, usually employed or subcontracted by the tour operator who accompanies a tour from departure to return, acting as a troubleshooter. This term is often incorrectly interchanged with courier, conductor, host, manager, director, or leader, since each term designates different duties although they do perform the escort function.

escorted tour: (1) a prearranged travel program, usually for a group, escorted by a tour manager or leader. In a fully conducted tour, the escort will also provide guide service throughout.

escrow accounts: funds placed in the custody of licensed financial institutions for safekeeping. Many contracts in travel require that agents and tour operators maintain customers deposits and prepayments in escrow accounts until the time of service.

ethnic tour: tour designed for people usually of the same heritage travelling to their native origin, or to a destination with ethnic relevance.

European plan: a type of rate that consists of the price of the room only, no included meals.

Evolutionary theories: Theories of tourism which see destinations evolving, in the sense that the types of tourists change, or evolve, over time.

excursion: journey where the traveller returns to the original point of departure.

executive coach: a luxury motorcoach with seating of 25 or fewer with upscale amenities.

Exotic plants: Plants whose genetic stock comes from beyond the area in which they are found.

extensions : an arranged sub-tour offered optionally before or after a tour or cruise at an extra charge.

Externalities: Those costs or benefits arising from production or consumption of goods and services which are not reflected in market prices.

FAM tour: an abbreviation for familiarization tour which is often a complimentary or reduced-rate travel program for travel agents, tour operators, travel writers or others to acquaint them with a specific destination or attraction, thereby helping to stimulate sales.

fixed expense: an expense related to the tour as a whole, which does not vary with the number of passengers such as a meal or a per person entrance to an attraction.

flag carrier: a transportation carrier designated by a country to serve international routes.

flora: all the plants of a particular area.

folio: an itemized record of a guest's charges and credits, maintained in the front office till departure, and can be referred to as guest bill or guest statement.

food cover: a unit of food service provided to a customer. The term is not synonymous with meal because a food cover may comprise only a cup of coffee or bowl of soup.

Force majeure: This is an unforeseeable or uncontrollable situation or train of events that would excuse a breach of contract.

foreign flag: any carrier not registered in the USA (applies to air and sea transportation).

franchise: the right to market a product or service, often exclusively for a specified area by a manufacturer, developer, or distributor in return for a fee.

Frequent Independent Traveller: FIT: custom designed, pre-paid tour with many individualized arrangements. Also used as foreign independent traveller.

full house: a hotel with all guest rooms occupied.

full-service restaurant: a food-service establishment with several menu selections and table service.

function room: room used for functions, also called banquet room.

function: a prearranged, catered group activity, usually held in private room/area.

gateway: the point of access to a country or region, usually an airport or seaport, although certain frontier points and railway stations can be given the designation.

gateway city: city with an international airport.

gateway: city, airport, or area from which a flight or tour departs.

Green Globe/Green Globe 21: GREEN GLOBE 21 is the worldwide benchmarking and certification programme which facilitates sustainable travel and tourism for consumers, companies and communities. It is based on Agenda 21 and principles for Sustainable Development endorsed by 182 governments at the United Nations Rio de Janeiro Earth Summit in 1992.

Greenhouse effect: The trapping of the sun's thermal radiation by gases and water vapour, keeping the surface of the earth warmer than it would be otherwise.

Greenhouse gases: Gases that contribute to the greenhouse affect. These include carbon dioxide, methane and water vapour. One source of greenhouse gases is the burning of fossil fuels, such as oil, gas and coal.

ground operator: a company or individual providing such services as hotel, sightseeing, transfers, and all other related services for groups. See receptive operator.

ground package: often expressed as a percentage (eg. 100% or 110%) of the lowest regular fare for the air travel scheduled.

group leader: an individual, acting as liaison to a tour operator, acts as escort.

group tour: a prearranged, pre-paid travel program for a group usually including all components. Also see packaged tour.

guaranteed tour: a tour guaranteed to operate.

guest account: an itemized record of a guest's charges and credits.

guide: (1) a person qualified to conduct tours of specific localities or attractions (many reliable guides are licensed), (2) an airline, bus, railroad, or ship manual of schedules and fares, usually printed seasonally.

guided tour: a local sightseeing trip conducted by a guide.

head tax: fee charged for arriving and departing passengers in some foreign countries.

heritage: a very broad expression that describes anything that has a link with some past event or person (e.g. cultural heritage refers to past customs and traditions with the unspoken implication that these are worthwhile or creditable).

heritage site: a place that capitalises on its connection with heritage.

Heritage: Things of value that are inherited which people want to keep. Heritage can be natural, cultural, tangible, intangible, personal or collective. Natural heritage is often conserved in places such as reserves and national parks. Cultural heritage practices are often conserved through ongoing traditions and practices.

Heritage: Today's perception of a pattern of events in the past.

High conservation value: Recognition of the great significance of a natural or cultural site.

History: A pattern of events in the past.

host: (1) a representative of the group (organizer) that may arrange optional excursions and answer questions but does not have escort authority (2) liaison to the tour operator or tour manager, or (3) a representative who provides only information or greeting services or who assists at the destination with ground arrangements without actually accompanying the tour.

HRM: Human Resource Management, concerned with the strategic management of human resources to achieve a competitive advantage.

hub and spoke tours: tours which utilize a central destination with side trips of varying length to nearby destinations.

immigration: the process by which a government official verifies a person's passport, visa or origin of citizenship.

Impacts: Effects, which may be either positive or negative, felt as a result of tourism-associated activity. Tourists have at least three kinds of impacts on a destination: economic, sociocultural and environmental. Tourism also has effects on tourists, in terms of possible attitude and behaviour changes.

Impromptu Travel: No arrangements booked in country of destination prior to travel. (Another name for FIT travel).

inbound tour operator: company specializing in domestic tours for foreign visitors in the strictest sense. Can also be used interchangeably with receptive operator.

inbound tour: group of travellers whose trip originated in another city or country.

incentive or incentive commission: See override.

incentive tour: (1) a trip offered as a prize, particularly to stimulate the productivity of employees or sales agents, or (2) the business of operating such travel programs.

incidentals: charges incurred by participants of a tour, but are not included in the tour price.

inclusive tour: tour in which all specific elements – transportation, airfare, hotels, transfers, and other costs – are offered for a flat rate. An inclusive tour does not necessarily cover all costs such as personal items and telephone.

independent contractor: a person contractually retained by another to perform certain specific tasks The other person has no control over the independent contractor other than as provided in the contract. In the context of group travel, a tour manager is often retained by the tour operator, or tour brochure designer/writer might be hired in this capacity.

independent tour: an unescorted tour sold through agents to individuals. For one price, the client guaranteed air travel, hotel room, attraction admissions and (typically) a car rental.

Indigenous people: Indigenous peoples are those who are descendants of the ...

Indigenous species: A species that occurs at a place within its historically known natural range, and forms part of the natural biological diversity of a place.

info-mediaries: Organisations which provide websites/electronic guides as an information resource, sharing other resources such as web links to organisations that sell tourism/travel. The infomediary may be an organisation or company in its own right, or may form part of an individual company's or organisation's customer service.

Information systems: Systems that use information technology to capture, transmit, store, retrieve, manipulate, or display information.

Infrastructure: Construction needed to support economic development.

Innovative best practice: A practice that is considered to be of the highest quality, excellence, or standing – a leader in the field.

Intangibility: The characteristic of not being touchable: a good is tangible whereas a service is intangible.

Intermediary: An organisation within the chain of distribution whose function is to facilitate the supply of a given product from producers to consumers. In the travel industry examples are travel agencies and tourism information offices.

intermediate carrier: a carrier that transports a passenger or piece of baggage as part of an inter-line movement, but on which neither the point of origin or destination is located.

intermodal tour: tour using several forms of transportation such as airplanes, motorcoaches, cruise ships, and trains to create a diversified and efficient tour package.

Interpretation: An educational process that is intended to stimulate and facilitate people's understanding of place, so that empathy towards, conservation, heritage, culture and landscape is developed.

Interpretation: Revealing the significance and meanings of natural and cultural phenomena to visitors, usually with the intent of providing a satisfying learning experience and encouraging more sustainable behaviour.

Introduced species: A translocated or alien species found at a place outside its historically known natural range, as a result of the intentional or accidental dispersal by human activities. Includes genetically modified organisms.

itinerary: the travel schedule provided by a travel agent or tour operator for the client. A proposed or preliminary itinerary may be rather vague or very specific. A final itinerary spells out all details, including flight numbers, departure times, and similar data, as well as describing planned activities.

land operator: a company that provides local services, see also ground/receptive operator.

lead time: advance time between initiating a tour and its departure date.

Leadership: Influencing and directing the performance of group members towards the achievement of organisational goals

leg: portion on a journey between two scheduled stops.

Leisure travel: Travel undertaken for pleasure and unrelated to paid work time.

Length of stay: No of nights spent in one destination. Most tourist boards seek to find ways of increasing visitors' length of stay.

letter of agreement: a letter from the buyer to the supplier accepting the terms of the proposal. This may also be the suppliers initial proposal that has been initialed by the buyer.

Lifecycle: The particular pattern through which a destination evolves.

Limits of acceptable change: Environmental indicators that can monitor changes over time as a consequence of tourism.

load factor: average number of seats occupied, e.g. motorcoach or air.

local: belonging to a particular place or region.

low season: that time of the year at any given destination when tourist traffic, and often rates, are at their lowest. Also referred to as off-peak or off-season.

macro business: a large, formal business that employs many people.

manifest: final official listing of all passengers and/or cargo aboard a transportation vehicle or vessel.

Market orientated pricing: A method of pricing that benchmarks prices against competitors when deciding on price.

market segment: the concept of dividing a market in parts.

Market segmentation: Market segmentation is a marketing approach that encompasses the identification of different groups of customers with different needs or responses to marketing activity. The market segmentation process also considers which of these segments to target.

Mass tourism: Traditional, large scale tourism commonly, but loosely used to refer to popular forms of leisure tourism pioneered in southern Europe, the Caribbean, and North America in the 1960s and 1970s.

master account: the guest account for a particular group or function that will be paid by the sponsoring organization

master bill: all items contracted by the operator and supplier that will be paid by the operator.

MAVERICS: Characterisation of tourists of the future as multi-holidaying, autonomous, variegated, energised, restless, irresponsible, constrained and segmented.

Mediation: An attempt to settle a dispute using a neutral third party.

micro business: a small, often informal, business that employs very few people.

Minimal impact practices: Deliberate human behaviour that reduces the negative impact of people or objects on the environment to a minimum.

minimum charge: the amount that each customer must pay no matter what is consumed. For example: a two-drink minimum in a club.

minimum land package: the minimum tour expressed in terms of cost and ingredients that must be purchased to qualify for an airline inclusive tour, or contract bulk inclusive tour fare. Such packages usually include a certain number of nights lodging, other specified ingredients such as sightseeing tours and/or entertainment and/or car rental. The minimum rate for the combined air fares and

Mode of travel: The type of transport used to make a journey between an origin and a destination, and can include walking and cycling as well as all forms of mechanical transport.

Monitoring: The ongoing review and assessment of the natural or cultural integrity of a place in order to detect changes in its condition with reference to a baseline condition.

Motivation: Internal and external forces and influences that drive an individual to achieving certain goals.

motorcoach tour operator: a company that creates tours in which group members are transported via motorcoach on a planned itinerary of stops.

motorcoach: a large, comfortable, well-powered bus that can transport groups and their luggage over long distances

mystery tour: a tour to an unpublished destination — passengers get a surprise!

nationwide tour: sold to people throughout the nation.

Natural area: Areas that exist in or are formed by nature which are not artificial, and can include cultural aspects.

natural attraction: a tourist attraction that has not been made or created by people.

natural disaster: a destructive force (e.g. earthquake, flood, volcanic eruption).

Nature Tourism (Nature-based tourism): Ecologically sustainable tourism with a primary focus on experiencing natural areas.

Negligence: Failing to exercise what is legally considered to be reasonable care.

net wholesale rate: a rate usually slightly lower than the wholesale rate, applicable to groups when components are specifically mentioned in a tour brochure. The rate is marked up by wholesale sellers to cover tour costs.

no show: guest with confirmed reservations who does not arrive and has not cancelled.

No-frills: A low-cost scheduled travel package based on minimising operator service and costs, which are passed to the consumer as a low price.

Non-profit: Non-profit organisations are those which are driven by non-financial organisational objectives, i.e. other than for profit or shareholder return.

occupancy: the percentage of available rooms occupied for a given period. It is computed by dividing the number of rooms occupied for a period by the number of rooms available for the same period.

off-peak: a period in which a hotel or attraction is not in its busiest season.

Off-site management: Provision of pre-visit (or otherwise off-site) educational and interpretive materials to raise awareness of management issues and encourage minimal impact behaviour.

on-demand public transportation: transportation services, such as taxicabs that do not have regular schedules.

On-site assessment: A site-visit by a quality systems member to verify material submitted during the accreditation application.

On-site management: Management of visitor impacts and behaviour on-site through the use of signs, formed tracks or board-walks, barriers and the physical presence of management staff.

Operations management: "The ongoing activities of designing, reviewing and using the operating system, to achieve service outputs as determined by the organization for customers" (Wright, 1999).

operations: performing the practical work of operating a tour or travel program. Operations usually involves the in-house control and handling of all phases of the tour, with both suppliers and clients.

option date: the date agreed upon when a tentative agreement is to become a definite commitment by the buyer

option: tour feature extension or side trip offered at extra cost.

Organisation: A deliberate arrangement of people to achieve a particular purpose.

outbound operator: a company which takes groups from a given city or country to another city or county.

outbound tour: any tour that takes groups outside a given city or country, opposite of inbound.

outfitter: a business that provides services or equipment at a recreational facility.

overbook: accepting reservations for more space than is available.

override: a commission over and above the normal base commission percentage.

pacing: The scheduling of activities within an itinerary to make for a realistic operation and give a certain balance of travel time, sightseeing, events and free time.

package tour: a combination of several travel components provided by different suppliers, which are sold to the consumer as a single product at a single price.

packager: an individual or organization that coordinates and promotes the package tours and establishes operating guidelines for the tour.

passport: government document permitting a citizen to leave and re-enter the country.

pax: industry abbreviation for passengers.

peak fare, rate, or season: highest level of charges assessed during a year.

Perishability: The characteristic of being perishable. In tourism the term is used to describe, for example, a particular hotel room on a specific night or a particular seat on a specific flight: they cannot be 'stored' and sold later, so they are perishable.

Personal disposable income: The amount an individual has left over for personal expenditure on goods and services, after payment of personal direct taxes, national insurance and pension contributions.

Person-trip: A Person-trip for non-residents begins each time a non-resident traveller enters Canada. The person-trip concludes when the traveller leaves Canada. For residents, each time a person departs from Canada a person-trip begins. It ends when the traveller returns to Canada.

Physical evidence: The tangible evidence of a service, including everything which can be seen, touched, smelt and heard.

Pollution: Harmful effects on the environment as a by-product of tourism activity. Types include: air; noise; water; and aesthetic.

port of entry: point at which persons enter a country where customs and immigration services exist.

Positioning: The process of ensuring potential customers have a desired perception of a product or service, relative to the competition.

pre-and post-trip tours: optional extension packages before or after a meeting, tour or convention.

preformed group: a tour group in existence prior to the tour, the members of which share a common destination and purpose.

Price elasticity of demand: A measure of the variability that can be expected in sales when prices are changed. Unity elasticity would see equal increase in sales to in reaction to a decrease in price. Inelastic demand would not change when prices went down or up.

Price elasticity of demand: A relationship between the changes in prices charged for a good or service (here taken as hotel rooms) and the change in the amount demanded.

primary market: a country in which the US Travel & Tourism Admin (USTTA) maintains an office.

Process control: A systematic use of tools to identify significant variations in operational performance and output quality, determine root causes, make corrections and verify results (Evans and Lindsay, 1999:345).

Process design: Involves specifying all practices needed, flowcharting, rationalisation and error prevention (Rao et. al., 1996:540-541).

Process improvement: A proactive task of management aimed at continual monitoring of a process and its outcome and developing ways to enhance its future performance (James, 1996:359).

Process: "A set of interrelated or interacting activities which transforms inputs into outputs" (ISO, 2000a:7).

Product: "The result of a process" (i.e. output), which may be either a service, or a good (hardware or processed materials) or software (e.g. information) or their combination (ISO, 2000a:7).

Profit: The excess of revenue over expenses, if expenses exceed revenues in a given period the organisation will make a loss.

proof of citizenship: a document, necessary for obtaining a passport, that establishes one is nationality.

Protected area: Any area of land and/or sea dedicated to the conservation, protection and maintenance of biodiversity and natural and cultural resources, which is managed through legal or other means.

protected: guarantee by a supplier or wholesaler to pay commissions, plus all refunds to clients, on pre-paid, confirmed bookings regardless of subsequent cancellation of a tour or cruise.

Public policy: Is whatever governments choose to do or not to do (Thomas Dye 1992: 2). Such a definition covers government action, inaction, decisions and non-decisions as it implies a very deliberate choice between alternatives (see Hall and Jenkins 1995).

Quality: The degree to which a set of inherent characteristics of a product fulfils customer requirements (ISO, 2000a).

Qualmark: Classification and grading system for the New Zealand tourism industry, using 5 star system.

Rack Rate: Retail price of accommodation, airfares, activities/attractions.

Regulation: Control through formalised processes.

release: (1) signed form giving the tour operator permission to use a persons name, picture or statement in an advertisement; (2) to give up space, as in returning unsold airline reservations.

Renewable energy: Energy sources that are practically inexhaustible. For example solar, hydro and wind energy.

Requirements: Stated, generally implied (as a custom or common practice for the organisation, its customers and other interested parties) or obligatory needs (ISO, 2000a).

resort: a hotel, motel or condominium complex located in an area associated with recreation and leisure, such as the mountains or the seashore. Normally offer facilities for sports and recreational activities.

responsibility clause: that section of a brochure that spells out the conditions under which a tour is sold. The clause should name the party responsible for the tour financially.

Responsible tourism: Type of tourism which is practised by tourists who make responsible choices when choosing their holidays. These choices reflect reponsible attitudes to the limiting of the extent of the sociological and environmental impacts their holiday may cause.

Restoration: Returning existing habitats to a known past state, or to an approximation of the natural condition, through repairing degradation, removing introduced species, and revegetating using native locally occurring species.

retailer: (1) travel agents or (2) one who sells directly to the consumer.

Revenue expenditure: The cost of resources consumed or used up in the process of generating revenue, generally referred to as expenses.

Revenue management: Revenue management is a management approach to optimising revenue, often based on managing revenues around capacity and timing (yield management), for different market segments or from different sources of funding.

risk monies: funds that an agency would not recoup should a tour not take place, such as nonrefundable deposits, promotional expenses, and printing costs.

room rates: day rate: usually one-half the regular rate for a room during the day up to 5 pm; flat rate: a specific room rate for a group agreed upon by the hotel/group in advance; group rate: rate based on an agreed upon minimum number of rooms used, also called flat rate; net group rate: a wholesale rate for group business (usually a minimum of 10 and 15 people) to which an operator may add a markup if desired; net wholesale rate: a rate usually lower than the group rate, applicable to groups or individuals when a hotel is specifically mentioned in a tour folder; published rate: a full rate available to or advertised to the public, The rate can change, depending upon the season. Also known as rack rate.

room service: food or beverages served in a guest's room.

run-of-the-house rate: flat rate for which a hotel or motel agrees to offer any of its available rooms to a group. Final assignment of the rooms is the discretion of the hotel.

Sales: Revenue from ordinary activities: not necessarily cash.

Seasonality: A phenomenon created by either tourism supply or demand (or both) changing according to the time of the year.

sector: a part or branch of the whole industry that provides particular goods and/or services.

series operator: a travel agent, wholesaler, tour operator, or broker who blocks space in advance for a series of movements over a given period of time, not necessarily on a back-to-back basis.

service: work done for the benefit of another.

service charge: (1) a specified percentage of a hotel's daily rate (usually 10% or 15 %) charged to the guest, who in return is relieved of the responsibility for tipping; (2) a fee charged to a client by a travel agent in addition to the commissions paid to him or her by the principals.

service delivery: the manner in which customer needs are met.

Service encounter: The moments of interface between customer and supplier.

Service marketing mix: The addition of People, Physical Evidence and Process to the four areas of activity more usually associated with marketing products,: Price, Place, Promotion and Product.

service provider: a person or company that supplies a particular service.

service: non-physical, intangible attributes that management controls, including friendliness, efficiency, attitude, professionalism, and responsiveness.

Servicescape: The location in which the service encounter takes place.

shore excursion: a land tour, usually available at ports of call and sold by cruise lines or tour operators to cruise passengers.

short haul: 1-3 hour flight.

shoulder season: period when there is neither a high nor low demand for a destination, usually falling in the spring or fall months for most areas.

single supplement: an extra charge assessed to a tour purchased for single accommodations.

site destination selection company: company that investigates and suggests potential meeting sites to suit corporate or association needs.

Skills gaps: Employers perceive existing employees have lower skill levels than needed to achieve business objectives, or where new, apparently trained and qualified for specific occupations, entrants still lack requisite skills.

Skills shortages: Lack of adequately skilled individuals in the labour market due to low unemployment, sufficiently skilled people in the labour market but not easily geographically accessible or insufficient appropriately-skilled individuals.

Small business: A small business is one which has a small number of employees, profit and/or revenue. Often these are owner-managed, with few specialist managers. Some definitions of small businesses distinguish between businesses with under 10 employees, which are micro-businesses, and those with 10-49 employees, which are classified as small businesses.

SME(s): Small and Medium Enterprises.

Social: Relating to human society and interaction between its members.

souvenir: a product purchased by a tourist as a reminder of a holiday.

special event tour: a tour designed around a particular event, e.g.: Mardi Gras.

special interest tour: a tour designed to appeal to clients with a curiosity or concern about a specific subject. Most special interest tours provide an expert tour leader and usually visit places and/or events only relevant to that interest.

special market: a foreign country with high potential for US inbound travel which does not have an office of the US Travel and Tourism Administration (USTTA).

Stakeholder: Any person, group or organisation with an interest in, or who may be affected by, the activities of another organisation.

state travel office: an official government agency or privately run, non-profit organization responsible for travel development and promotion of a state or province.

Statute: The law as made by parliament, e.g. in the UK, the Disability Discrimination Act (1995). A statute is made up of many parts called 'sections' or 'provisions'.

Statutory instrument: The vast majority of delegated legislation in the UK is in the form of statutory instruments governed by the Statutory Instruments Act 1946.

step-on guide: an independent guide who comes aboard a motorcoach to give an informed overview of the city or attraction to be toured.

Strategic information systems: Systems designed to support the strategic management decision processes and implementation.

Strategy pyramid: A visual way of representing the different levels of the strategy conceptualisation and implementation process. The most general assumptions are shown at the apex and the practical, implementation actions are at the base.

subcontractor: a local operator who provides services for a wholesaler.

supplier: the actual producer of a unit of travel merchandise or service such as a hotel or restaurant.

Suppliers: Individuals, companies or other organisations which provide goods or services to a recognisable customer or consumer.

surety bond: insurance to guarantee that an insure will carry out the specific work he or she was hired to do.

sustainable: something which can be kept in the same or a better condition for the future.

Sustainable development: Development carried out in such a way as to meet the needs of the present without compromising the ability of future generations to meet their needs.

Sustainable tourism: According to the World Tourism Organisation, this is "envisaged as leading to management of all resources in such a way that economic, social and aesthetic needs can be fulfilled with maintaining cultural integrity, essential ecological processes, biological diversity, and life support systems."

Sustainable tourism: Tourism that can be sustained over the long term because it results in a net benefit for the social, economic, natural and cultural environments of the area in which it takes place.

Sustainable tourism: Tourism that is economically, socioculturally and environmentally sustainable. With sustainable tourism, sociocultural and environmental impacts are neither permanent nor irreversible.

themed tour: a tour designed around a specific theme such as fall foliage, also a special interest tour.

tour basing fare: a reduced-rate excursion fare available only to those who buy pre-paid tours or packages. Tour basing fares include inclusive tours, group inclusive tours, incentive tours, contract bulk inclusive tours, and group round-trip inclusive tours.

tour broker: a person or company which organizes and markets tours.

tour catalog: a publication by tour wholesalers listing their tour offerings.

tour conductor: see tour manager/director.

tour consultant: individual within an agency selling and advising clients regarding a tour. The consultant is sometimes a salesperson with particular expertise in escorted tour sales.

tour departure: the date of the start by any individual or group of a tour program, also used in referral to the entire operation of that single tour.

tour escort: the tour company staff member or independent contractor who conducts the tour. Often called the tour manager or tour director. It is technically a person that only escorts the group and does not have charge of the commentary portion.

tour leader: usually a group leader, also see escort.

tour manager: a person employed as the escort for a group of tourists, usually for the duration of the entire trip, perhaps supplemented by local guides. The terms tour director, leader, escort,

tour manual: (1) a summary of facts about a companys rules, regulations, and official procedures; (2) a compendium of facts about a destination, including its attractions, accommodations, geography, and special events, used by destination marketing organizations to attract tour operators and visitors and their area.

tour menu: a menu that limits group clients to two or three choices at a special price.

tour operator: a person or company which creates and/or markets inclusive tours and subcontracts with suppliers to create a package. Most tour operators sell through travel agents and/or directly to clients.

tour option: any component of a package tour that is not included in the package price, but may be purchased as an added feature to extend the length of the package or enhance the trip.

tour order: a coupon given to the purchaser of a tour package, identifying the tour, the seller, and the fact that the tour is pre-paid. It is used as a form of proof of payment and receives vouchers for meals, porterage, transfers, entrance fees, and other expenses. Also see tour vouchers.

tour organizer: person who locates and creates groups for preformed tours. The tour organizer is often compensated only with a free trip.

tour vouchers: documents issued by tour operators to be exchanged for tour components, also called coupons.

tour: any prearranged journey to one or more destinations.

Tourism Commodity: Tourism Commodity is one for which a significant part of its total demand in Canada comes from visitors.

Tourism Demand: Tourism Demand is defined as the spending of Canadian and non-resident visitors on domestically produced commodities. It is the sum of tourism domestic demand and tourism exports.

Tourism Domestic Demand: Tourism Domestic Demand is the spending in Canada by Canadian visitors on domestically produced commodities.

Tourism Employment: Tourism Employment is a measure of employment in tourism and non-tourism industries. It is based on an estimate of jobs rather than "hours of work". Thus, someone who works 10 hours a week counts for as much, by this measure, as someone who works 50 hours a week.

Tourism Exports: Tourism Exports is spending by foreign visitors on Canadian-produced goods and services. It includes spending that may take place outside of Canada, for instance, the purchase of an airline ticket from a Canadian international carrier, to travel to Canada.

Tourism flows: The major movements of tourists from specific home areas to destinations.

tourism geography: the knowledge of countries, regions, major cities, gateways, famous icons, monuments, building structures, and geographical features such as rivers, seas, mountains, deserts and time zones.

Tourism income multiplier (TIM): Exaggerated effect of a change in tourism expenditure on an area's income.

tourism industry: a group of businesses that provide services and facilities for consumption by tourists.

Tourism Industry: Tourism Industry is an industry that would cease to exist or would continue to exist only at significantly reduced levels of activity in the absence of tourism.

tourism infrastructure: roads, railway lines, harbours, airport runways, water, electricity, other power supplies, sewerage disposal systems and other utilities to serve not only the local residents but also the tourist influx (suitable accommodation, restaurants and passenger transport terminals form the superstructure of the region).

tourism product: different things to the various members of the tourism industry. To the hotel it is 'guest-nights'. To the airline it is the 'seats flown' and the 'passenger miles'. To the museum, art gallery or archaeological site, the product is measured in terms of the number of visitors. For the tourist the product is the complete experience resulting from the package tour or travel facility purchased, from the time they leave home until their return.

Tourism satellite account: System of accounting at national or regional level which reveals the total direct impact of tourism on the economy.

Tourism System: A framework that identifies tourism as being made up of a number of components, often taken to include the tourist, the tourist generating region, the transit route region, the tourist destination and the tourism industry (Leiper, 1990).

tourism: the business of providing and marketing services and facilities for leisure travellers. Thus, the concept of tourism is of direct concern to governments, carriers, and the lodging, restaurant, and entertainment industries, and of indirect concern to virtually every industry and business in the world.

Tourism: The definition of tourism used in the national tourism indicators (NTI) is that adopted by the World Tourism Organization and the United Nations Statistical Commission: "the activities of persons travelling to and staying in places outside their usual environment for not more than one consecutive year for leisure, business and other purposes."

tourist: one who travels for a period of 24 hours or more in a place other than that in which he or she usually resides, whose purpose could be classified as leisure (whether for recreation, health, sport, holiday, study or religion), business, family, mission or meeting.

Tourist attractions: Tourist attractions are defined as being destinations for visitors' excursions which are routinely accessible to visitors during opening hours. Visitors can include local residents, day-trippers or people who are travelling for business or leisure purposes. Formal definitions exclude shops, sports stadia, theatres and cinemas, as these meet a wider purpose, although in practice tourists may consider the excluded categories to be tourist attractions.

tourist card: a kind of visa issued to tourists prior to entering a country (required in addition to a passport or other proof of citizenship).

tourist facility: a feature created for utilisation by tourists.

tourist route: a route developed to attract tourists to an area to view or experience something unique to that area (e.g. wine route, whale route, heritage route, battlefield route).

tourist trend: a general tendency to visit a country, region or destination or to pursue a specific tourist activity.

Tourist: Anyone who spends at least one night away from home, no matter what the purpose.

TOWS matrix: Uses a SWOT analysis to develop strategies by matching strengths with opportunities, using opportunities to reduce weaknesses, using strengths to overcome threats, and reducing weaknesses and avoiding threats.

Tracking Research: Ongoing research conducted at regular intervals to track changes in specific factors, for example, potential customers' intention to travel to NZ.

tracking: a cause of action or method of monitoring, such as tracking the number of tours that come into a specific destination.

transfer: local transportation, sometimes including porterage, as from one carrier terminal to another, from terminal to a hotel, or from a hotel to an attraction.

transit visa: visa allowing the holder to stop over in a country to make a travel connection or brief visit.

transit: process of changing planes without going through security and/or customs.

travel agent/agency: a person or firm qualified to arrange for all travel components.

trip director: an escort for an incentive company. Larger companies reserve this title for the person who directs all personnel and activities for a trip.

upgrade: to move to a better accommodation or class of service.

value season: a time of year when prices are lower than peak, also called low or off-season.

Variability: Because the production and the consumption of a tourism experience are inseparable and because differing circumstances and people will affect each experience, those experiences are prone to variance and create a challenge for tourism managers to achieve consistency of standards.

variable cost: a cost that changes according to how many people take a tour, such as motorcoach expenses.

Virtual organisation: Organisation in which major processes are outsourced to partners.

visa waiver: a program to eliminate the visa requirement for selected countries.

visa: stamp of approval recorded in a passport to enter a country for a specific purpose.

Visitors: A broader category than 'tourist', includes tourists and same-day visitors.

Visitors: Visitors are persons who undertake tourism as defined above. They are referred to as either tourists (those who stay overnight or longer in the place visited), or same-day visitors.

volume incentive: see override.

waitlist: list of clients awaiting transportation or accommodations at times when they are not available, confirmed as a result of subsequent cancellations.

Working Capital: Operational assets and liabilities needed for everyday operation, e.g. cash or bank overdraft, stock and trade creditors, known as net current assets/liabilities.

World Heritage Area: Land of cultural and/or natural significance inscribed on the World Heritage List.

world heritage site: a site designated by UNESCO as being of special historical, cultural or natural importance.

Yield Management: "A revenue maximization technique which aims to increase net yield through the predicted allocation of available ... capacity to predetermined market segments at optimal price" (Donaghy et al., 1997a).

Zoning: Different eco-systems may be zoned in terms of their robustness to pressures from tourism in an attempt to mitigate environmental damage.

Bibliography

Andrew, N; Flanagan, S & Ruddy, J: *Tourism Destination Planning*, Dublin, Dublin Institute of Technology, 2002.

Apostolopous, Y and Leivadi, S: *Sociology of Tourism, The: Theoretical And Empirical Investigations*, London, Retailed, 1996.

Ashworth, G J and Dietvorst, A G J: *Tourism and Spatial Transformations: Implications For Policy and Plan*, Wallingford, CAB International, 1995.

Ashworth, Greg and Larkham, P J: *Building a New Heritage: Tourism, Culture & Identity in the New Europe*, London, Routledge,1994.

Baum, Tom: *We're all Going on a Summer Holiday: Images of Tourism Past and Person*, Buckingham, University of Buckingham, 1995.

Beeho, A & Prentice, R: *Conceptualising The Experiences of Heritage Tourists*, 1997.

Beeton, Sue:: *Film-Induced Tourism*, Clevedon, Channel View, 2005.

Belie et al.: *Tourism and the Inner City: An Evaluation of / Impact of Grant Assist*, London, HMSO, 1990.

Benefice, Brian G, and Cooper, Chris: *Geography of Travel and Tourism*, The, London, Heinemann, 1987.

Bolshevism, Germy: *Coping with Tourists: European Reactions to Mass Tourism*, Oxford, Berghahn Books, 1995.

Boniface, Priscilla and Fowler, Peter: *Heritage and Tourism: In the Global Village*, London, Retailed, 1993.

Bosselman, Fred P: *In The Wake of the Tourist: Managing Special Places in Eight Countries*, Washington, DC, Conservation Foundation, The, 1978.

Briguglio, L and Vella, Leslie: *Competitiveness of the Maltese Islands in Mediterranean in Tourism*, Chichester, John Wiley, 1995.

Brown, Dona: *Inventing New England: Regional Tourism in the Nineteenth Century*, Washington DC, Smithsonian Institution, 1995.

Brunt, Paul: *Market Research in Travel and Tourism*, Oxford, Butterworth Heinemann, 1997.

Burkart, A and Medlik, S: *Management of Tourism*, The, London, Heinemann, 1975.

Chambers, Erve: *Native Tours: The Anthropology of Travel and Tourism*, Prospect Heights, Waveland Press, 2000.

Chandler, Harry and Carter, John: *Chandler's Travels: A Tour of the Life of Harry Chandler*, London, Quiller Press, 1985.

Clark, Colin: *Tourist Services and Guidance: Heritage and Information*, Strasbourg, Council of Europe Press, 1989.

Coccosis, Harry and Nijkamp, Peter: *Sustainable Tourism Development*, Aldershot, Avebury, 1995.

Cohen, Erik: *Towards a Sociology of International Tourism*, 1972.

Dann, Graham M S: *Language of Tourism*, The, Wallingford, CAB International, 1996.

Davidson, R and Maitland, R: *Tourism Destinations, London*, Hodder and Stoughton, 1997.

Davidson, Rob: *Travel and Tourism in Europe*, Harlow, Addison Wesley Longman, 1998.

Ecotec: *Calderdale: Tourism Impact Study*, Calderdale, ECOTEC/Calderdale Council, 1990.

Edensor, Tim: *Tourists at the Taj*, London, Retailed, 1998.

Edgell, David L: *International Tourism Policy, New York*, Van Nostrand and Reinhold, 1990.

Elliott, James: *Tourism: Politics and Public Sector Management*, London, Retailed, 1997.

Fairgrieve, James: *Geography in School*, London, University of London Press, 1926.

Foster, Douglas: *Travel and Tourism Management*, London, Macmillan Educational, 1985.

Frechtling, Douglas C: *Practical Tourism Forecasting*, Oxford, Butterworth Heinemann, 1996.

Gamble, P. R: *The Educational challenge for Hospitality and Tourism Studies*, Tourism Management, 13, 1992.

Ghimire, Krishna: *The Native Tourist*: Mass Tourism within Developing Regions, London, Earthscan, 2001.

Goeldner, C. R: *The Evaluation of Tourism as an Industry and a Discipline, Paper Presented to*, International Conference for Tourism Educators, Guildford, University of Surrey, 1988.

Gunn, Clare and Var, Turgut: *Tourism Planning*, London, Retailed, 2002.

Hall, C Michael *Tourism Planning: Policies, Processes and relationships*, Harlow, Prentice Hall, 2000.

Hall, Colin and Jenkins, John: *Tourism and Public Policy*, London, Retailed, 1995.

Hall, Colin Michael: *Tourism and Politics*: Policy, Power, & Place, Chichester, Wiley, 1994.

Harrison, Lyndon: *Tourism Means Jobs*, Chester, Lyndon Harrison, 1996.

Harron, S and Weiler, B: *Ethnic Tourism*, Belhaven/Wiley, 1992.

Inkpen, G: *Information Technology for Travel and Tourism*, Harlow, Addison Wesley Longman, 1998.

Inskeep, Edward *National and Regal Tourism Planing*: Methodologies & Case Studies, London, Routledge/WTO, 1994.

Irwin, William *The New Niagara*: *Tourism, Technology, And the Landscape of Niagara Fal*, University Park, PA, University of Pennsylvania, 1996.

Jack, G and Phipps, A: *Tourism and Intercultural Exchange*: *Why Tourism Matters*, Clevedon, Channel View, 2005.

Jakle, John: *Tourist, The: Travel in Twentieth Century North America*, University of North Nebraska, 1985.

Jennings, Gayle: *Tourism Research*, Chichester, Wiley, 2001.

Judd, D R: *Promoting Tourism* in US Cities, 1995.

Karski, A: *Urban Tourism* - A Key to Urban Regeneration?, 1990.

Kotler, Philip et al: *Marketing Places*: *Attracting Investment, Industry & Tourism etc*, New York, free press, 1993.

Labarge, Margaret Wade: *Medieval Travellers*: *The Rich and Restless*, London, Hamish Hamilton, 1982.

Laws, Eric: *Tourist Destination Management: Issues, Analysis & Policies*, London, Routledge, 1995.

Leed, Eric J: *Mind of the Traveller, The: From Gilgamesh to Global Tourism*, New York, 1991.

MacCannell, Dean: *Tourist, The: A New Theory of the Leisure Class*, London, Macmillan, 1976.

Machin, Alan: *Retracing the Steps: Tourism as Education, Janus*, Fin, ATLAS / FUNTS, 2001.

Opperman, Martin and Chon, Kye-Sung: *Tourism in Developing Countries, London*, International Thomson Business Press, 1997.

Patullo, Polly: *Last Resorts*: *The Cost of Tourism in the Caribbean*, London, Cassell, 1996.

Pearce, Douglas: *Tourism Today*: *A Geographical Analysis*, Harlow, Longman, 1995.

Pearce, P L: *Social Psychology Of Tourist Behaviour*, The, Oxford, Pergamon, 1982.

Peters, M: *International Tourism*, London, Hutchinson, 1969.

Ringer, Greg: *Destinations: Cultural Landscapes of Tourism*, London, Routledge, 1998.

Ritchie, Brent: *Managing Educational Tourism*, Clevedon, Channel View, 2003.

Robinson, H: *Geography of Tourism*, A, London, Macdonald and Evans, 1976.

Robinson, M, Evans, E & Chalazion, P: *Tourism and Cultural Change, Sunderland*, Business Education Publishers Ltd, 1996.

Rogers, H Anthea and Slinn, Judy A: *Tourism: Management of Facilities*, London, Pitman: M & E, 1993.

Schwaninger, M: *Trends in Leisure and Tourism for 2000 - 2010*, Prentice Hall, 1989.

Scottish Tourist Board: *Visitor Attractions: A Development Guide*, Edinburgh, Scottish Tourist Board, 1991.

Seaton, A V et al: *Tourism: The state of the Art*, Chichester, John Wiley, 1994.

Shaw, G and Williams, A: *Tourism and Tourism Spaces*, London, Sage, 2004.

Stevens, Terry: *Island Tourism*: Malta, , WTO, 1993.

Trench, R: *Travellers in Britain*, London, Aurum, 1990.

Tribe, John *Corporate Strategy for Tourism, London*, International Thomson Business Press, 1997.

Urry, John: *Tourist Gaze*, The, London, Sage, 1990.

Van den Berg et al: *Urban Tourism: Performance and Strategies in Eight European Cities*, Aldershot, Avebury, 1995.

Van Harssel, Jan: *Tourism: An Exploration*, New York, Prentice Hall, 1994.

Veal, A: *Leisure and Tourism*: Policy and Planning, Wallingford, CABI, 2001.

Wahab, S A: *Tourism Management*, Tourism International Press, 1975.

Walle, Alfred H: *Cultural Tourism*: A Strategic Focus, Boulder, Co, Westview Press, 1998.

Wilkinson, Paul: *Tourism Policy and Planning: As Studies from the Caribbean*, Elmsford New York, Cognizant Communications Corporation, 1997.

Yale, Pat: *From Tourist Attractions to Heritage Tourism*, Huntingdon, Elm, 1991.

Zarkia, Cornelia: *Philoxenia: Receiving Tourists*-but *not Guests-on a Greek Island*, Oxford, Berghahn Books, 1996.

Index

V

W

□□□